THE TEN MAHAVIDYA'S: GODDESSES OF THE KALI AGE

Aurealia Nelson (Amba Siddhi)

Copyright © 2025 Aurealia Nelson

All rights reserved.

No part of this publication may be reproduced, distributed, or transmitted in any form or by any means, including photocopying, recording, or other electronic or mechanical methods, without the prior written permission of the publisher, except in the case of brief quotations embodied in critical reviews and certain other non-commercial uses permitted by copyright law.

Although the publisher and the author have made every effort to ensure that the information in this book was correct at press time and while this publication is designed to provide accurate information in regard to the subject matter covered, the publisher and the author assume no responsibility for errors, inaccuracies, omissions, or any other inconsistencies herein and hereby disclaim any liability to any party for any loss, damage, or disruption caused by errors or omissions, whether such errors or omissions result from negligence, accident, or any other cause.

979-8-89778-052-5

Staten House

Contents

Dedication 10
The Ten Mahavidyas An Overview 11
Shaktism and the Devi Gita A Foundational Framework 15
The Significance of Kali Yuga and the Mahavidyas 19
Methodology and Approach 23
Interpreting the Mahavidyas in the 21st Century 27
Kalis Iconography and Attributes 31
Kalis Role in the Cosmos and Religious Practices 35
Kali and the Concept of Time 39
Kali in Modern Interpretations 43
Kalis Relevance in Contemporary Society 47
Taras Manifestations and Iconography 51
Tara as a Protector and Guide 55
Taras Connection to Compassion and Liberation 59
Tara in Different Cultural Contexts 63
Taras Relevance in the Modern World 67
Tripura Sundaris Iconography and Symbolism 71
Tripura Sundaris Role in Tantric Practices 75
Tripura Sundari and the Concept of Divine Beauty 79
Tripura Sundari in Different Religious Traditions 83
Tripura Sundari and Contemporary Spirituality 87
Bhuvaneshvaris Iconography and Attributes 91
Bhuvaneshvaris Role in Cosmic Order 96
Bhuvaneshvari and the Concept of Sovereignty 100
Bhuvaneshvari in Different Textual Sources 104
Bhuvaneshvari and Contemporary Challenges 108
Bhairavis Iconography and Attributes 112
Bhairavis Association with Power and Transformation 116
Bhairavis Role in Tantric Rituals 120

Bhairavi in Different Literary and Artistic Traditions 124
Bhairavi and the Power of Transformation 128
Chhinnamastas Unique Iconography 132
Chhinnamasta and the Concept of SelfSacrifice 136
Chhinnamastas Role in Tantric Practices 140
Chhinnamasta in Various Textual Sources 144
Chhinnamasta and the Path of SelfRealization 148
Dhumavatis Iconography and Attributes 152
Dhumavati and the Embracing of Solitude..........................157
Dhumavatis Role in Tantric Practices 161
Dhumavati in Different Textual Sources 165
Dhumavati and the Acceptance of Impermanence 169
Bagalamukhis Iconography and Attributes 173
Bagalamukhi and the Power of Speech..............................177
Bagalamukhis Role in Tantric Practices 181
Bagalamukhi in Different Textual Sources.........................185
Bagalamukhi and the Power of Communication 189
Matangis Iconography and Attributes..............................193
Matangi and the Power of Music and Art...........................197
Matangis Role in Tantric Practices 201
Matangi in Different Textual Sources.............................205
Matangi and Creative Expression..................................209
Kamalatmikas Iconography and Attributes 213
Kamalatmika and the Lotus Symbolism 217
Kamalatmikas Role in Tantric Practices...........................221
Kamalatmika in Different Textual Sources 225
Kamalatmika and Spiritual Growth 229
Similarities and Differences in Iconography 233
Comparative Analysis of Their Roles and Functions...............237
Comparing Their Associations with Different Deities 241

Comparative Analysis of Their Mantras and Yantras 245

Synthesizing the Mahavidyas Collective Message 249

Archetypal Energies and Psychological Processes 253

The Shadow Self and the Mahavidyas.............................257

The Mahavidyas and Healing Practices 261

The Mahavidyas and Personal Growth 265

Integrating the Mahavidyas into Modern Contexts.................270

Kalis Role in Social Transformation 275

Taras Compassion and Social Action 279

The Mahavidyas and Feminist Perspectives.......................283

The Mahavidyas and Environmental Activism 287

Harnessing the Mahavidyas for Positive Social Change 291

Recapitulation of Key Themes..295

The Enduring Relevance of the Mahavidyas 299

Future Directions for Research 303

Practical Applications and Personal Reflections..................307

A Final Contemplation on Divine Feminine Power................311

Acknowledgments 315

Appendix A...316

   Kali 316

   Tara 316

   Tripura Sundari 316

   Bhuvaneshvari 317

   Bhairavi 317

   Chhinnamasta...317

   Dhumavati 317

   Bagalamukhi 317

   Matangi 318

   Kamalatmika 318

Appendix B 319
    Kali 319
    Tara 319
    Tripura Sundari 319
    Bhuvaneshvari 320
    Bhairavi 320
    Chhinnamasta 320
    Dhumavati 320
    Bagalamukhi 321
    Matangi 321
    Kamalatmika 321
    General Guidance for Tantric Practices 321
Appendix C 324
    Kali Yantra 324
    Tara Yantra 324
    Tripura Sundari Yantra 324
    Bhuvaneshvari Yantra 324
    Bhairavi Yantra 324
    Chhinnamasta Yantra 325
    Dhumavati Yantra 325
    Bagalamukhi Yantra 325
    Matangi Yantra 325
    Kamalatmika Yantra 325
Glossary 327
References 328
Author Biography 329

Dedication

This book, a journey into the heart of the ten Mahavidyas, is dedicated to the unwavering spirit of the Divine Feminine, in all its multifaceted glory. It is an offering to the boundless Shakti, the energy that animates the cosmos and resides within each of us. My deepest gratitude extends to the countless scholars, practitioners, and devotees who have, throughout the ages, preserved and illuminated the path of understanding these powerful goddesses.

Their tireless efforts in translating ancient texts, interpreting intricate symbolism, and sharing their lived experiences have been the bedrock of this work.

Specifically, this dedication is to those who have felt the transformative power of the Mahavidyas in their own lives. To those who have sought solace, strength, and guidance in the face of adversity through their devotion. To those who have found inspiration in their intricate iconography, and those whose lives have been enriched by their mantras and practices. This work is intended as a bridge, connecting the ancient wisdom of the Mahavidyas with the complexities of the modern world. It seeks to honor their timeless messages and empower individuals to embrace the potent energies they represent.

It is also dedicated to the future generations of scholars and spiritual seekers, those who will continue to explore the profound depths of these goddesses and contribute to our collective understanding of the divine feminine. May this work serve as a stepping stone for their own explorations, inspiring further research, illuminating hidden meanings, and fostering a deeper appreciation for the multifaceted power of the Mahavidyas. This offering is a testament to the enduring power of these goddesses and the eternal wisdom they embody, a wisdom that continues to resonate and transform lives across time and cultures. May it inspire a renewed understanding of their potent energies and their lasting relevance in our lives today and into the future, illuminating the path toward a more compassionate, empowered, and spiritually fulfilling world. May this work serve as a catalyst for the ongoing unfolding of their wisdom.

The Ten Mahavidyas An Overview

The ten Mahavidyas represent a fascinating and complex aspect of Hindu Tantra, particularly within the framework of Shaktism. Understanding their significance requires delving into the rich tapestry of Hindu cosmology, the evolution of Tantric traditions, and the interplay between textual interpretations and archaeological findings. These goddesses are not merely mythological figures; they embody powerful archetypal energies, each representing a unique facet of the divine feminine, Shakti. Their combined power reflects the multifaceted nature of the cosmos and the human experience.

The Mahavidyas – Kali, Tara, Tripura Sundari, Bhuvaneshvari, Bhairavi, Chhinnamasta, Dhumavati, Bagalamukhi, Matangi, and Kamalatmika – emerged within the Tantric tradition, a branch of Hinduism that emphasizes ritual practices, mantra recitation, and the harnessing of subtle energies for spiritual growth and transformation. While their origins are shrouded in some mystery, their worship and iconography are richly documented in various texts, including the Devi Mahatmya, various Puranas, and specialized Tantric manuals. These texts offer diverse interpretations of their attributes, powers, and roles within the cosmic order.

Archaeological evidence, albeit limited in direct representation of the Mahavidyas, provides valuable contextual information. Sculptures, temple architecture, and inscriptions from various historical periods reveal the evolution of their iconography and the geographical spread of their worship. The interplay between textual accounts and archaeological findings helps us trace the development of their cults and understand how their image and symbolism have changed over time, adapting to diverse cultural and regional contexts.

The iconography of the Mahavidyas is remarkably diverse. Each goddess displays a unique set of attributes, reflecting her specific nature and powers. Kali, for example, is often depicted as a fierce, dark-complexioned goddess, wielding weapons and adorned with skulls, representing her power over death and destruction. In contrast, Tripura Sundari is characterized by exquisite beauty and grace, symbolizing the alluring and captivating aspect of the divine feminine. Tara, a prominent figure in Vajrayana Buddhism as well as Shaktism, is often depicted with serene and compassionate features, embodying protection and guidance. These diverse representations emphasize the multifaceted nature of Shakti, reflecting the dynamic energies that shape the cosmos and the human experience.

The relationship between the Mahavidyas and other significant deities within the Hindu pantheon, particularly Shiva and Shakti, is crucial to understanding their place in Hindu cosmology. Shaktism, as a distinct tradition within Hinduism, emphasizes the power and independence of the divine feminine, Shakti. The Mahavidyas represent the most potent manifestations of this energy, embodying its diverse aspects and capacities. The Devi Gita, a crucial text for understanding Shaktism, frequently mentions and illuminates the powers and roles of the Mahavidyas. Their connection to Shiva, the male principle, often represents the dynamic interplay between opposing forces – creation and destruction, preservation and transformation – essential for maintaining cosmic equilibrium. The union of Shiva and Shakti is often depicted symbolically, signifying the fundamental unity underlying the apparent duality of the universe.

The historical context of the Mahavidyas is equally important. Their emergence and evolution are intertwined with the broader development of Tantra, which itself underwent various transformations over centuries. Different schools of Tantric thought emphasized different aspects of the Mahavidyas, leading to variations in their iconography, worship practices, and associated mantras and yantras. The development of Tantra also influenced the relationship between the Mahavidyas and other Hindu deities and traditions, leading to the syncretic blend of beliefs and practices observed in many regions and communities. Tracing this historical evolution provides invaluable insights into the multifaceted nature of the Mahavidyas and their place within the broader context of Hindu religious thought.

The study of the Mahavidyas goes beyond the simple recounting of myths and legends. Their symbolism resonates profoundly with modern psychological and spiritual concepts. For instance, Kali's destructive power can be interpreted as the necessary dismantling of outdated belief systems or societal structures that no longer serve us. Tara's protective and compassionate nature reflects the need for empathy and support in a world often characterized by conflict and uncertainty. Tripura Sundari's exquisite beauty represents the importance of appreciating the beauty and grace within ourselves and the world around us. Each Mahavidya offers a unique lens through which to examine the complexities of the human condition and the challenges we face in the 21st century.

Understanding the Mahavidyas requires a multidisciplinary approach. The analysis presented in this book will draw upon various sources, including Sanskrit texts, archaeological evidence, and scholarly interpretations, providing a holistic understanding of these complex goddesses. The approach will integrate scholarly rigor with spiritual insight, offering a perspective that is both academically sound and spiritually meaningful. The book acknowledges the limitations of solely relying on written sources, emphasizing the need to consider the broader cultural and historical context in which the Mahavidyas emerged and continue to be worshipped.

Moreover, the book aims to engage a broad spectrum of readers. While it aims to provide detailed analyses that will resonate with academic scholars, it will also be accessible to spiritual practitioners and general readers interested in mythology, goddesses, and Eastern spirituality. The approach will be to weave together scholarly interpretations with engaging narratives and relatable examples, making the complex concepts of Tantra and the Mahavidyas more accessible to a wider audience. Analogies to contemporary situations will be used, connecting the archetypal energies embodied by the Mahavidyas to the challenges and opportunities of the 21st century. This approach aims to bridge the gap between academic scholarship and spiritual understanding, enriching the reader's appreciation for these powerful goddesses and their enduring relevance. Finally, the inclusion of relevant mantras or practices, always presented within a proper academic framework, will cater to those seeking a deeper engagement with the spiritual aspects of the Mahavidyas. The ultimate goal is to provide a comprehensive, yet engaging, exploration of the ten Mahavidyas, facilitating a deeper understanding and appreciation of their rich symbolism and enduring significance.

Shaktism and the Devi Gita A Foundational Framework

Shaktism, the dominant tradition within Hinduism that focuses on the divine feminine principle, Shakti, provides the crucial lens through which we must understand the Mahavidyas. Shaktism doesn't merely relegate Shakti to a subordinate role; instead, it elevates her to the supreme position, acknowledging her as the ultimate creative and transformative force of the cosmos. This emphasis on the independent power and agency of the divine feminine stands in contrast to other Hindu traditions where the divine masculine, represented by Shiva or Vishnu, often holds a more prominent position. Within the Shaktic framework, the
Mahavidyas emerge as the most potent manifestations of this supreme energy, each embodying a distinct aspect of Shakti's multifaceted nature. This perspective is vital for comprehending the individual powers and unique symbolism of each Mahavidya.

The Devi Gita, a pivotal scripture within Shaktism, serves as an invaluable text for understanding the Mahavidyas and their significance. Embedded within the larger work of the Devi Bhagavata Purana, the Devi Gita offers a direct dialogue between the Goddess and her devotee. This intimate conversation reveals profound insights into the nature of Shakti, the path to spiritual liberation, and the essential qualities of a true devotee. It is not merely a mythological narrative; it's a profound philosophical discourse that lays bare the core principles of Shaktic thought. The Devi Gita explicitly mentions several Mahavidyas, enriching our comprehension of their roles and attributes beyond their depictions in iconography and ritual practices. Understanding the Devi Gita's teachings is crucial for grasping the deeper spiritual meanings associated with each Mahavidya.

The Devi Gita emphasizes the dynamic interplay between the divine feminine and masculine, Shiva and Shakti. It doesn't present them as opposing forces but rather as two complementary aspects of a single, unified reality. The union of Shiva and Shakti is frequently portrayed symbolically, signifying the fundamental unity
underlying the apparent duality of the universe. This concept of *adi-shakti*, the primordial energy, as the source of all creation, is

central to the Devi Gita's teachings. This primordial energy manifests in diverse forms, and the Mahavidyas are among its most significant and powerful expressions. The Goddess, in her various manifestations, embodies both the fierce and the gentle, the destructive and the creative, the terrifying and the nurturing – all essential facets of the cosmic dance. The Devi Gita elucidates this intricate dance of energies, highlighting the essential role each Mahavidya plays in maintaining cosmic equilibrium.

The concept of Shakti itself is multifaceted and complex. It is not simply a single entity but a dynamic force manifesting in myriad ways. It is the creative power that brings the universe into being, the sustaining power that preserves it, and the transformative power that leads to its eventual dissolution and rebirth. Shakti can be understood as the energy that animates all things, the life force that permeates every aspect of existence. In the context of the Mahavidyas, Shakti's manifestations take on unique and powerful forms. Each Mahavidya represents a particular aspect of this cosmic energy, reflecting its diverse expressions within the universe and within the human experience. Their diverse iconography, attributes, and associated mantras are all manifestations of this fundamental energy, each offering a unique pathway for spiritual aspirants to connect with the divine feminine.

The Devi Gita's relevance to the Mahavidyas extends beyond simple mention; it provides a deeper understanding of their individual characteristics. For instance, Kali, often depicted as a fierce and terrifying figure, is also revealed in the Devi Gita as the ultimate liberator, destroying ignorance and illusion to reveal the true nature of reality. Her seemingly destructive nature is not merely chaotic; it is a necessary process of transformation and purification. Similarly, the Devi Gita illuminates Tara's compassionate nature, highlighting her role as a protector and guide for those who seek liberation.

Tara's protective power is not merely physical; it extends to the spiritual realm, safeguarding the devotee from the pitfalls of ignorance and delusion. The Gita underscores that while Tara's demeanor is compassionate, her power is immense and unwavering.

Tripura Sundari, depicted as a radiant goddess of beauty and grace, is shown in the Devi Gita to represent the ultimate bliss and fulfillment that comes from realizing one's true nature. Her beauty is not merely superficial; it reflects the inherent beauty and perfection of the divine within each individual. Similarly, the Devi Gita reveals the transformative power of Bhuvaneshvari, the goddess of the universe. Bhuvaneshvari's dominion over the entire cosmos symbolizes the interconnectedness of all things and the ultimate unity that underlies the apparent diversity of the universe.

Through her, the devotee understands the wholeness and interconnectedness of creation. The Devi Gita's verses, carefully analyzed, reveal the nuanced meanings of the Mahavidyas, extending beyond their superficial iconographic representations.

The Devi Gita also provides a framework for understanding the seemingly contradictory aspects of the Mahavidyas. Goddesses like Chhinnamasta, with her self-decapitated image, initially appear shocking and violent, yet the Devi Gita interprets this iconography as representing the transcendence of ego and the realization of one's true self. The act of self-sacrifice signifies the surrender of the individual will to the divine will, a crucial step on the path to liberation. Similarly, Dhumavati, the goddess of widowhood and desolation, might appear initially negative; however, the Devi Gita reveals her as a powerful force representing the acceptance of impermanence and the ability to find strength and wisdom even in the face of adversity. Her seemingly bleak attributes point to the ability to find inner strength during challenging times.

Bagalamukhi, known for her ability to bind enemies and conquer adversaries, is presented in the Devi Gita not solely as a goddess of victory but as a symbol of inner strength and self-mastery. The ability to "bind" refers to controlling negative thoughts and emotions, thus paving the way for inner peace and spiritual growth. Matangi, the goddess of wisdom and learning, is not only the patron of the arts but also a symbol of the power of knowledge to illuminate the path to liberation. Her association with knowledge transcends mundane learning and encompasses spiritual insight.

Finally, Kamalatmika, the goddess of creation and fulfillment, represents the ultimate realization of one's potential and the complete manifestation of one's true self. The Devi Gita explains that her lotus-like qualities denote the unfolding of one's spiritual potential.

The philosophical underpinnings of Shaktism, as illuminated by the Devi Gita, highlight the importance of self-realization and the transcendence of the ego. The path to liberation, according to the Devi Gita, involves a process of self-discovery and the eventual union with the divine feminine. This process requires devotion, self-discipline, and a deep understanding of one's own nature. The Mahavidyas serve as powerful guides on this path, each embodying a specific aspect of the divine feminine that can assist the devotee in their journey towards self-realization. Through the study and contemplation of the Mahavidyas and their association with the Devi Gita, one can gain profound insights into the nature of Shakti, the complexities of the human condition, and the path towards liberation. The Devi Gita, therefore, is not merely a religious text; it is a profound philosophical and spiritual guidebook for navigating the complexities of life and realizing one's full potential. The
following chapters will delve into the individual Mahavidyas, drawing upon the insights provided by the Devi Gita and other relevant texts to provide a comprehensive understanding of these powerful goddesses.

The Significance of Kali Yuga and the Mahavidyas

The Hindu cosmology operates within a cyclical framework of time, divided into four Yugas – Satya Yuga, Treta Yuga, Dvapara Yuga, and Kali Yuga. Each Yuga represents a distinct era, characterized by specific moral, spiritual, and societal characteristics. Kali Yuga, the current age, is often described as an era marked by a decline in dharma (righteousness), an increase in adharma (unrighteousness), and a prevalence of materialism and egoism. This doesn't imply a purely negative connotation; rather, it suggests a specific set of challenges and opportunities. Understanding Kali Yuga's unique attributes is essential for grasping the particular relevance and significance of the Mahavidyas in the present day.

The scriptures describe Kali Yuga as an age of diminished lifespan, diminished strength, and diminished spiritual understanding.

However, this decline is not absolute. It indicates a shift in the dominant energies and values of the era. The emphasis on material pursuits and the prevalence of conflict, as depicted in traditional accounts, should not be interpreted as an indication of an inevitable moral collapse. Rather, it points to the need for a stronger adherence to spiritual practices and a deeper understanding of the inner self, a need acutely relevant to our modern times. The inherent challenges of Kali Yuga, such as the overwhelming presence of technology, consumerism, and rapid societal change, create a fertile ground for spiritual questioning and the need for a renewed sense of purpose.

The Mahavidyas, as potent manifestations of Shakti, are especially relevant during Kali Yuga. Their symbolic attributes directly address the spiritual and societal challenges of this age. Kali, the primordial goddess, serves as a powerful example. Her terrifying form, often associated with death and destruction, symbolizes the necessary process of dismantling old structures and beliefs that no longer serve our growth. Her association with time itself emphasizes the transient nature of all things, reminding us of the importance of embracing impermanence. In Kali Yuga's whirlwind of rapid change, Kali's message of transformation and acceptance of cycles becomes particularly potent. The fearsome aspects of Kali represent the necessary destruction of ego, ignorance, and delusion – hindrances to spiritual growth that are particularly pronounced in the materialistic aspects of Kali Yuga.

Tara, the compassionate savior, is crucial in navigating the turbulent waters of Kali Yuga. Her ability to rescue from danger reflects the need for compassion, protection, and guidance amidst overwhelming societal chaos. Her compassionate nature offers solace and hope, a vital counterpoint to the often-overwhelming negativity of the present age. In a world increasingly characterized by anxiety and uncertainty, Tara's protective presence offers a sense of security and spiritual resilience. The power of her compassion extends beyond the purely physical, providing strength to confront personal and societal challenges.

Tripura Sundari, the goddess of beauty and grace, embodies the power of inner beauty and spiritual fulfillment, providing a counterbalance to the emphasis on superficiality and materialism characterizing Kali Yuga. Her radiant beauty reminds us of the inherent divinity within each individual, encouraging us to seek inner peace and joy, independent of external validation. The pursuit of inner beauty transcends the fleeting pleasures of the material world, providing a more enduring source of fulfillment in a world obsessed with appearances and transient gratification.

Bhuvaneshvari, the goddess of the universe, embodies the interconnectedness of all things. Her wisdom helps us understand the larger context of our actions and choices, guiding us toward compassionate and responsible behavior. In a world grappling with global issues such as climate change and social inequality, Bhuvaneshvari's holistic perspective is especially important. Her reminder of our interconnectedness emphasizes the importance of collective responsibility and mindful actions that promote harmony and sustainability.

Chhinnamasta, with her self-decapitated image, represents the transcendence of ego and the importance of self-sacrifice. This radical act symbolizes the surrender of the individual will to the divine will, a crucial path to liberation. In an age marked by self-centeredness and materialism, Chhinnamasta's iconography serves as a reminder of the need to transcend ego and embrace a larger purpose. The act of self-sacrifice, though seemingly extreme, points to a profound truth: true liberation lies in surrendering to something larger than oneself.

Dhumavati, the goddess of widowhood and desolation, encourages acceptance of impermanence and the ability to find strength and wisdom in challenging times. Her seemingly negative attributes offer a paradoxical message of resilience and inner strength. In a world grappling with loss, uncertainty, and the impermanence of all things, Dhumavati's message of acceptance becomes profoundly relevant. Her image offers a pathway to accepting the inevitable cycles of life, death, and rebirth, thus fostering inner peace.

Bagalamukhi, the goddess who binds enemies, represents the mastery of inner negativity and the ability to control destructive thoughts and emotions. In a world prone to conflict and discord, Bagalamukhi's power signifies the importance of inner peace and self-mastery. The "binding" of enemies is not limited to external adversaries; it extends to the internal battles waged against negative emotions and destructive thoughts. The inner peace achieved through self-mastery is a valuable asset in navigating the complexities of Kali Yuga.

Matangi, the goddess of learning and wisdom, highlights the importance of knowledge and education as tools for spiritual growth. Her association with the arts also underscores the importance of creativity and self-expression as pathways to spiritual insight. In an age of rapid technological advancements and access to vast amounts of information, Matangi's message of discerning knowledge and wisdom takes on particular importance. The ability to sift through vast quantities of data and find meaningful understanding becomes crucial for personal and societal progress.

Kamalatmika, the goddess of creation and fulfillment, reminds us of the potential for positive change and the importance of embracing our full potential. Her association with the lotus flower symbolizes growth and spiritual development even in challenging environments. In an age characterized by uncertainty and challenges, Kamalatmika's message of creative potential and fulfillment becomes an inspiration. The ability to realize our full potential in the midst of adversity offers a powerful message of hope and resilience.

In conclusion, the Mahavidyas offer a unique and powerful framework for understanding and navigating the complexities of Kali Yuga. Their diverse attributes and symbolism directly address the challenges and opportunities of our time, providing guidance and inspiration for spiritual growth and societal transformation. Each goddess offers a unique perspective and set of tools to help us cultivate inner strength, compassion, wisdom, and acceptance in the face of an ever-changing world. The Devi Gita, as a key text illuminating the nature of Shakti, helps us understand these goddesses' diverse roles and their relevance in the context of the current age. By studying and contemplating the Mahavidyas, we can gain profound insights into the human condition and discover a path toward self-realization and liberation, even within the unique context of Kali Yuga.

Methodology and Approach

This book employs a multifaceted methodology, drawing upon a rich tapestry of sources to illuminate the ten Mahavidyas. Our approach integrates rigorous scholarly analysis with a contemplative, spiritual understanding, acknowledging the inherent complexities of interpreting ancient religious traditions. The primary textual sources include the Devi Gita, a pivotal scripture within Shaktism that provides profound insights into the nature of Shakti and its diverse manifestations. We also draw upon a wide range of related Tantric texts, including the Devi Mahatmya, various Puranas (specifically those containing narratives or descriptions related to the Mahavidyas), and relevant Upanishads, which offer philosophical underpinnings for understanding the cosmic energies embodied by these goddesses. These texts are not treated as monolithic authorities but rather as a collection of diverse perspectives that offer a nuanced understanding of the Mahavidyas' evolving interpretations across different schools of thought and historical periods.

Beyond textual sources, we engage with scholarly interpretations of these texts. This includes a critical examination of existing academic work on Shaktism, Tantra, and the Mahavidyas, taking into consideration various perspectives and schools of thought. The interpretations presented in this book are not intended to be definitive or exclusive; rather, they are offered as insightful explorations within a broader scholarly conversation. We acknowledge the inherent limitations in interpreting ancient texts, particularly those with complex symbolic language and varying interpretations across different traditions and time periods. We strive to present a balanced view, acknowledging multiple perspectives and potential ambiguities.

Our interpretive framework is informed by both academic scholarship and a spiritual understanding cultivated through years of study and practice within the Hindu and Tantric traditions. This approach aims to bridge the gap between objective academic analysis and the subjective, experiential dimension of spiritual practice. It is understood that the Mahavidyas are not simply intellectual concepts but powerful, living deities whose energy and influence continue to shape the spiritual lives of countless devotees. This understanding informs our approach, striving to capture both the intellectual and experiential dimensions of their significance.

The book's structure is designed to facilitate a comprehensive exploration of the ten Mahavidyas. Following this introductory chapter, each subsequent chapter is dedicated to a single Mahavidya. Each chapter follows a consistent structure, beginning with an overview of the goddess's iconography, mythology, and primary attributes. This is followed by a detailed analysis of the relevant scriptures and scholarly interpretations, exploring the goddess's symbolism and significance within the broader context of Shaktism and other religious traditions. Furthermore, each chapter will analyze the relevance of the particular Mahavidya in the context of Kali Yuga, examining how her attributes and teachings offer guidance and support in navigating the challenges and opportunities of this era.

The book's approach goes beyond a simple recounting of myths and legends; it actively engages with the philosophical and spiritual implications of the Mahavidyas. We explore the relationship between their symbolic representations and their profound psychological and spiritual meanings. We delve into the practical applications of their teachings, exploring how their messages can be integrated into contemporary spiritual practice and personal growth. We also analyze the role of the Mahavidyas in addressing various societal challenges. The book explicitly considers the societal implications of the Mahavidyas' energies and symbolism. How have their teachings impacted various communities and social structures throughout history? This investigation extends to exploring the contemporary relevance of their wisdom in addressing societal challenges, such as social justice, environmental sustainability, and the ethical use of technology. The book explores the interplay between the personal spiritual practice and the broader societal application of the Mahavidyas' teachings.

The study also incorporates a comparative approach, analyzing the Mahavidyas within the context of other related deities and concepts within Hindu and Buddhist traditions. This comparative lens helps to highlight the unique characteristics of each Mahavidya while simultaneously illuminating the broader themes and interconnections within the broader divine landscape. This analysis draws parallels and contrasts, identifying both shared attributes and distinct characteristics across different traditions and interpretations.

A limitation of this study lies in the inherent complexity and ambiguity surrounding the interpretations of ancient Tantric texts. The meaning and symbolism of the Mahavidyas often depend on the specific tradition, school of thought, and individual practitioner's interpretation. Therefore, this book cannot claim to provide an entirely exhaustive or definitive account of the Mahavidyas.

Instead, it aims to offer a thoughtful exploration of their diverse attributes and symbolic meanings, acknowledging the multifaceted interpretations that have arisen throughout history.

The use of archaeological evidence is limited due to the nature of the subject matter. While archaeological findings can offer valuable contextual information about the historical periods in which the Mahavidyas were worshipped, the specific iconography and symbolic representations are primarily conveyed through textual sources. However, where relevant, we will incorporate available archaeological evidence, such as depictions of goddesses in temple art and sculptures, to enrich our understanding of their visual representation and cultural significance across different periods and regions.

This book recognizes the limitations of a purely academic approach to understanding the Mahavidyas. While scholarly analysis is crucial, the spiritual dimension is equally important. Therefore, the book attempts to strike a balance between rigorous scholarship and contemplative insight. It acknowledges the role of personal experience and intuitive understanding in appreciating the deeper meanings of these goddesses. The book's overall approach encourages the reader to engage with the Mahavidyas not only intellectually but also through personal reflection and spiritual practice.

Finally, the subsequent chapters will provide in-depth explorations of each Mahavidya, following the structure outlined above. Each chapter will delve into the specific iconography, mythology, textual references, scholarly interpretations, and contemporary relevance of each individual goddess. This detailed analysis will allow for a rich and nuanced understanding of the unique power and significance of each Mahavidya, concluding with a synthesis that integrates the insights gathered from the individual chapters to provide a comprehensive overview of the ten Mahavidyas as a whole and their relevance in the Kali Yuga.

Interpreting the Mahavidyas in the 21st Century

Interpreting the multifaceted symbolism and archetypal energies of the Mahavidyas within the contemporary context requires a nuanced approach that bridges the gap between ancient traditions and modern realities. The 21st century presents a unique set of challenges and opportunities, marked by rapid technological advancements, globalization, and profound shifts in societal structures and values. While the scriptures and traditional interpretations offer invaluable insights, a meaningful engagement with the Mahavidyas necessitates an exploration of their relevance to these contemporary circumstances. This isn't about forcing a modern interpretation onto ancient deities, but rather understanding how their archetypal energies resonate with the human condition, regardless of the temporal context.

The Devi Gita, for example, offers profound insights into the nature of Shakti, the divine feminine energy. This energy isn't confined to a specific historical period; it's a fundamental force that underpins the cosmos and manifests in diverse ways throughout human experience. The Mahavidyas, as manifestations of this energy, can be understood as archetypal representations of various aspects of Shakti – aspects that remain profoundly relevant today.

Consider Kali, the embodiment of primordial energy, often depicted as terrifying yet liberating. In a world grappling with existential threats like climate change and social injustice, Kali's fierce energy can be seen as a call for radical transformation. Her willingness to destroy limitations and outdated systems can be interpreted as a prompt for decisive action in the face of global challenges. The destructive aspect of Kali is not simply about violence, but about dismantling that which prevents growth and liberation—whether personal or societal. In this interpretation, Kali doesn't encourage mindless destruction; she encourages a conscious dismantling of negative patterns, both internally and externally. This conscious dismantling can be seen in various modern contexts, such as activism that confronts systemic issues or personal journeys that involve overcoming deeply ingrained self-limiting beliefs.

Similarly, Tara, the saviour goddess, offers a potent message of compassion and protection in a world increasingly fractured by conflict and inequality. Her ability to navigate perilous situations and rescue those in distress resonates with the need for empathy and collaborative action to address humanitarian crises, social injustices, and environmental degradation. Tara's compassion transcends geographical boundaries, mirroring the global interconnectedness of modern society. Her image as a protector, often depicted with a serene yet resolute demeanor, speaks to the strength and resilience required to face the challenges of our time. The compassion she embodies is not passive; it is a powerful force that motivates individuals and communities to work towards a more just and equitable world.

Tripura Sundari, the goddess of beauty and bliss, reminds us of the importance of nurturing inner peace and joy amid the chaos and stress of modern life. Her emphasis on aesthetic appreciation and the cultivation of positive emotions provides a vital counterpoint to the often-overwhelming negativity that permeates contemporary society. The emphasis on beauty doesn't imply superficiality; it speaks to the intrinsic beauty that is present in all of existence, and the ability to appreciate that beauty even in the midst of suffering.

In a digital world saturated with superficial images, Tripura Sundari's message calls for a deeper appreciation of genuine beauty, both internal and external, promoting a mindful engagement with the world.

Bhuvaneshvari, the goddess of the world, represents the interconnectedness of all beings and the importance of ecological responsibility. Her embodiment of the material world highlights the need for sustainable practices and responsible stewardship of the planet. In an age of environmental crisis, Bhuvaneshvari's message of holistic awareness encourages us to consider the consequences of our actions on the larger ecosystem. Her association with the earth signifies the profound connection between human society and the natural world, emphasizing the urgency of environmental protection and harmonious coexistence with nature. The preservation of biodiversity and the fight against climate change directly address the inherent message of Bhuvaneshvari.

Bhairavi, the embodiment of dynamic energy, challenges us to confront our fears and embrace the transformative potential of change. Her association with death and rebirth symbolizes the cyclical nature of life and the importance of letting go of old patterns and embracing new beginnings. In a rapidly changing world, the energy of Bhairavi empowers us to embrace the uncertainties inherent in life's journey and see change as an opportunity for growth and transformation. Her image encourages individuals to step outside of their comfort zones, pushing personal boundaries and making conscious choices regarding their lives.

Chhinnamasta, the goddess with self-severed head, represents the power of self-sacrifice and the ability to transcend ego-centric limitations. Her symbolism encourages detachment from materialistic desires and the pursuit of spiritual liberation. In a world often obsessed with material gain, Chhinnamasta's message of detachment can be profoundly liberating. The act of self-sacrifice doesn't necessarily refer to literal self-harm, but rather to the willingness to let go of attachments that hinder spiritual growth. This can be seen in various acts of selflessness, from philanthropic endeavors to personal sacrifices made for the benefit of others.

Dhumavati, the goddess of widowhood and solitude, reminds us to embrace the darker aspects of life and find strength in adversity. Her association with loneliness and hardship encourages resilience and the ability to find inner peace in challenging circumstances. In a world that often values outward success and social conformity, Dhumavati's message of embracing solitude and accepting adversity provides a vital counterpoint. Her strength lies in her ability to find peace and acceptance even in the most challenging situations, reminding us that solitude can be a source of empowerment and inner growth. The resilience she embodies can be a guiding force during personal hardships and times of collective crisis.

Bagalamukhi, the goddess of speech and victory, embodies the power of communication and the importance of using our voice to effect positive change. In an age of misinformation and social division, her message encourages clear and compassionate communication, promoting understanding and cooperation. The power of speech is not just about winning arguments; it is about using one's voice to promote truth, understanding, and positive change in the world. This is particularly relevant in an age where digital platforms and mass media have such a significant impact on public discourse and social justice movements.

Matangi, the goddess of music and learning, inspires creativity, artistic expression, and the pursuit of knowledge. In a world that values innovation and intellectual curiosity, her message highlights the importance of continuous learning and the power of the arts to inspire and transform. The arts in all forms have the power to express profound truths, inspire change, and offer a pathway to understanding. The pursuit of knowledge and understanding is a vital part of navigating the complexities of the modern world.

Kamalatmika, the goddess of fulfillment and abundance, represents the potential for spiritual and material well-being. Her message is a reminder that true fulfillment comes not just from material possessions but from inner peace and harmony. In a consumer-driven society, Kamalatmika's message underscores the importance of mindful consumption, gratitude, and appreciation for the blessings in our lives. It challenges the consumerist mindset and reminds us that true abundance comes from inner peace and harmonious relationships, rather than solely from material wealth.

In conclusion, the Mahavidyas, far from being relics of a bygone era, offer a rich tapestry of archetypal energies that remain profoundly relevant in the 21st century. Their messages resonate deeply with the challenges and opportunities of our time, providing guidance and inspiration for navigating the complexities of modern life. Their timeless wisdom offers a pathway to personal transformation and collective progress, encouraging us to engage with the world with compassion, courage, and a deep understanding of our interconnectedness. The following chapters will delve deeper into each Mahavidya, exploring their individual attributes and providing further insights into their contemporary relevance.

Kalis Iconography and Attributes

Kali, the primordial goddess of time and destruction, presents a visual complexity that mirrors the multifaceted nature of her energy. Her iconography is not static; it varies across different schools of thought, geographical regions, and historical periods.

Understanding her diverse depictions is crucial to grasping the depth and breadth of her symbolism. One common representation portrays her as a dark-skinned, four-armed goddess, adorned with a garland of skulls and standing on the prostrate Shiva, her consort.

This image immediately conveys her power over death and her transcendence of even the most powerful of deities. The skulls are not merely gruesome ornaments; they symbolize the cyclical nature of life and death, the constant renewal and transformation that underpins the cosmic process. The subjugation of Shiva, usually depicted as the supreme god in many traditions, underscores Kali's sovereignty over even divine power. This isn't an act of aggression but a symbolic representation of Shakti's ultimate authority over all creation, including its creator.

The number of arms Kali is depicted with varies. Sometimes she is shown with two arms, sometimes four, and occasionally even more.

The additional arms signify the multiplicity of her powers and functions. Each hand typically holds a symbolic weapon or object: a sword to sever attachments, a trident to pierce illusion, a skull to represent the transience of life, and a khaṭvāṅga (a club topped with a skull) representing death and liberation. The specific items and their arrangement may differ slightly depending on the particular artistic tradition and the specific text being referenced.

Yet, the overarching message remains consistent: Kali wields the power to sever bonds, destroy illusions, and confront death itself.

Beyond the weapons, Kali's adornments are equally significant. The garland of skulls, previously mentioned, is a recurring motif, emphasizing her association with death and the cyclical nature of existence. She is often depicted with a protruding tongue, symbolizing her ecstatic nature and the consumption of ego and ignorance. Her necklace, frequently made of severed human hands, illustrates her mastery over karma and her power to liberate from the cycle of rebirth. The garments she wears are often minimal or nonexistent, representing her primordial nature and her transcendence of material concerns. The absence of clothing signifies her purity, her connection to the raw energy of creation, untouched by the constraints of societal norms.

The posture of Kali also contributes to the overall symbolism. Her dancing posture, known as *tandava*, is a dynamic expression of cosmic energy and the inherent movement and transformation within the universe. It is an active dance, not a static pose, suggesting a constant state of creation and destruction. This contrasts with depictions of more static goddesses, highlighting Kali's powerful, dynamic energy. The earth goddess, for instance, is often shown seated or standing calmly, symbolizing stability and groundedness, whereas Kali's dancing posture represents an unstoppable force. Another aspect is her often dishevelled appearance, emphasizing her wild, untamed nature. She is not constrained by rules or societal norms; she is the embodiment of pure, unadulterated energy.

Different Puranas and Tantric texts offer varying descriptions of Kali's iconography, leading to regional variations in her portrayal.

For instance, some texts emphasize her terrifying aspect, highlighting her ferocity and destructive power. These depictions might portray her with fierce eyes, bared teeth, and a blood-soaked appearance. Other texts, however, focus on her nurturing and compassionate side, emphasizing her ability to protect devotees and grant liberation. In these representations, the emphasis shifts from terror to tenderness, highlighting a gentler aspect of her personality. This duality, the coexistence of the terrifying and the benevolent, is a key feature of Kali's complexity.

The Devi Mahatmya, a section of the Markandeya Purana, narrates several stories of Kali's intervention, which further inform her visual representations. In the story of the buffalo demon, she is depicted as a powerful warrior, effortlessly slaying her opponent. This portrays her active role in maintaining cosmic order, vanquishing demonic forces that threaten dharma. This powerful image is often reflected in iconography depicting her in a fierce battle stance, weapon at the ready, demonstrating her ability to act decisively and swiftly. The victory over the demon is not just a physical triumph but also a symbolic representation of overcoming inner obstacles and negativities.

The Tantric texts often depict Kali in a more intimate and esoteric manner. They describe practices of ritual worship dedicated to Kali, emphasizing the transformative power of her energy. The visualizations and mantras associated with these rituals often guide specific iconographic representations, focusing on particular details and emphasizing specific aspects of her energy. These depictions, intended for specific ritual contexts, may differ significantly from those meant for public display, reflecting the esoteric nature of Tantric practice. They might emphasize certain features, such as her specific adornments or mudras (hand gestures), according to the aim of the ritual.

The variations in Kali's iconography should not be interpreted as contradictions, but rather as diverse facets of the same powerful archetype. Each representation reflects different aspects of her energy and resonates with various aspects of human experience.

Her terrifying aspect embodies the necessary destruction that precedes creation; her compassionate aspect reveals the underlying nurturing power of primordial energy. The different iconographic details – weapons, adornments, postures – all contribute to the complex narrative of Kali's multifaceted nature. Her imagery offers a profound exploration of the interplay between creation and destruction, life and death, and ultimately, the ever-shifting nature of reality itself. Understanding her iconography is therefore a key to comprehending the deeper significance of this powerful and multifaceted goddess. The analysis of her various representations moves beyond a simple catalogue; it offers a lens through which we can understand the complexities of the divine feminine energy and its relevance to the human condition. The variations are not imperfections, but rather a testament to the rich tapestry of cultural and spiritual interpretations that have shaped our understanding of this powerful goddess over millennia. This multiplicity serves as a powerful reminder of the ever-evolving and complex nature of the divine, reflecting the ever-shifting landscapes of human experience. The seemingly contradictory aspects – ferocious and compassionate, destroyer and nurturer – are not mutually exclusive but rather interconnected aspects of a single, all-encompassing reality.

Kalis Role in the Cosmos and Religious Practices

Kali's role extends far beyond the battlefield of mythological narratives. She is not merely a destroyer of demons, but a fundamental cosmic force, deeply interwoven into the fabric of creation, preservation, and destruction within the Hindu cosmology.

Her association with *Kala*, time itself, positions her as a dynamic participant in the eternal cycle of existence. Unlike static deities representing singular aspects of reality, Kali embodies the ever-flowing river of time, its relentless current sweeping away the old to make way for the new. This continuous process of destruction and renewal is not chaotic but rather a vital element of cosmic order, mirroring the cyclical nature of life, death, and rebirth.

Understanding Kali's function within this grand cosmic drama necessitates exploring the concept of *Maya*, illusion. Kali, as the primordial energy, is capable of piercing the veil of Maya, revealing the underlying truth of reality. Her destructive power is not arbitrary violence but the dismantling of false beliefs, attachments, and ego-driven illusions that bind individuals to the cycle of Samsara (rebirth). The destruction she brings is not an end, but a necessary prelude to liberation. By shattering the ego's clinging to the material world, she clears the path for spiritual awakening and the realization of one's true self, or Atman.

The Devi Gita, a pivotal text within Shaktism, provides crucial insights into Kali's cosmic role. While not explicitly focusing on Kali as much as other forms of the Goddess, the underlying principles of Shakti's dynamic power resonate strongly with Kali's attributes. The Devi Gita emphasizes the transformative power of the divine feminine, her capacity to both create and destroy, to nurture and to fiercely protect her devotees. Kali's actions, viewed through this lens, become manifestations of this fundamental cosmic energy, her seemingly destructive acts ultimately contributing to the larger cosmic balance.

Kali's association with time finds expression in her iconography. The garland of skulls, often misinterpreted as mere macabre ornamentation, symbolizes the relentless march of time, consuming all things in its path, yet simultaneously representing the cyclic nature of existence. Each skull represents a moment, a life, a death, all ultimately absorbed into the vast expanse of time. This cyclical nature is not something to fear, but to understand and accept as an inherent part of the cosmic order. It is within this acceptance that liberation from the fear of death and the cycle of rebirth can be achieved.

The religious practices surrounding Kali's worship are multifaceted and often deeply personal, varying considerably depending on the tradition and the individual practitioner. Yet, certain core elements remain consistent. The recitation of specific mantras, often containing potent sounds with vibratory energy, is central to many Kali rituals. These mantras are not merely repetitive chants but powerful tools for focusing the mind, invoking Kali's energy, and accessing deeper states of consciousness. The mantras, coupled with focused visualization and meditation, aim to connect the practitioner with Kali's energy, experiencing her as a transformative force within their own being.

The use of yantras, geometric diagrams imbued with sacred symbolism, is another important aspect of Kali worship. These complex designs are often meticulously constructed according to precise specifications, each line and symbol carrying a profound spiritual significance. The yantra acts as a focal point for meditation, allowing practitioners to concentrate their energy and connect with the specific energy associated with Kali. The visual complexity of the yantra can help facilitate a deeper understanding of Kali's multifaceted nature. The yantra, often associated with a particular mantra, can be seen as a visual representation of the mantra's energy, creating a potent synergy between sound and form.

The ritualistic offerings made to Kali also hold significant symbolic meaning. While some traditions involve elaborate offerings, others emphasize the simplicity and sincerity of the offering itself. The symbolic acts of offering food, flowers, or other items are not merely acts of appeasement, but representations of surrendering to the cosmic flow, recognizing Kali's sovereignty over all aspects of existence. These offerings can be understood as symbolic acts of self-sacrifice, mirroring the surrender of the ego that is necessary for spiritual growth. The act of giving, of relinquishing attachment to material possessions, underscores the ephemeral nature of worldly things.

The worship of Kali is not always confined to formal temple rituals. Many practitioners incorporate elements of Kali worship into their daily lives, viewing her presence in the seemingly ordinary events of life. The challenges and difficulties encountered daily can be viewed as opportunities for spiritual growth, the opportunities for testing faith and fortitude. The understanding of Kali's power to overcome obstacles and triumph over adversity provides strength and resilience in the face of hardship.

The importance of understanding the context within which Kali is worshiped is crucial. The focus shouldn't be on seeking a simplistic understanding, but on grasping the depth and richness of her symbolism and its implications for spiritual growth. This requires a deeper understanding of Tantric philosophy and its emphasis on the inherent duality of creation and destruction, life and death. These seemingly opposing forces are not at odds with each other but inextricably linked, representing the fundamental dynamics of the cosmos.

Furthermore, the role of Kali in the current era, within the context of Kali Yuga, requires careful consideration. The Kali Yuga, the present age in Hindu cosmology, is often associated with decline and moral decay. However, this perception is not without its complexities. Kali, as the embodiment of the Kali Yuga, is also seen as a powerful force for transformation and liberation. Her energy, while potentially disruptive, can also serve as a catalyst for spiritual awakening, prompting individuals to confront their inner darkness and overcome their limitations. This tumultuous energy can be utilized for self-reflection and spiritual growth rather than being seen merely as negative and challenging.

The association of Kali with destruction, therefore, should not be interpreted solely as negativity or violence. Her destructive power represents the necessary purging of that which hinders spiritual progress, the breaking down of ego-driven attachments and illusions that prevent the realization of the true self. This destructive energy paves the way for spiritual rebirth and transformation, echoing the cyclical nature of time and the continuous process of creation and destruction that underpins the cosmos.

Therefore, understanding Kali's role in the cosmos and the various religious practices associated with her worship offers a profound insight into the fundamental principles of the Hindu cosmology. Her presence extends beyond the confines of mythological narratives, encompassing the intricate interplay between creation, preservation, and destruction, the cyclical nature of existence, and the ultimate goal of liberation from the cycle of rebirth. Her worship is not merely about appeasing a powerful goddess but about engaging with a fundamental cosmic principle, and utilizing her energy for spiritual transformation. The seemingly contradictory aspects of her nature highlight the complex interplay of forces within the cosmos and within the individual human experience. The understanding of Kali is therefore a path to understanding the depths of the universe and the nature of reality itself. It's a journey of self-discovery, guided by the power of a goddess who embodies both the terrifying and the tender, the destroyer and the nurturer, all aspects of the one cosmic reality.

Kali and the Concept of Time

Kali, the fearsome and awe-inspiring goddess, is inextricably linked to the concept of time, a connection that deepens when considering her namesake, the Kali Yuga. This current age, according to Hindu cosmology, is often characterized by moral decline and societal upheaval. However, to view Kali Yuga solely through a lens of negativity is to misunderstand its profound significance and the role Kali plays within it. Instead of simply representing decay, Kali, as the embodiment of this Yuga, acts as a powerful catalyst for transformation, a force that compels both introspection and action.

The relentless flow of time, symbolized by Kali's garland of skulls, is not arbitrary chaos but a fundamental aspect of cosmic order. Each skull represents a fleeting moment, a life lived, and a death accepted, all contributing to the continuous cycle of creation and destruction. This cycle is not a linear progression towards some ultimate end, but a continuous renewal, a constant interplay of birth, death, and rebirth. This understanding counters the prevalent modern anxiety surrounding the relentless march of time, offering a framework for acceptance and even celebration of life's impermanence. By acknowledging the transient nature of all things, we can free ourselves from the attachments that bind us to suffering. This resonates deeply with the Buddhist concept of *Anicca* , the impermanence of all phenomena, a central tenet that encourages detachment from material possessions and transient experiences.

Kali's iconography reinforces this cyclical understanding of time.

Her dark complexion, often associated with night, symbolizes the unknown and the mysterious depths of existence. The night, devoid of the sun's blinding light, allows for introspection, for a deeper examination of the self and the universe. Just as the night gives way to the dawn, Kali's destructive force ultimately paves the way for renewal and rebirth. This duality, the darkness giving rise to light, mirrors the cyclicality of time and the constant flux of reality. This isn't to romanticize suffering but to contextualize it within a larger cosmic framework, providing a perspective that helps us process challenging experiences and find meaning within them.

The Kali Yuga, in its association with moral decline, presents unique challenges. The rapid advancements in technology, the acceleration of globalization, and the growing environmental crisis all reflect the potential for both immense progress and catastrophic consequences. Kali's energy, as a catalyst for change, can be seen in these very developments. The destructive aspects of these processes—environmental degradation, social inequality, and the erosion of traditional values—mirror Kali's destructive power. Yet, simultaneously, these challenges present opportunities for profound transformation. The very awareness of these issues, the impetus to address them, represents a potential for positive change, a movement towards a more sustainable and equitable future.

This transformative potential necessitates a conscious engagement with Kali's energy. Passive acceptance of the challenges of the Kali Yuga is insufficient. Instead, active participation in addressing these issues, guided by ethical principles and a commitment to positive change, becomes essential. This calls for a shift in perspective, viewing challenges not as insurmountable obstacles but as opportunities for growth and transformation. Kali's energy, when harnessed correctly, can provide the strength, resilience, and determination necessary to navigate these complex times.

The concept of *Karma Yoga* , selfless action, finds particular resonance within the context of Kali Yuga. The performance of duty without attachment to results becomes a powerful tool for navigating the uncertainties and challenges of this age. By focusing on actions that contribute to the greater good, individuals can channel Kali's transformative energy into positive change, mitigating the negative aspects of this era. This active engagement counters the potential for apathy and despair, converting the challenges of Kali Yuga into opportunities for spiritual growth and societal betterment.

The spiritual practices associated with Kali's worship provide further insight into this transformative potential. The recitation of Kali's mantras, the meticulous creation and use of yantras, and the symbolic offerings all serve as powerful tools for connecting with her energy. These rituals are not merely outward expressions of devotion but inward journeys of self-discovery, enabling practitioners to confront their inner darkness and overcome their limitations. The mantras, through their vibratory energy, can help to break down mental barriers, while the yantras offer a visual framework for focusing the mind and deepening meditation. The offerings, through acts of self-sacrifice, symbolize a letting go of attachments, paving the way for spiritual liberation.

However, understanding Kali's connection to time and the Kali Yuga necessitates a nuanced approach. It's crucial to avoid simplistic interpretations that reduce Kali's role to mere destruction or solely associate the Kali Yuga with negativity. The complexities of both must be understood within a larger framework of cyclical time, acknowledging both the destructive and transformative aspects of Kali's energy and the potential for both decline and renewal within the Kali Yuga. The narratives of destruction are balanced by the narratives of renewal and transformation.

Furthermore, the focus should not solely remain on the individual level. The collective action to address the challenges of Kali Yuga—environmental destruction, social injustice, and political instability—is vital. Kali's energy can inspire collective action, promoting collaboration and cooperation in addressing global challenges. The individual's spiritual journey must be intertwined with a commitment to social responsibility and environmental stewardship. This collective effort, guided by ethical principles and a deep understanding of interconnectedness, represents a powerful response to the challenges of our times.

This approach challenges the conventional interpretations of Kali Yuga as an era of decline. By viewing the challenges of the age not as signs of inevitable decay but as opportunities for transformation, we can harness Kali's energy for positive change. The seemingly contradictory nature of Kali, the destroyer and the nurturer, reflects the inherent duality of existence. It is in recognizing and embracing this duality, in acknowledging both the destructive and the creative forces at play, that we can find a path to navigate the complexities of Kali Yuga and create a future that embraces both individual and collective transformation. The acceptance of this inherent duality is key to understanding the essence of Kali's energy and its relevance in navigating the contemporary world. The cyclical nature of time itself offers both the possibility of destruction and the inevitability of renewal. It is in this dynamic interplay that we find the true meaning of Kali and her place within the human experience in the Kali Yuga. The future, therefore, is not a predetermined trajectory, but a space for conscious creation, guided by the energy of Kali herself.

Kali in Modern Interpretations

The enduring power of Kali lies not only in her ancient scriptures and iconography but also in her capacity for continuous reinterpretation and appropriation within modern contexts. Her image, initially terrifying and profoundly spiritual, has migrated from the secluded sanctums of temples to the vibrant canvases of contemporary artists, the pages of bestselling novels, and even the screens of popular media. This evolution of Kali's representation reflects a complex interplay between reverence, misinterpretation, and the ever-shifting cultural landscape.

One striking aspect of Kali's modern interpretations is the shift in her perceived aesthetic. While traditional depictions often emphasize her ferocious aspects – bared fangs, multiple arms wielding weapons, a garland of severed heads – contemporary artists frequently explore a more nuanced portrayal. Some emphasize her fierce protective nature, her role as a destroyer of negativity and ignorance, rather than focusing solely on violence. These depictions often showcase Kali with a more serene or compassionate expression, even bordering on beauty, highlighting her role as a source of empowerment and liberation rather than pure terror. This altered aesthetic speaks volumes about changing cultural perceptions of femininity and power. The "fearsome mother" archetype gives way to a more complex understanding of a powerful feminine force that is both destructive and creative, terrifying and nurturing. This transformation isn't necessarily a rejection of traditional iconography, but rather an expansion of its meaning, reflecting the evolving understanding of gender roles and the diverse expressions of divine power.

The literary realm has also embraced Kali's image with varying degrees of reverence and accuracy. She has appeared as a central figure or a powerful symbol in numerous contemporary novels, poems, and short stories, showcasing the continued fascination with her powerful persona. These portrayals are often influenced by the author's individual perspective and understanding of the Goddess. Some remain faithful to the traditional narratives, emphasizing Kali's destructive power and its ultimate purpose in cosmic renewal.

Others weave her into completely new contexts, using her as a metaphor for societal change, female empowerment, or the darker aspects of human nature. In these diverse representations, Kali serves as a flexible symbol that can be adapted to suit a wide variety of themes and narratives. This flexibility, however, necessitates a careful approach, ensuring the nuances of her symbolism are not lost in the pursuit of literary effect. A superficial understanding can lead to misrepresentation, transforming the Goddess into a mere symbol of violence devoid of her deeper spiritual meaning.

Popular culture presents a more ambiguous relationship with Kali. While some artistic expressions remain sensitive and respectful, others trivialize or commercialize her image, reducing her to a mere aesthetic choice or a marketable commodity. This often involves the appropriation of her imagery without any real comprehension of her spiritual significance. The use of Kali's iconography in fashion, music videos, and other forms of media can contribute to a superficial understanding, separating her from her deep spiritual significance. This lack of contextual understanding risks turning the powerful Goddess into a mere fashion statement or trendy symbol, stripping her of the profound spiritual essence that has sustained her worship for millennia. This phenomenon highlights the crucial role of education and critical analysis in navigating the modern interpretations of spiritual figures, ensuring their reverence and preventing their misappropriation for trivial purposes.

The appropriation and potential misrepresentation of Kali requires critical examination. The ease with which her image can be detached from its spiritual context and employed for commercial or artistic purposes without a deep understanding necessitates careful consideration of its implications. The potential for misinterpretations extends beyond casual use; misconceptions have historically fueled inaccurate and prejudicial portrayals of Hinduism and its associated deities. This necessitates a conscious effort to understand and respect the religious and cultural context of Kali's symbolism. Scholarly interpretations, careful engagement with primary source materials (scriptures and traditional practices), and a commitment to avoiding sensationalist portrayals are crucial to ensure responsible engagement with Kali's image in modern contexts. Simply put, utilizing Kali's iconography requires a profound understanding of her symbolism, a respect for her religious context, and a conscious effort to avoid reducing her to a mere aesthetic or commercial element.

The evolution of Kali's representation also reveals a fascinating interplay between tradition and modernity. While some contemporary interpretations strive to maintain fidelity to traditional narratives and iconography, others deliberately challenge or reimagine established interpretations. This can lead to a rich tapestry of representations, showcasing the multifaceted nature of the Goddess and the ongoing dialogue between tradition and contemporary understandings. However, this process must be guided by a profound respect for the religious and spiritual context of Kali's worship, ensuring that any reinterpretation avoids trivialization or misrepresentation. It is crucial to remember that Kali is not merely an aesthetic motif but a powerful spiritual force with a deeply rooted history and a complex symbolism that demands thoughtful engagement.

The responsibility, therefore, lies with both creators and consumers of these modern interpretations. Artists and writers must approach their work with a deep understanding of Kali's multifaceted nature, avoiding simplistic or stereotypical representations. Audiences, in turn, must be critically engaged, seeking to understand the nuances of the symbolism, and recognizing the potential for misinterpretation and appropriation. This critical engagement necessitates a move beyond mere aesthetic appreciation to a deeper exploration of the spiritual and philosophical underpinnings of Kali's mythology. Only through such rigorous scrutiny can we ensure that Kali's powerful image continues to inspire and enlighten, rather than being misused or trivialised in the modern age.

Moreover, the scholarly community plays a vital role in addressing the challenges of modern interpretations. Academic discourse surrounding Kali should actively strive to provide a balanced perspective, contextualizing her image within its rich historical and religious framework, while acknowledging the validity of contemporary reinterpretations that arise from respectful engagement. Such scholarly work can serve as a corrective to misleading or superficial representations, offering a deeper understanding for both specialists and the wider public. This scholarly engagement extends beyond academic papers to include public lectures, workshops, and accessible publications aimed at broadening understanding and promoting respectful engagement with Kali and her complex symbolism.

This exploration of Kali's presence in the modern world highlights the continuous negotiation between tradition and contemporary expression. Her enduring power lies in her adaptability, her ability to be reinterpreted and reimagined across different cultures and contexts. However, this adaptability necessitates a cautious and respectful approach. The risk of misinterpretation and misappropriation necessitates critical vigilance, ensuring that the profound spiritual and philosophical significance of Kali is not lost in the translation from ancient scripture to contemporary expression. The future of Kali's portrayal depends on a conscious effort to balance artistic freedom with a deep understanding of her sacredness, ensuring that her image continues to inspire awe, reverence, and a deeper engagement with the complexities of the divine feminine. This conscious engagement, guided by both scholarly insight and spiritual sensitivity, is the key to ensuring that Kali's enduring presence in the modern world remains a source of inspiration, empowerment, and profound spiritual understanding, rather than a source of misrepresentation and trivialization. The careful navigation of these complexities is vital to preserving the integrity of Kali's powerful symbolism for generations to come. The path forward lies in fostering a responsible and respectful dialogue between tradition and contemporary expression, ensuring that the profound spiritual force of Kali continues to resonate with modern audiences while maintaining her sacred significance.

Kalis Relevance in Contemporary Society

Kali's enduring appeal in contemporary society stems from her potent symbolism of destruction and transformation, resonating deeply with the inherent challenges and uncertainties of the modern world. Her power is not merely one of annihilation, but rather a potent force for necessary change, a catalyst for breaking down old structures and making way for new beginnings. This resonates profoundly in a world grappling with constant flux – technological advancements, societal shifts, and environmental crises – all demanding adaptation and often, the dismantling of outdated systems.

Unlike benevolent deities who offer comfort and reassurance, Kali confronts us with the uncomfortable truths of existence. She demands we acknowledge the darkness within ourselves and the world around us, urging us to confront our shadows rather than shy away from them. This confrontation, though initially unsettling, is a crucial step towards growth and transformation. The act of destruction, in Kali's context, is not an act of nihilism, but rather a necessary prelude to creation. Just as the dismantling of old, decaying cells allows for the growth of new, healthy ones, so too does Kali's destructive energy pave the way for renewal and regeneration.

This understanding of Kali's transformative power offers a powerful framework for navigating personal challenges. When faced with adversity – the loss of a loved one, a career setback, or a personal crisis – the energy of Kali can be channeled to dismantle limiting beliefs, unhealthy patterns, and emotional baggage that hinder growth. Her fierce energy can empower individuals to confront their fears, release ingrained negativity, and embrace the opportunity for profound personal transformation that arises from these challenging experiences. Instead of succumbing to despair or clinging to the past, Kali's energy inspires us to acknowledge the pain, accept the change, and actively engage in the process of rebuilding and reimagining our lives.

The collective challenges faced by contemporary society also find resonance in Kali's symbolism. The global issues of climate change, social inequality, and political polarization require a radical shift in mindset and action. Kali's energy, in this context, can be seen as a call to dismantle the systems and structures that perpetuate these problems. It is an invitation to confront the root causes of suffering, to challenge the status quo, and to actively participate in creating a more just and sustainable world. This involves not only acknowledging the pervasive darkness and injustice but also summoning the courage and determination to actively dismantle the systems and mindsets that sustain them. This is not a passive process, but one demanding active engagement and a willingness to confront difficult truths.

The relevance of Kali's worship in contemporary society is evident in the burgeoning interest in her iconography and symbolism across diverse communities. While traditional worship continues in temples and ashrams, a new wave of engagement reflects the adaptability of her symbolism in modern settings. This expanded reach includes artists incorporating Kali's imagery in their work, exploring themes of female empowerment, challenging societal norms, and confronting the darker aspects of human nature. The versatility of Kali's symbolism allows for interpretations spanning feminist movements, environmental activism, and even discussions on the darker aspects of technology and its impact on society. Each of these interpretations is a testament to the enduring power of Kali to inspire and challenge, demonstrating her timeless relevance.

The empowerment inherent in Kali's energy resonates strongly with the contemporary feminist movement. Her fierce independence, her unwavering power, and her rejection of patriarchal structures make her a powerful symbol for women striving for autonomy and liberation. Kali's image challenges the traditional portrayal of the feminine as passive and subservient, instead embodying a strength and resilience that inspires women to claim their power and challenge societal norms. This symbolism transcends simple aesthetics and taps into a profound yearning for liberation from oppressive structures.

Furthermore, Kali's role as a destroyer of illusion and ignorance is increasingly relevant in a world saturated with information. In the age of misinformation and "fake news," Kali's energy offers a powerful tool to discern truth from falsehood, to cut through the noise, and to cultivate clarity and insight. Her ability to sever the head of ignorance empowers us to question dominant narratives, to challenge biases, and to seek truth, even when it is uncomfortable or challenging. This discernment is crucial in navigating the complex information landscape of the modern world, and Kali's symbolism provides a powerful framework for cultivating critical thinking and independent judgment.

Beyond these specific applications, Kali's relevance extends to the broader human experience of confronting mortality and impermanence. Her association with death and destruction forces us to acknowledge our own finitude and the transient nature of all things. This confrontation with impermanence, however challenging, can paradoxically be a source of profound liberation.

By accepting the inevitable cycle of birth, death, and rebirth, we can live more fully in the present moment, appreciating the preciousness of life and embracing the inherent changes it brings. This acceptance of impermanence, inspired by Kali, fosters a more mindful and intentional approach to life, allowing us to appreciate the transient beauty of existence.

The contemporary interpretations of Kali often demonstrate a nuanced understanding of her symbolism, moving beyond the simplistic association with mere violence. This evolution reflects a deeper appreciation of the complexities of her character and the multifaceted nature of divine power. Contemporary artists and writers often explore the more compassionate aspects of Kali, recognizing her role as a protector and nurturer, while acknowledging her capacity for destruction. This broadened understanding enriches Kali's image, offering a powerful framework for understanding the complexities of existence and the interplay between opposing forces.

The study of Kali's relevance in contemporary society underscores the continuing evolution of her interpretations and the ways in which her symbolism adapts to the changing needs and perspectives of humanity. She is not a static figure frozen in time, but rather a dynamic force whose energy continues to resonate with and inspire

individuals and communities across the globe. This enduring power reflects her inherent ability to speak to fundamental aspects of the human condition, offering a powerful framework for confronting challenges, embracing change, and ultimately, discovering profound personal and collective transformation. The ongoing engagement with Kali's symbolism demonstrates the vital role of myth and archetype in providing meaning and purpose in a constantly
evolving world. The continuous interpretation and reinterpretation of Kali's image reflect the ongoing dialogue between tradition and modernity, ensuring that her potent energy remains a source of inspiration and empowerment for generations to come. This dynamic exchange is essential to preserving the richness and depth of her symbolism while ensuring its relevance in the modern era. Her enduring legacy lies in her ability to both challenge and inspire, to destroy and create, demonstrating the cyclical nature of existence and the power of transformation.

Taras Manifestations and Iconography

Tara, the saviour, the liberator, manifests in a breathtaking array of forms, each carrying unique symbolism and iconographic details. Understanding these diverse manifestations is key to grasping the multifaceted nature of her power and compassion. Unlike a singular, static deity, Tara exists as a constellation of forms, each reflecting a specific aspect of her boundless energy and the diverse needs of her devotees. This multiplicity, rather than signifying fragmentation, highlights the adaptability and universality of her protective essence.

One of the most common distinctions lies between the White Tara and the Green Tara. White Tara, often depicted in a serene, seated posture, embodies the peaceful aspect of Tara, representing longevity, healing, and spiritual enlightenment. Her gentle gaze and peaceful demeanor offer solace and comfort, symbolizing the nurturing and protective qualities that guide seekers on the path to liberation. She is often associated with the overcoming of obstacles through patience, perseverance, and inner peace. The color white itself is symbolic of purity, clarity, and the absence of suffering, reflecting the tranquil state achieved through spiritual practice and the unwavering devotion to the path. The specific mudras (hand gestures) she employs further enhance her iconography, often representing specific blessings or actions, such as the bestowing of long life or the granting of wisdom. Detailed depictions often include her seated on a lotus flower, signifying purity and spiritual awakening, and adorned with elaborate jewelry and adornments that further enhance her regal appearance and signify her divine status.

In contrast, Green Tara, often depicted in a more dynamic posture, embodies the active and wrathful aspects of Tara, representing swift action and the overcoming of obstacles with decisive intervention. Her vibrant green hue symbolizes vitality, growth, and the powerful energy that swiftly removes obstacles and protects against harm. While her energy may appear fierce, it is ultimately directed toward protection and liberation. Unlike the gentle serenity of White Tara, Green Tara's energy is characterized by speed and decisiveness, a force that actively intervenes to prevent suffering and guide practitioners towards enlightenment. Her iconography often depicts her standing in a graceful yet powerful pose, ready to act swiftly on behalf of her devotees. The specific attributes and adornments she possesses can vary depending on regional variations and specific artistic styles, but generally, she is depicted with fierce energy yet retaining a compassionate heart. The wrathful aspect is not meant to inspire fear but rather to demonstrate the fierce determination and unwavering power she wields to protect her devotees from harm.

Beyond White and Green Tara, numerous other manifestations exist, each with their own specific attributes and iconographic features. These variations are not contradictory but complementary, adding depth and nuance to Tara's multifaceted nature. For instance, some traditions depict Kurukulla Tara, a fierce form associated with the accomplishment of desires and the fulfillment of spiritual aspirations. Her intense energy and determined gaze signify the active pursuit of spiritual goals, and her iconography often includes weaponry and other symbolic elements that represent her ability to overcome obstacles in the pursuit of enlightenment. The Kurukulla aspect emphasizes that the path to spiritual attainment is not always peaceful, and sometimes, forceful action is necessary to overcome inner and outer obstacles.

The Eight-Armed Tara is another important manifestation, representing the various aspects of Tara's power and the multitude of ways she aids her devotees. Each of her eight arms carries a specific attribute or implements, often symbolizing different blessings or actions, each one representing a different aspect of her protectiveness. The detailed iconography of each hand gesture and the symbolic objects held within her grasp require careful study to fully grasp their meaning. These symbolic elements offer deeper insights into the varied ways she can intervene to aid her followers, and are not merely decorative features.

The numerous other forms, including the Four-Armed Tara and the Twenty-One Taras, each reflect a particular aspect of her boundless compassion and power. These manifestations emphasize the vastness of Tara's influence and her capacity to adapt to the specific needs of her devotees. The iconographic features unique to each of these Taras provide an intricate tapestry of meanings, highlighting diverse paths to liberation and demonstrating her adaptability to different spiritual practices and contexts.

Furthermore, the artistic representations of Tara reflect the cultural and temporal contexts in which they were created. The evolution of her iconography across different artistic traditions, spanning Tibetan thangkas, Nepalese metalwork, and Indian paintings, reveals fascinating variations in her depiction. These variations are not merely aesthetic choices, but rather reflect the diverse interpretations and spiritual understandings of Tara within different schools of thought and regions. The symbolic elements often vary, reflecting unique cultural and contextual interpretations of her power and significance. For example, the specific jewelry, ornamentation, and other stylistic details can significantly impact the overall impression and meaning of the depiction.

Examining these diverse artistic styles reveals how Tara's essence has been interpreted and adapted across different times and regions. Comparing a Tibetan thangka depicting a fierce Green Tara with a Nepalese statue of a serene White Tara highlights these regional and stylistic differences, emphasizing the multifaceted nature of Tara's iconography and its ability to transcend cultural boundaries.

The textual descriptions of Tara in various tantric texts also play a crucial role in understanding her iconography. These texts often provide detailed accounts of her attributes, appearance, and symbolic significance, offering further insights into the deeper meanings behind her diverse manifestations. A careful analysis of these texts reveals the spiritual and philosophical foundations of her various forms, and provide a richer understanding of the iconographic elements. Comparing different textual accounts from various schools of thought reveals further variations in the interpretations of Tara's iconography.

In conclusion, Tara's iconography is far more than mere visual representation. It is a dynamic and evolving system of symbols, each detail carrying deep meaning and reflecting the multifaceted nature of her power and compassion. Her various manifestations, from the serene White Tara to the fiercely protective Green Tara and her numerous other forms, offer a profound exploration into the different paths to liberation and the vastness of her protective energy. The artistic representations and textual descriptions further enhance our understanding, demonstrating the adaptability and universality of Tara's essence across diverse traditions and cultural contexts. By studying these diverse representations, we gain a richer understanding of Tara's complex symbolism, and the enduring appeal of this powerful and compassionate goddess in the modern world. The continued study and interpretation of her iconography will undoubtedly uncover further layers of meaning, ensuring that the veneration of this pivotal deity remains relevant and inspiring for future generations.

Tara as a Protector and Guide

Tara's unwavering compassion extends beyond mere benevolent observation; she actively intervenes to protect and guide her devotees. This protectiveness isn't limited to warding off physical harm; it encompasses the entire spectrum of suffering, from material hardship to spiritual stagnation. She acts as a steadfast guide, illuminating the path to liberation and offering solace amidst life's turbulent currents. This active role sets her apart from many other deities, who may offer blessings but not direct intervention in worldly affairs. Tara, however, is deeply involved in the lives of her followers, offering aid and protection in tangible ways.

Her protective role is especially pronounced in Vajrayana Buddhism, where she holds a position of supreme importance. Often considered a manifestation of the Buddha's wisdom, Tara is revered as a powerful bodhisattva, embodying the compassionate qualities of enlightenment. In this context, her protection is not simply a matter of warding off evil forces; it is an active participation in the process of spiritual awakening. She acts as a mentor, a shield, and a source of inspiration, guiding practitioners along their spiritual journey and assisting them in overcoming the obstacles that impede their progress. The very act of invoking her name, reciting her mantras, and engaging in practices dedicated to her are believed to create a protective shield, deflecting negative energies and
attracting positive influences.

The mantras associated with Tara are powerful tools for protection and spiritual growth. The most common mantra, "Om Tare Tuttare Ture Soha," is a potent invocation that resonates with her compassionate essence. Repeating this mantra is believed to invoke Tara's blessings, creating a protective aura and fostering inner peace. The rhythmic repetition of the mantra is not merely a mechanical act; it is a meditative practice that connects the practitioner to Tara's energy, facilitating a deeper understanding of her compassionate nature. The therapeutic potential of this mantra is considerable, reducing stress and anxiety, and promoting a sense of calm and well-being. Many practitioners find that regular recitation of Tara's mantras not only provides a sense of protection but also improves mental clarity and emotional stability.

Furthermore, various practices are associated with Tara, each designed to enhance her protective influence. These practices range from simple visualizations and offerings to complex tantric rituals. Visualizing Tara's form, focusing on her compassionate gaze, and contemplating her attributes can evoke her protective energy.

Offering flowers, incense, or light to her images is a common practice that is seen as a way of showing devotion and invoking her blessings. More advanced practices, common within Vajrayana Buddhism, involve intricate visualizations, mudra gestures, and the recitation of specific mantras, leading to a deeper connection with Tara's energy and enhancing her protective influence.

The efficacy of these practices lies not merely in the ritualistic actions themselves but in the devotion and faith that accompany them. Tara's power is amplified by the practitioner's unwavering belief in her compassion and ability to protect. It is a relationship of mutual trust and reliance, where the devotee opens themselves to Tara's grace, and Tara, in turn, extends her protective energy. This faith is not blind acceptance but rather a deep understanding of Tara's nature and her capacity to aid those who call upon her. The effectiveness of Tara's protection is often described as being
proportionate to the sincerity and dedication of the practitioner.

The specific forms of Tara, each with unique attributes and associated practices, reflect the diverse aspects of her protection. White Tara, for example, is associated with longevity, healing, and peaceful resolution, offering protection from illness and promoting well-being. Her serene countenance and gentle energy provide solace and comfort, guiding practitioners towards a state of inner peace. In contrast, Green Tara, with her dynamic posture and vibrant energy, represents swift action and the overcoming of obstacles. She is invoked for immediate protection from harm, offering a powerful force that swiftly removes obstacles and ensures safety. These two forms, while differing in their approach, both represent Tara's unwavering commitment to protecting her
devotees.

The numerous other forms of Tara, such as Kurukulla Tara, Eight-

Armed Tara, and the Twenty-One Taras, each offer different forms of protection, tailored to specific needs and situations. Kurukulla Tara, for instance, is invoked for the fulfillment of desires and the attainment of spiritual goals, providing protection on the path to enlightenment. The Eight-Armed Tara, with her multiple arms wielding various implements, represents the multifaceted nature of her protection, offering aid in a wide range of circumstances. The Twenty-One Taras represent a more complete manifestation of her capabilities, each offering unique protection and guidance. These varied forms highlight the vastness of Tara's compassion and her ability to adapt to the diverse needs of her devotees.

The study of Tara's protective role extends beyond the realm of religious practice. Her iconography, mantras, and associated practices offer a rich source of therapeutic and psychological benefits. The act of visualizing her peaceful form, for example, can reduce anxiety and promote relaxation. The repetition of her mantras can induce a state of meditative calm, improving focus and concentration. The underlying principles of devotion and faith fostered through Tara's worship can cultivate inner strength and resilience, helping individuals to overcome challenges and navigate life's uncertainties. The therapeutic potential of Tara's practice is a powerful testament to the enduring relevance of her protective role in the modern world.

Moreover, the concept of Tara's protection transcends simple avoidance of harm. It involves a deeper process of spiritual growth and transformation. Tara's protection acts as a catalyst, propelling practitioners towards self-discovery and spiritual awakening. By overcoming obstacles and challenges with her assistance, devotees develop resilience, inner strength, and a deeper understanding of their own potential. This transformative aspect of Tara's protection is crucial, extending beyond mere physical safety to encompass the journey toward spiritual liberation. Her intervention isn't a passive act of shielding but an active participation in the devotee's path towards self-realization.

Tara's protective energy is not limited to individuals; it extends to the collective well-being of communities and even the entire world. In various traditions, she is invoked for the protection of nations, the prevention of calamities, and the promotion of peace and harmony. This broader scope of her protective power emphasizes her role as a benevolent force working for the overall betterment of humanity. This collective aspect of her protection speaks to the universal nature of her compassion, highlighting her role as a protector not just of individuals, but of the entire world.

The study of Tara's protective role, therefore, offers a profound and multifaceted exploration of compassion, guidance, and the transformative power of devotion. Her role extends far beyond a simple shield against harm; she serves as a guide, a teacher, and a source of unwavering support on the path to spiritual liberation and collective well-being. Her diverse forms, mantras, and practices offer a rich tapestry of approaches to seeking her protection, revealing the enduring power and relevance of her devotion in the contemporary world. The continued exploration of these practices will undoubtedly uncover further layers of meaning, revealing the depth and breadth of Tara's compassionate guidance and unwavering protection. Her enduring appeal and efficacy lie not only in her power to protect, but also in her ability to guide and transform, nurturing the spirit and fostering a journey towards lasting peace and liberation.

Taras Connection to Compassion and Liberation

Tara's compassionate nature is not merely a passive attribute; it's an active force that intervenes in the lives of her devotees, guiding them through the labyrinthine paths of existence towards liberation. This intervention isn't limited to shielding them from external harm; it encompasses a profound spiritual guidance, assisting in the dismantling of internal obstacles that hinder their progress on the path to enlightenment. The very essence of Tara is intertwined with the concept of *karuna* , the boundless compassion that seeks the alleviation of suffering for all beings. This compassion isn't a sentimental emotion, but a powerful force capable of transforming lives.

The Devi Gita, while not explicitly focused on Tara, provides a framework for understanding the power of divine compassion. The Devi, as the supreme manifestation of the divine feminine, embodies an all-encompassing compassion, a characteristic that is deeply mirrored in Tara's essence. The Devi Gita's emphasis on the transformative power of divine grace aligns perfectly with Tara's role as a guide and protector. The Devi's ability to bestow liberation, to transcend the cycle of samsara, is directly reflected in Tara's capacity to assist her devotees in achieving the same goal.

The unwavering devotion and surrender encouraged within the framework of the Devi Gita find a powerful echo in the trust and faith that are essential aspects of invoking Tara's aid.

In Vajrayana Buddhism, Tara's compassion is deeply entwined with the concept of Bodhisattvahood. As a Bodhisattva, Tara embodies the aspiration for enlightenment, not for herself alone, but for all sentient beings. This selfless dedication to the liberation of others is central to her being. Her compassion manifests not as mere sympathy but as active intervention, providing guidance and support to those striving for spiritual awakening. The numerous forms of Tara, each with specific attributes and mantras, highlight the multifaceted nature of this compassionate intervention. White Tara, for instance, embodies peaceful compassion, offering solace and healing. Green Tara, on the other hand, represents active compassion, swiftly intervening to overcome obstacles and offer immediate assistance.

The mantras associated with Tara are more than mere incantations; they are powerful tools for accessing her compassionate energy. The widely used mantra, "Om Tare Tuttare Ture Soha," is a potent invocation that resonates with her essence, connecting the practitioner to her compassionate power. The rhythmic repetition of the mantra fosters a meditative state, promoting inner peace and facilitating a deeper connection with Tara's energy. This connection is crucial, as it allows the devotee to tap into the vast reservoir of compassion Tara embodies. The mantra is not merely a verbal ritual; it's a pathway to accessing a state of heightened awareness and compassion, aligning the practitioner's energy with Tara's benevolent force.

Further deepening the understanding of Tara's compassionate influence are various visualizations and practices associated with her worship. Visualizing Tara's form, focusing on her compassionate gaze, and contemplating her attributes can evoke her protective energy and internalize her compassion. The act of offering flowers, incense, or light to her image is not just a symbolic gesture; it is an act of devotion that creates a channel for her grace to flow. These practices, when undertaken with sincerity and devotion, create a powerful resonance with Tara's compassionate energy, facilitating a transformation of the practitioner's inner landscape.

The efficacy of these practices is inseparable from the devotee's faith and devotion. Tara's power isn't autonomous; it's amplified by the unwavering belief and surrender of the practitioner. This faith isn't passive acceptance; it's an active engagement with Tara's energy, a deep understanding of her compassionate nature and a sincere trust in her capacity to guide and protect. This mutual relationship between the devotee and the deity fosters a powerful synergy, amplifying the transformative potential of the practice.
The deeper the devotion, the more profound the experience of Tara's compassionate guidance.

Beyond individual practice, Tara's compassion extends to the collective well-being of humanity. Various traditions depict her involvement in protecting communities, averting calamities, and promoting peace and harmony. This broader application of her compassionate energy highlights her role as a benevolent force working towards the betterment of all beings. Her influence transcends individual needs, encompassing the well-being of society as a whole. This aspect underlines the universal nature of her compassion, a boundless energy that seeks the alleviation of suffering on all levels.

The concept of liberation within the context of Tara's compassion goes beyond a simple escape from suffering; it involves a profound transformation of consciousness. Tara's guidance doesn't just shield her devotees from harm; it leads them on a transformative journey toward self-discovery and spiritual awakening. Through overcoming obstacles with her assistance, devotees cultivate resilience, inner strength, and a deeper understanding of their own potential. This transformative process is essential, leading to a liberation that extends far beyond the material realm.

Tara's assistance in achieving liberation encompasses various levels. It begins with shielding from immediate dangers and difficulties, providing refuge and solace amidst life's turmoil. It then progresses to a deeper level, assisting in the unraveling of karmic patterns and the transcendence of limiting beliefs. Finally, it culminates in a profound spiritual awakening, leading to a state of lasting peace and liberation from the cycle of samsara. This journey is not a passive one; it requires active participation from the devotee, a sincere commitment to the practice, and a deep trust in Tara's compassionate guidance.

The study of Tara's connection to compassion and liberation offers a profound exploration of the transformative power of faith, devotion, and the unwavering support of a compassionate divine presence. Her role extends far beyond a mere protector; she acts as a guide, a mentor, and a source of unwavering support on the journey to self-realization and ultimate liberation. Her enduring appeal lies in her ability to not only shield from harm but also to nurture, guide, and transform, leading her devotees towards lasting peace and the profound realization of their inherent Buddha-nature. The exploration of Tara's compassionate energy continues to unveil deeper layers of meaning, offering timeless wisdom and enduring guidance on the path to liberation. Her influence resonates powerfully in the modern world, offering solace, strength, and a path to spiritual growth amidst the complexities of contemporary life. The continued study of Tara's teachings offers a profound opportunity for spiritual growth and a deeper understanding of the boundless nature of compassion. Her enduring legacy is one of unwavering support and guidance on the path to liberation, a beacon of hope and compassion in a world often shrouded in suffering.

Tara in Different Cultural Contexts

Tara's adaptability as a deity is perhaps most strikingly evident in the diverse ways she is worshipped and represented across different cultural contexts. While her core essence – that of compassionate action leading to liberation – remains constant, the specific manifestations of this essence are remarkably varied, reflecting the unique cultural landscapes in which she is revered. The interplay between established religious narratives and local beliefs, customs, and traditions creates a rich tapestry of Tara worship, underscoring the fluid and dynamic nature of religious expression.

In Tibet, Tara holds a position of unparalleled importance within Vajrayana Buddhism. Here, she is not merely a goddess but an embodiment of the very essence of enlightenment, a powerful Bodhisattva whose compassion extends to all beings. The numerous forms of Tara found in Tibetan Buddhism, each with their unique attributes, mantras, and iconography, reflect the multifaceted nature of her compassionate action. White Tara, for instance, is often invoked for longevity, healing, and protection from harm, while Green Tara is associated with swift and decisive intervention in times of crisis. These variations are not merely aesthetic differences; they reflect the nuanced ways in which compassion can manifest in the lives of devotees, addressing their individual needs and circumstances. The elaborate mandalas and intricate rituals surrounding Tara's worship in Tibetan Buddhism highlight the profound reverence and spiritual significance she holds within this tradition. The use of specific hand gestures (mudras), symbolic objects (vajras, bells), and the recitation of specific mantras in conjunction with visualizations further personalize the devotee's engagement with Tara's energy. The integration of Tara's worship into the broader context of Tibetan Buddhist philosophy and practice emphasizes her role as a powerful force for spiritual growth and liberation. The lineage of Tara's teaching and empowerment ceremonies are carefully preserved, passed down through generations of lamas, safeguarding the authenticity and integrity of her practice. This emphasis on lineage reinforces the importance of authentic guidance in accessing Tara's transformative power.

Moving eastward, into Nepal, Tara's worship blends seamlessly with the indigenous animistic beliefs and practices of the region. While retaining the core tenets of Buddhist teachings, the local interpretations of Tara often incorporate elements of folk religion, resulting in a unique syncretic form of worship. This fusion is evident in the various local manifestations of Tara, often depicted with attributes specific to the region's cultural landscape. These local forms often integrate elements of nature worship, reflecting the deep connection between the Nepali people and their natural environment. In this context, Tara is not merely a divine being; she is a protector of the land, a guardian of the community, and a symbol of the harmonious relationship between humans and nature.

The festivals and rituals associated with Tara in Nepal are often characterized by vibrant colors, music, and dance, reflecting the lively and expressive nature of the local culture. These celebrations are not just religious events; they are occasions for community bonding, reaffirming social cohesion and cultural identity. The incorporation of local traditions into Tara's worship demonstrates the remarkable adaptability of her symbolism to different cultural settings.

The worship of Tara in India, particularly within the Himalayan regions and those bordering Nepal, shows a similar blending of Buddhist and Hindu traditions. While Tara's origins are firmly rooted in Buddhism, her image and attributes have been readily absorbed into the wider Hindu pantheon, often being identified with various aspects of the Devi, the Divine Mother. This syncretism underscores the fluidity of religious boundaries and the capacity of religious beliefs to adapt and evolve over time. The integration of Tara into the Hindu tradition further highlights the universality of her compassionate essence, demonstrating that her message resonates across different religious frameworks. In some regions of India, Tara's iconography merges with local folk deities, resulting in unique hybrid forms, showcasing the dynamic interaction between different religious systems. This fusion often strengthens local identities while retaining the fundamental compassionate attributes associated with Tara.

In contrast to the integration of Tara into established religious structures, her presence in certain pockets of South and Southeast

Asia sometimes presents a more folk-religious aspect. Here, Tara might be worshipped not as a prominent figure within an established religious system but as a local protector, associated with specific geographical areas, natural elements, or particular aspects of life, such as health, wealth, or prosperity. Her image might be simpler, less elaborate than the detailed depictions found in Tibetan or Nepalese art, reflecting the localized and less formalized nature of her worship. These less formal practices often highlight a more immediate, personal connection between the devotee and the deity, reflecting a more direct response to community needs. The rituals and offerings associated with these localized forms of Tara often reflect the particular concerns of the community, ranging from protecting crops and livestock to ensuring the well-being of individuals and families. This reflects the adaptability of Tara's symbolism to address a vast array of human needs and concerns.

The variations in Tara's representation extend beyond her iconography; they also encompass the mantras and rituals associated with her worship. While the "Om Tare Tuttare Ture Soha" mantra is widely known and used, different regions and traditions have developed their own specific mantras and invocations, reflecting the unique cultural nuances and spiritual preferences of the devotees. These variations in practice demonstrate the rich diversity within Tara's worship while preserving the essence of her compassionate power. The practice of visualization, a cornerstone of Tara's worship, also varies, with different traditions emphasizing different aspects of her form and attributes. These differences reflect the diverse ways in which individuals connect with the divine, demonstrating the flexibility and inclusivity of Tara's worship. The fluidity of these practices speaks to the adaptable nature of the spiritual connection with Tara, capable of meeting the diverse needs and expressions of devotion across various cultures.

The adaptability of Tara's symbolism doesn't imply a lack of coherence or consistency in her essence. On the contrary, the ability of her image and practice to adapt to different cultural settings highlights the universality of her compassionate message and its enduring relevance across diverse contexts. The variations observed in her worship do not diminish her core attributes; rather, they enrich our understanding of the multifaceted nature of compassion and its varied manifestations. The different forms of Tara, the diverse mantras, and the regionally specific rituals all testify to the richness and complexity of her legacy, demonstrating her capacity to resonate with people from diverse cultural backgrounds and spiritual perspectives. This adaptability is not a sign of inconsistency but a testament to the profound and enduring power of her compassionate essence. The study of Tara's presence in various cultures offers a valuable insight into the dynamic nature of religious expression and the ability of powerful symbols to adapt and evolve while retaining their core meaning.

The different cultural contexts of Tara's worship offer a fascinating case study in the interplay between global religious traditions and localized beliefs. It underscores the dynamic nature of religious expression and the capacity of spiritual symbols to adapt and evolve while retaining their core essence. Tara's enduring popularity across vast geographical areas, from the high Himalayas to the plains of India and beyond, demonstrates the universality of her compassionate message, providing a powerful example of religious syncretism and adaptation. The study of Tara's diverse manifestations reveals a depth of spiritual meaning and practice that far transcends geographical boundaries, offering valuable insights into the enduring power of faith and devotion. The rich tapestry of Tara's worship, woven from diverse cultural threads, offers a compelling example of the adaptability and enduring relevance of religious traditions in the modern world. The continued study of Tara's cultural expressions promises to reveal further layers of meaning, highlighting the profound and transformative power of compassion in a world that desperately needs it. The ongoing exploration of Tara's influence across various cultures serves as a testament to the enduring appeal of a deity whose essence resonates across time and across different belief systems.

Taras Relevance in the Modern World

Tara's enduring appeal lies not merely in her ancient origins and rich mythology, but also in her remarkable capacity to resonate with the anxieties and aspirations of the modern world. Her compassionate energy, readily accessible through prayer, meditation, and ritual, offers solace and strength in the face of contemporary challenges. While her iconography and mantras may vary across cultures, the underlying message of liberation remains powerfully consistent. In an era defined by rapid technological advancement, global interconnectedness, and escalating environmental concerns, Tara's protective and guiding presence continues to offer a beacon of hope and resilience.

One of the most significant aspects of Tara's relevance in the modern world lies in her potent symbolism of overcoming obstacles. The very etymology of her name, derived from the Sanskrit word *tarā*, meaning "she who liberates," points to her inherent power to guide individuals through difficult times. In a world often characterized by uncertainty and instability, Tara's unwavering compassion offers a sense of security and assurance. Her devotees find solace in her protective energy, perceiving her as a guiding force capable of navigating them through life's inevitable trials. This is particularly relevant in a globalized world where individuals often face challenges related to displacement, migration, and cultural adaptation. Tara's image serves as a reminder that even amidst adversity, there is hope for liberation and transformation.

Tara's message of compassion also holds significant relevance in addressing the prevalent social injustices and inequalities that plague modern societies. Her unwavering empathy for all beings transcends boundaries of race, religion, gender, and social status. In a world marked by conflict, discrimination, and systemic oppression, Tara's compassionate presence serves as a powerful counterpoint, inspiring acts of kindness, empathy, and social justice. Devotees may find inspiration in her example to engage in acts of service, promoting peace and harmony within their communities and beyond. This active engagement with Tara's teachings can lead to meaningful societal changes, fostering a more just and equitable world for all. Her image can inspire action, urging followers to actively address the challenges of their time and work towards a more compassionate society.

Furthermore, Tara's symbolism resonates deeply with the growing awareness of environmental issues that define the 21st century. In many of her manifestations, she is closely associated with nature, often depicted amidst lush landscapes or with elements of the natural world integrated into her iconography. This connection underscores the importance of environmental stewardship and highlights the interconnectedness of all beings. In a time when climate change and environmental degradation pose existential threats, Tara's message serves as a timely reminder of the need for ecological responsibility and sustainable practices. Devotees can find inspiration in her protective energy to become active participants in preserving the environment, fostering a more harmonious relationship between humanity and the natural world.

This echoes the ancient traditions where Tara is revered as a protector of the land and its inhabitants.

The practice of Tara's worship, too, finds resonance in the modern context. The recitation of her mantras, particularly the well-known "Om Tare Tuttare Ture Soha," offers a powerful tool for stress reduction and emotional regulation. In our increasingly fast-paced and demanding world, finding moments of calm and inner peace is essential for maintaining mental and emotional well-being. The repetitive chanting of the mantra can act as a meditation practice, helping individuals to focus their minds, quiet their anxieties, and cultivate a sense of serenity. This practice not only fosters individual well-being but also cultivates a sense of connection to something larger than oneself, facilitating spiritual growth and personal transformation. The accessibility of this practice, needing only a quiet space and a focused mind, makes it adaptable to the lifestyles of individuals across varied settings.

The visualization practices associated with Tara's worship also provide a valuable tool for modern individuals seeking self-improvement and personal growth. The act of visualizing Tara's compassionate presence can serve as a powerful means of cultivating inner strength, resilience, and self-compassion. By focusing on her attributes of wisdom, courage, and unwavering kindness, individuals can draw upon her energy to overcome personal challenges and develop a more positive self-image. This focus on self-cultivation complements other contemporary wellness practices, reinforcing the message of self-care and personal responsibility in navigating life's complexities. This approach complements broader mindfulness practices and contributes to an overall sense of well-being.

The adaptability of Tara's symbolism and practices across different cultural contexts also reflects her relevance in an increasingly globalized world. Her multifaceted manifestations – from the fierce warrior goddess to the gentle mother figure – illustrate the ability of religious symbolism to address a wide range of human experiences and needs. In a world characterized by cultural diversity and religious pluralism, Tara's capacity to transcend boundaries and resonate with individuals from diverse backgrounds speaks to the universality of her compassionate message. The blending of Tara's worship with various local traditions underscores the adaptability of spiritual practices in addressing the unique concerns of different communities. This inherent flexibility makes Tara's message more accessible and relatable to a wider audience, fostering a sense of inclusivity and shared spiritual experience.

The modern world, often characterized by uncertainty and rapid change, requires individuals to develop resilience, compassion, and a strong sense of inner peace. Tara, in her many forms and through diverse practices, offers a pathway towards achieving these essential qualities. Her unwavering compassion, protective energy, and potent symbolism provide a source of strength and guidance in navigating life's challenges. The ongoing relevance of Tara's message lies in her ability to address the profound human needs for security, hope, and liberation, thereby empowering individuals to live more meaningful and fulfilling lives in the modern era.

The accessibility of Tara's teachings, whether through mantra recitation, visualization practices, or engaging with her diverse iconography, makes her a powerful force for positive change in the present day. Her compassionate energy, capable of inspiring both personal transformation and social action, continues to offer profound insights and transformative power to those who seek her guidance. Tara's enduring relevance is not merely a matter of historical significance; rather, it is a testament to her ability to address the fundamental spiritual and emotional needs of humanity across time and cultures. Her teachings provide a timeless framework for navigating the complexities of modern life with compassion, resilience, and a deep sense of purpose. The continued exploration and study of Tara and her teachings promise to reveal further layers of meaning and relevance in the ever-evolving context of our current times, making her a compelling figure for study and devotion. The profound wisdom embedded within Tara's symbolism and practices continues to offer a beacon of hope and empowerment to individuals seeking spiritual solace and social transformation.

Tripura Sundaris Iconography and Symbolism

Tripura Sundari, the third Mahavidya, presents a captivating enigma within the pantheon of Hindu goddesses. Unlike the fierce and overtly powerful imagery associated with some of her sisters, Tripura Sundari embodies a more subtle, yet profoundly potent, form of divine energy. Her iconography, rich in symbolism, offers a nuanced exploration of beauty, grace, power, and the ultimate realization of the divine feminine principle. Understanding her visual representation is key to grasping the depth of her spiritual essence.

One of the most striking aspects of Tripura Sundari's iconography is her depiction as the epitome of beauty. She is often portrayed as a young, radiant woman, possessing exquisite features, graceful posture, and an alluring presence. This representation doesn't simply convey physical attractiveness; it symbolizes the ultimate beauty of the cosmos, the inherent perfection and harmony that underlies all creation. This beauty is not superficial; it is a reflection of the divine, an expression of the supreme consciousness manifesting in its most aesthetically pleasing form. Different artistic schools subtly vary this portrayal. Some emphasize a more delicate, almost ethereal beauty, while others highlight a more vibrant, regal radiance. These variations, however, are not contradictory; they represent the multifaceted nature of the divine, capable of manifesting in diverse yet equally valid forms.

The color most frequently associated with Tripura Sundari is red, or sometimes a deep crimson. This hue is not merely an aesthetic choice; it carries significant symbolic weight. Red is associated with energy, passion, vitality, and the primal life force. In Tantric traditions, it's often linked to Kundalini Shakti, the potent energy residing at the base of the spine. The red color in Tripura Sundari's depictions emphasizes her connection to this powerful energy, highlighting her ability to awaken and channel this force for spiritual transformation. The use of red also connects her with the concept of *rajas* in the three Gunas – the inherent qualities of nature– signifying action, movement, and dynamism, all necessary aspects in the path of spiritual evolution. The intensity of the red can also vary, sometimes hinting at a more fiery, passionate energy, while at other times suggesting a more subtle, yet equally powerful, inner radiance.

Another prominent feature of Tripura Sundari's iconography is the presence of various adornments. She is often depicted wearing exquisite jewelry, fine garments, and carrying symbolic objects. These ornaments are not simply decorative; they hold profound meaning, representing different aspects of her power and attributes. The jewelry, for example, can symbolize the richness and abundance of the cosmos, the splendor of creation, and the inherent beauty of the divine. The garments might be richly embroidered, hinting at the complexity and multifaceted nature of the divine experience. The specific objects she holds – such as lotuses, weapons, or other auspicious symbols – further enhance the narrative of her divine essence, adding another layer of meaning to her visual representation. Detailed analyses of these adornments and associated symbolism could constitute a study of their own, with scholars continuing to uncover new interpretations from their nuances.

The number three is often associated with Tripura Sundari, reflected both in her name – Tripura meaning "three cities" – and in her visual representations. This number represents the three gunas (Sattva, Rajas, and Tamas), the three worlds (Bhu, Bhuva, and Sva), and the threefold nature of reality (creation, preservation, and destruction). Her connection to the number three emphasizes her holistic nature, her ability to encompass and transcend the limitations of duality. Artistically, this might be portrayed through triptych arrangements of images, or by subtly incorporating the number three into her adornments or the composition of the artwork. Careful study reveals how these artistic decisions are not accidental; rather, they are carefully chosen to amplify the symbolic significance of her form.

Her posture and overall demeanor also contribute to the rich symbolism. She may be depicted in a seated posture radiating grace and tranquility, or in a standing posture that exudes strength and power. These varying postures aren't arbitrary but rather reflect her multifaceted nature, her ability to embody both the passive and active principles of creation. A seated posture may emphasize her contemplative nature, her ability to guide and nurture, while a standing posture might highlight her power to protect and liberate.

The subtle tilt of her head, the gentle curve of her lips, the positioning of her hands – all these elements contribute to the overall narrative, giving insights into her various facets. Even minute details in various artistic schools show a consistent underlying philosophy but with a unique expression.

Tripura Sundari is also frequently depicted in the context of her consort, Shiva. This connection signifies the union of the divine masculine and feminine principles, the ultimate harmony and integration of opposing forces. The depiction of this union emphasizes the transformative potential inherent in the relationship between Shiva and Shakti. This is not a simple union of equals, but a dynamic interplay where Shiva's consciousness provides the stage for Shakti's energy to manifest. The subtle nuances in these depictions, ranging from a tender embrace to a powerful, almost fierce togetherness, add significant depth to the interpretation of her iconography. This interplay is central to understanding the tantric philosophy underlying her worship.

Different schools of art have their own particular interpretations and styles of depicting Tripura Sundari. The variations in iconography across regional and temporal differences highlight the evolving understanding and interpretation of her divine form. Some schools emphasize her regal bearing and adorned magnificence, others showcase a more intimate and compassionate aspect, and still others focus on her fierce protective power. These diverse representations do not contradict each other; rather, they complement each other, illustrating the boundless and multifaceted nature of her divinity. Each artistic interpretation offers a unique lens through which to understand the complexities of this powerful goddess.

The symbolism within Tripura Sundari's iconography goes beyond simply visual representation. The careful study of her various attributes – her color, adornments, posture, and relationship to Shiva – offers a profound meditation on the nature of the divine feminine, the power of creation, and the path of spiritual transformation. Her beauty is not merely superficial but reflects the inherent perfection of the cosmos. Her energy, represented by the color red, symbolizes the potent life force within us all. Her adornments signify the richness and complexity of the divine experience. And her union with Shiva exemplifies the ultimate harmony of opposing forces. The analysis of her iconography serves as a powerful tool for spiritual understanding, offering a pathway toward realizing our own divine potential.

In the current era, understanding Tripura Sundari's iconography remains as relevant as ever. Her representation of beauty, power, and grace resonates deeply with contemporary aspirations for wholeness and balance. In a world characterized by rapid change and increasing complexity, her image offers a visual anchor – a reminder of the inherent harmony and perfection that underlies even the most challenging circumstances. Her embodiment of both fierce protection and nurturing compassion can provide strength and solace in facing life's difficulties. The diverse representations across different schools of art highlight the adaptability and inclusiveness of the divine, reminding us that the path to spiritual realization can be approached in many ways. Therefore, the continued study and contemplation of Tripura Sundari's iconography provides an invaluable resource for spiritual growth and self-discovery in the 21st century and beyond. Her image becomes a powerful tool for meditation and contemplation, guiding us towards the realization of our inherent divinity. It is a living testament to the enduring power of the divine feminine principle in the ever-evolving landscape of spiritual understanding. The ongoing engagement with her symbolism allows for a continuous rediscovery of her profound message, reinforcing its timeless relevance and profound impact.

Tripura Sundaris Role in Tantric Practices

Tripura Sundari's profound beauty and grace, as explored in her iconography, are not merely aesthetic qualities; they are integral to her role within Tantric practices. Her worship transcends passive admiration; it's an active engagement with a potent divine energy designed to facilitate spiritual transformation. This engagement primarily occurs through the utilization of specific rituals, mantras, and yantras, all meticulously crafted to channel her energy and unlock hidden potentials within the practitioner.

One of the core aspects of Tripura Sundari's Tantric practice involves the use of *mantras* . These sacred sounds, when chanted with proper pronunciation, intention, and understanding, are believed to resonate with the divine energy of Tripura Sundari, activating specific chakras and facilitating spiritual awakening. The repetition of her mantra is not merely a mechanical act; it's a process of aligning oneself with her vibration, gradually transforming the practitioner's consciousness. Different schools and lineages within Tantra may employ variations in the mantra used, reflecting diverse interpretations and traditions. However, the underlying principle remains the same: the mantra acts as a conduit, connecting the practitioner to the divine power of Tripura Sundari. The potency of the mantra is amplified by the practitioner's unwavering focus and devotion, leading to a deeper connection with the goddess. The experience is often described as a gradual purification of the mind, a process that calms mental chatter, replacing it with a profound sense of serenity and inner peace. Advanced practitioners may report more profound experiences, such as visions, profound shifts in perspective, or a heightened sense of connection with the divine.

Further enhancing the effectiveness of mantra recitation are the accompanying *yantras* . These geometric diagrams are not mere symbols; they are complex energetic configurations designed to focus and direct the energy of the mantra. Each line, angle, and symbol within the yantra is imbued with symbolic meaning, creating a visual representation of Tripura Sundari's divine essence. The practitioner often meditates upon the yantra, allowing its complex geometry to imprint itself on their consciousness. This visual meditation deepens the impact of the mantra, further refining the practitioner's subtle energy body and increasing their receptivity to the divine. The specific yantra used in conjunction with Tripura Sundari's mantra may vary depending on the lineage and tradition.

However, the general principle of utilizing the yantra as a visual focus point remains constant, augmenting the mantra's power and facilitating a deeper meditative state. The intricacy of the yantra demands careful and focused attention, forcing the practitioner to quiet the mind and allow for a deep immersion into the sacred geometry.

The rituals associated with Tripura Sundari are multifaceted and complex, varying considerably across different Tantric traditions. They often involve elaborate preparations, including specific timings, offerings, and meticulous adherence to prescribed procedures. These rituals are not performed mechanically; they are acts of devotion, aimed at creating a sacred space where the practitioner can connect with the divine energy of Tripura Sundari. Offerings, ranging from flowers and incense to specific types of food and drink, are presented to the goddess as a sign of reverence and gratitude. These offerings are not simply material items; they represent the practitioner's offering of their own energy and devotion to the divine.

The performance of *puja*, a ritualistic form of worship, is a central aspect of Tripura Sundari's Tantric practice. Puja involves a series of carefully orchestrated steps, each with its own symbolic significance. The practitioner's involvement is not merely external; rather, it involves an internal process of self-purification and spiritual growth. As the practitioner performs the puja, they are simultaneously purifying their own energy body, aligning themselves with the divine energy of Tripura Sundari. The elaborate process is often seen as a microcosm of the larger spiritual journey, mirroring the practitioner's own transformation. The experience is deeply personal and transformative, leaving the practitioner with a profound sense of peace, connection, and renewed spiritual purpose.

Beyond specific rituals, mantras, and yantras, the Tantric practice involving Tripura Sundari emphasizes the importance of *sadhana*, a dedicated spiritual practice or discipline. This involves a commitment to self-discipline, ethical conduct, and constant self-reflection. Sadhana is not merely a set of prescribed actions; it's a journey of self-discovery, involving the progressive purification of the practitioner's mind and body. The goal is not simply to achieve spiritual power; rather, it is to realize one's inherent divinity and achieve liberation (moksha). This integration of ritualistic practices with personal spiritual development provides a comprehensive framework for spiritual growth, ensuring the practitioner is not simply performing rituals but undergoing a genuine internal transformation.

The study of these Tantric practices requires a deep understanding of their symbolic significance and their underlying philosophical framework. It is not simply a matter of mechanically following prescribed steps; it's about engaging with a complex system of symbolism and ritual that aims to awaken the practitioner's latent spiritual potential. The effectiveness of these practices is dependent not only on the correct performance of rituals but also on the practitioner's sincere devotion, self-discipline, and unwavering commitment to spiritual growth. These practices are not meant to be taken lightly; they demand a deep commitment, patience, and a willingness to engage in self-reflection and personal transformation. Improper execution or lack of sincere devotion can lead to negative results, which underscores the importance of guidance from qualified teachers experienced in these practices.

The application of Tripura Sundari's energy in Tantric practices extends beyond personal spiritual development. Certain practices aim to harness her energy for specific purposes, such as healing, protection, or achieving specific goals. However, the use of such practices requires a deep understanding of ethical considerations and the potential consequences of manipulating energies that are profoundly powerful. The misuse of such knowledge is viewed as a serious transgression, and responsibility for its ethical application rests squarely with the practitioner. The subtle nuances of intention and the ethical ramifications associated with these advanced practices demand a high level of spiritual maturity and responsibility.

Furthermore, the integration of Tripura Sundari's principles within the broader context of Tantra emphasizes the balance between the active and passive, the dynamic and the serene. While some Mahavidyas are associated with more overtly powerful and fierce aspects of the divine, Tripura Sundari embodies a more subtle and refined approach, representing the beauty and grace that underpins the transformative power of the divine feminine. Her role highlights that spiritual growth is not simply about accumulating power but about cultivating inner harmony, balance, and a deep understanding of the interconnectedness of all things.

In conclusion, Tripura Sundari's role in Tantric practices is central to the understanding of the Devi Mahatmyam and the spiritual path it illuminates. Her practices are not merely rituals; they are a journey of self-discovery, transformation, and union with the divine feminine. The use of mantras, yantras, and rituals, when performed with proper understanding, intention, and devotion, can facilitate profound spiritual growth and lead the practitioner towards self-realization. The continued study and practice of these traditions provide a pathway toward a deeper understanding of the goddess, her symbolism, and her empowering influence on the spiritual journey. This engagement is not merely academic; it's a living practice that demands commitment, responsibility, and a lifelong pursuit of spiritual understanding. The ongoing exploration of her multifaceted nature continues to reveal new layers of depth,
ensuring her enduring relevance in the contemporary spiritual landscape.

Tripura Sundari and the Concept of Divine Beauty

Tripura Sundari, the supremely beautiful Goddess, transcends the conventional understanding of aesthetics. Her beauty is not merely a superficial attribute; it's a potent symbol imbued with profound spiritual significance. It's a beauty that radiates from within, a luminosity that illuminates the path toward spiritual realization. This divine beauty serves as a powerful catalyst for transformation, drawing the devotee inward on a journey of self-discovery and ultimately, union with the divine. Understanding Tripura Sundari's beauty requires moving beyond a purely sensual appreciation to grasp its deeper, mystical essence.

The scriptures depict Tripura Sundari's beauty using rich, evocative language, often employing metaphors and similes to convey its inexpressible nature. Her form is described as perfect, flawless, radiating a captivating aura that transcends the limitations of physical description. Her radiant complexion, often likened to molten gold or the morning sun, symbolizes enlightenment and the inner brilliance of the awakened self. Her eyes, described as captivating and luminous, often represent the wisdom and insight that accompany spiritual growth. Her graceful posture and elegant movements express the effortless ease and poise that characterize a life lived in harmony with the divine. This is not simply a visual beauty; it encompasses the totality of her being – a harmonious blend of physical perfection, radiant energy, and boundless compassion.

The association of Tripura Sundari with beauty is not arbitrary. In the context of Tantric philosophy, beauty acts as a powerful instrument of spiritual transformation. The experience of aesthetic beauty, whether through art, nature, or the divine form of a goddess like Tripura Sundari, can trigger profound emotional and spiritual responses. It can awaken a sense of wonder, awe, and reverence, opening the heart and mind to higher realms of consciousness. This aesthetic experience serves as a gateway, gently guiding the devotee towards deeper states of meditation and spiritual awareness. The captivating allure of Tripura Sundari's beauty serves to draw the devotee's attention away from the distractions of the material world, gently leading them toward a state of meditative focus and introspection.

However, the concept of beauty within the context of Tripura Sundari's worship is not merely about passive appreciation. It's an active engagement, a process of aligning oneself with the divine energy that her beauty embodies. The experience of her beauty isn't solely visual; it's an internal transformation, a gradual refinement of the practitioner's consciousness. This refinement mirrors the process of spiritual growth, a gradual stripping away of the illusions and attachments that obscure the true self. The practitioner's journey, in this context, becomes a process of becoming more beautiful, internally as well as externally, in reflection of the divine beauty they strive to attain.

The visual representations of Tripura Sundari, found in her various iconographic forms, serve as powerful tools in this process. These depictions, often intricate and richly symbolic, are not merely artistic expressions; they are carefully constructed visual aids designed to focus and direct the practitioner's attention and energy. The colors, gestures, and symbols utilized in these representations carry deeper symbolic meanings, each component serving to enhance the meditative experience and facilitate spiritual transformation. Studying and contemplating these images isn't simply an aesthetic exercise; it's a form of spiritual practice, a pathway to deeper connection with the goddess.

Moreover, the very act of creating these images, whether through painting, sculpture, or other art forms, is itself a form of Tantric practice. The artist, through their devotion and skill, channels the divine energy of Tripura Sundari, imbuing the artwork with her potent essence. The resulting artwork is more than a mere artistic creation; it's a sacred object, a vessel containing the divine energy of the goddess. Engaging with this artwork, through contemplation, meditation, or puja, becomes a potent means of accessing and connecting with Tripura Sundari's power.

The experience of beauty in the context of Tripura Sundari extends beyond the visual. It encompasses the auditory, olfactory, and even the tactile senses, creating a multi-sensory experience designed to immerse the practitioner completely in the divine presence. The sounds of devotional chants and mantras, the fragrance of incense and flowers offered during puja, the texture of sacred objects—all contribute to a holistic engagement that enhances the meditative state and facilitates spiritual growth. This multi-sensory immersion creates a powerful and transformative experience, leaving a lasting impression on the practitioner's consciousness.

This comprehensive approach to beauty highlights its profound spiritual impact. It is not simply a superficial appeal; it serves as a conduit, connecting the practitioner to the divine energy of Tripura Sundari and fostering a profound transformation of consciousness. Through the careful engagement with her iconography, mantras, and rituals, the practitioner gradually transcends the limitations of the physical world, experiencing a deeper connection with their inner self and the ultimate reality. This spiritual blossoming, this internal transformation, is the true manifestation of Tripura Sundari's divine beauty – a beauty that transcends the limitations of the physical and resides in the heart of the devotee.

The concept of divine beauty in Tripura Sundari's context also points to the interconnectedness of all things. Her beauty is not isolated; it's a reflection of the underlying harmony and unity that pervades the cosmos. Her form embodies the perfect balance and integration of all aspects of existence, representing the ultimate synthesis of opposites. This inherent harmony, reflected in her captivating beauty, reminds the devotee of the underlying unity of all creation, fostering a sense of interconnectedness and compassion that extends beyond the self.

Furthermore, Tripura Sundari's beauty challenges the conventional notions of beauty often imposed by societal standards. Her beauty is not confined to a particular physical form or aesthetic ideal; it transcends such limitations, representing a higher, more universal beauty that resides within the heart and soul. This universal beauty is accessible to all, regardless of their physical appearance or social status, underscoring the inclusivity and universality of spiritual practice. It emphasizes the intrinsic beauty that resides within each individual, waiting to be discovered and cultivated through spiritual practice and self-realization.

The exploration of Tripura Sundari's beauty thus becomes a journey of self-discovery. By engaging with her divine form and the symbols associated with her, the practitioner embarks on a path of self-transformation, gradually refining their inner being and aligning themselves with the divine. This journey is not easy; it demands dedication, discipline, and a willingness to confront and overcome inner limitations. But the reward is profound – the realization of one's own inherent divinity, reflected in the radiant beauty of the awakened self.

In conclusion, Tripura Sundari's beauty is not a mere aesthetic quality; it's a potent spiritual force, a catalyst for transformation, and a symbol of the inherent divinity within each individual. Her radiant form serves as a powerful reminder of the beauty that lies within us all, waiting to be revealed through dedicated spiritual practice and a deep engagement with the divine feminine.

Understanding the multifaceted nature of her beauty opens the door to a deeper appreciation of the Tantric path and the transformative power of the divine feminine energy. The continued contemplation of her beauty becomes a continuous journey of self-discovery, leading to the blossoming of the inner radiance that mirrors the radiant beauty of Tripura Sundari herself. The exploration of her beauty is, ultimately, a journey towards the realization of our own inherent divinity and the ultimate harmony of the self with the divine.

Tripura Sundari in Different Religious Traditions

The multifaceted nature of Tripura Sundari's worship extends beyond the confines of a single religious tradition. While Shaktism forms the bedrock of her veneration, her presence resonates profoundly within Saivism and Vaishnavism, albeit with nuanced variations in her attributes and symbolism. Understanding these diverse interpretations unveils the syncretic nature of Hindu religious thought and the remarkable adaptability of the divine feminine principle.

Within Shaktism, Tripura Sundari reigns supreme as the ultimate manifestation of Adi Shakti, the primordial cosmic energy. She embodies the fullness of the divine feminine, encapsulating power, beauty, grace, and compassion. Her iconography often depicts her as a radiant, youthful goddess adorned with exquisite jewelry and celestial ornaments. The five-faced representation, particularly prevalent in Srikula traditions, highlights her mastery over the five elements and the five senses, signifying a complete and harmonious integration of the physical and spiritual realms. Each face embodies a distinct aspect of her divine power, allowing for a multi-faceted approach to devotion and meditation.

In this context, the Devi Gita, a pivotal text in Shaktism, plays a crucial role in understanding Tripura Sundari's significance. The Devi Gita, a dialogue between the Goddess and the devotee, elevates the role of Shakti, the divine feminine principle, to the highest level of cosmic authority. It elaborates on her limitless power, her compassion, and her role in creation, preservation, and destruction. The text doesn't just describe her; it invites intimate communion, emphasizing the transformative power of devotion and surrender. This intimate dialogue serves as a roadmap for devotees, guiding them towards self-realization through the grace and guidance of the Goddess. The text illuminates the path to liberation, showcasing how Tripura Sundari's grace can dissolve the illusions of the material world, leading to the ultimate union with the divine.

However, Tripura Sundari's influence extends beyond the exclusive domain of Shaktism. Within Saivism, a tradition predominantly focused on the worship of Shiva, she is often viewed as the divine consort of Shiva, albeit not always explicitly named as Tripura Sundari. In this context, she is seen as the dynamic energy (Shakti) that complements and empowers Shiva's static, contemplative nature. The union of Shiva and Shakti, the masculine and feminine principles, represents the fundamental cosmic duality that underpins creation and sustains the universe. She embodies the creative force, the dynamic energy that animates the universe. The inherent duality emphasizes that true liberation requires a balance and harmonious interaction between both principles.

The integration of Tripura Sundari within Saivite theology often manifests subtly. Instead of direct worship under her name, she might be perceived as an embodiment of Parvati, Shiva's consort, or other powerful goddesses within the Shaivite pantheon, representing the divine feminine energy inherent in the cosmic dance of creation and destruction. This subtle integration underscores the fluidity of Hindu religious thought, where deities are often viewed through multiple lenses, their attributes merging and overlapping within different traditions. The reverence for Shakti, even within Saivite contexts, emphasizes that the worship of the feminine principle is not confined to a particular religious system; rather, it represents a fundamental aspect of the cosmic order itself.

The Vaishnava tradition, predominantly focused on the worship of Vishnu, incorporates the feminine principle in various manifestations. While Tripura Sundari is not as centrally featured as in Shaktism, her presence resonates implicitly within the broader Vaishnava cosmology. The idea of Lakshmi, Vishnu's consort, often encapsulates aspects of Tripura Sundari's beauty, grace, and auspiciousness. Lakshmi, the goddess of wealth and prosperity, reflects the abundance and fulfillment that Tripura Sundari represents in the Shakti tradition. Both goddesses embody the benevolent aspect of the divine feminine, bestowing blessings and nurturing devotion. This underlying convergence signifies that the divine feminine, in its various forms, transcends the boundaries of sectarian divisions, reflecting the universal cosmic energy that permeates all aspects of creation.

The syncretic nature of Tripura Sundari's worship is evident in the fluidity of her attributes and her ability to seamlessly integrate into diverse religious contexts. Her name itself, "Tripura Sundari," which translates to "the beautiful one of the three cities," hints at a cosmic significance extending beyond sectarian boundaries. The three cities, often interpreted symbolically as the three qualities of the mind— sattva, rajas, and tamas—also represent the three levels of consciousness. Tripura Sundari's triumph over these cities signifies her ability to overcome all limitations, and the conquest of these three cities represents the victory of consciousness over the illusionary nature of the material world, a theme relevant across various religious traditions. This profound significance extends beyond the realm of Shaktism, resonating deeply within the broader Hindu cosmology.

Furthermore, the various regional variations in the depiction of Tripura Sundari further illustrate this syncretic nature. Her iconography often adapts and blends with local traditions, incorporating elements of folk beliefs and regional aesthetics. The colors, ornaments, and specific gestures displayed can vary considerably depending on the geographic location and the prevailing cultural influences. This adaptability demonstrates the goddess's remarkable capacity to embrace diverse forms and interpretations, thus becoming an inclusive symbol that resonates with devotees from various backgrounds and cultural contexts.

The mantras associated with Tripura Sundari also reveal the remarkable syncretism of her worship. While specific mantras vary across different lineages and traditions, the underlying essence remains consistent: a profound invocation of her power and grace. These mantras, often chanted during puja (worship rituals), act as potent tools for connecting with the goddess's energy. The repetitive chanting allows devotees to access deeper meditative states and facilitate a profound spiritual transformation. These mantras, often infused with ancient Sanskrit sounds, are believed to resonate with the very fabric of creation, echoing the profound cosmic energy that Tripura Sundari embodies.

The rituals associated with Tripura Sundari's worship also showcase the syncretic nature of her veneration. While certain practices may be unique to specific lineages, the underlying principle of offering devotion and seeking blessings remains consistent. The offerings of flowers, incense, fruits, and other sacred items reflect a universal gesture of reverence and humility. The meticulously crafted rituals serve to create a sacred space for communion with the divine, fostering a sense of awe and reverence. This underlying unity underscores the universal language of devotion, irrespective of the specific religious context.

In conclusion, Tripura Sundari's presence transcends the limitations of a single religious tradition. While deeply rooted in Shaktism, her influence extends significantly into Saivism and Vaishnavism, highlighting the interconnectedness and syncretic nature of Hindu religious thought. The variations in her depiction and interpretation across different traditions, rather than contradicting her essence, enrich our understanding of the divine feminine principle and the multifaceted nature of spiritual practice. The adaptability of Tripura Sundari's iconography, mantras, and rituals only serve to underscore her universal appeal and the inclusive nature of her devotion. Her story transcends sectarian divisions, offering a pathway to spiritual realization for devotees across various religious backgrounds. The study of Tripura Sundari across these diverse religious traditions unveils the fluidity of Hindu religious thought and the remarkable capacity of the divine feminine principle to adapt and integrate into diverse cultural and spiritual landscapes. Her worship serves as a powerful testament to the unifying power of devotion and the ultimate interconnectedness of all things.

Tripura Sundari and Contemporary Spirituality

Tripura Sundari's enduring appeal lies not just in her historical significance within the rich tapestry of Hindu mythology but also in her potent relevance to contemporary spiritual seekers. Her symbolism, far from being confined to ancient texts and rituals, offers a powerful lens through which to examine and navigate the complexities of modern life. In an era characterized by rapid technological advancements, pervasive social anxieties, and a pervasive sense of uncertainty, Tripura Sundari's message of beauty, grace, and divine love provides a much-needed anchor for the soul.

Her name itself, "Tripura Sundari," the beautiful one of the three cities, carries a profound metaphorical weight applicable to our current times. The three cities, traditionally interpreted as the three gunas – sattva (goodness), rajas (passion), and tamas (ignorance) –can also be understood as representing the three dominant forces shaping our modern experience: the relentless pursuit of material success, the overwhelming tide of emotional entanglement, and the pervasive darkness of ignorance and fear. Tripura Sundari's conquest of these three cities, as depicted in various myths, translates into a powerful message of self-mastery and spiritual liberation in the 21st century. It signifies the possibility of transcending the limitations imposed by our materialistic desires, our emotional dependencies, and our self-imposed ignorance. The path to liberation, therefore, involves cultivating inner strength, emotional intelligence, and a deep understanding of oneself and the world around us.

This self-awareness, crucial for navigating the challenges of modern life, is closely intertwined with Tripura Sundari's aesthetic symbolism. Her depiction as a radiant, youthful goddess, adorned with exquisite jewelry and celestial ornaments, reflects the inherent beauty and grace that reside within each individual. This beauty is not merely superficial; it represents the innate divine spark within each of us, waiting to be awakened and nurtured. In a world obsessed with outward appearances and superficial achievements, Tripura Sundari's image serves as a potent reminder to focus on inner transformation and cultivate our inherent beauty from within.

This involves cultivating self-compassion, embracing our imperfections, and appreciating the unique gifts that each of us brings to the world.

The practical applications of Tripura Sundari's energy in contemporary spirituality are numerous and diverse. Her association with beauty and grace encourages us to approach life with elegance and poise, even amidst the inevitable storms and stresses of daily existence. This involves cultivating mindfulness, practicing self-care, and nurturing our creative potential. By embracing her energy, we can transform mundane tasks into acts of devotion, finding joy and fulfillment in the simplest of things.

Moreover, Tripura Sundari's association with the five elements –earth, water, fire, air, and ether – offers a profound pathway towards ecological awareness and environmental stewardship. Her mastery over these elements signifies the interconnectedness of all beings and the importance of living in harmony with nature. In a world grappling with the consequences of climate change and environmental degradation, Tripura Sundari's message serves as a clarion call for responsible environmental practices and a deeper appreciation for the planet's delicate ecosystem. Her energy can inspire us to make conscious choices that support sustainable living, reduce our environmental footprint, and promote ecological balance.

Furthermore, Tripura Sundari's connection with the five senses underscores the importance of mindful sensory engagement. In a world saturated with sensory overload, the ability to cultivate mindful awareness of our senses becomes a crucial tool for navigating the complexities of modern life. This involves paying attention to the subtle nuances of our sensory experiences, appreciating the beauty of nature, savoring the taste of food, and engaging with our surroundings with full presence. By cultivating mindful sensory engagement, we can reduce stress, enhance our creativity, and cultivate a deeper appreciation for the beauty of existence.

The application of Tripura Sundari's energy extends beyond individual practice to encompass social engagement and collective action. Her image as a radiant goddess representing beauty, grace, and divine love inspires us to extend compassion and understanding to others, particularly those who are marginalized and vulnerable.

Her energy can empower us to work towards social justice, fight against inequality, and create a more just and equitable society.

This involves embracing empathy, promoting inclusivity, and working collaboratively towards common goals.

In the context of navigating the challenges of modern relationships, Tripura Sundari's energy offers a profound pathway to cultivate healthier and more fulfilling connections. Her association with love and beauty inspires us to approach our relationships with greater compassion, understanding, and mutual respect. By cultivating inner balance and self-awareness, we can foster stronger bonds based on genuine connection and mutual appreciation. This involves practicing active listening, effective communication, and forgiveness, essential elements for navigating the complexities of interpersonal relationships.

Meditation practices focused on Tripura Sundari can be particularly potent tools for self-transformation and spiritual growth. Visualizing her radiant form, focusing on her beautiful attributes, and chanting her mantras can create a powerful space for inner transformation. This practice can help to reduce stress, improve focus, and cultivate a deeper sense of inner peace. The meditative focus on her various aspects—her five faces, her mastery over the elements, her connection to the three cities—can lead to a deeper understanding of oneself and the interconnectedness of all things.

In contemporary society, the pursuit of spiritual fulfillment often finds itself intertwined with the pressures and anxieties of daily life.

Tripura Sundari's message provides a way to integrate spiritual practice seamlessly into the everyday. This involves approaching mundane tasks with a sense of devotion, practicing mindfulness in our interactions, and fostering a spirit of gratitude and appreciation for the present moment. By embodying the qualities of beauty, grace, and divine love that Tripura Sundari represents, we can transform our daily lives into a path of spiritual growth and fulfillment.

In conclusion, Tripura Sundari's relevance extends far beyond the confines of historical religious contexts. Her symbolism resonates deeply with the spiritual aspirations and challenges of modern life.

Her energy, when tapped into consciously, provides a powerful resource for navigating the complexities of our times, fostering self-awareness, and promoting a more compassionate and fulfilling existence. By embracing her message of beauty, grace, and divine love, we can unlock our inner potential, cultivate healthier relationships, and contribute to the creation of a more just and harmonious world. The practices inspired by her iconography and energy offer a tangible pathway towards spiritual growth and self-realization within the context of our modern realities. Her enduring appeal stems from her capacity to inspire both individual transformation and collective action, making her a profoundly relevant figure for contemporary spirituality.

Bhuvaneshvaris Iconography and Attributes

Bhuvaneshvari, the "Mistress of the Universe," stands as a captivating figure amongst the Mahavidyas, her iconography reflecting the multifaceted nature of cosmic energy and the boundless potential of the feminine divine. Unlike some Mahavidyas whose depictions consistently adhere to a single, easily recognizable form, Bhuvaneshvari's visual representation demonstrates a remarkable degree of variation, hinting at the ever-shifting, protean nature of the cosmos itself. This diversity in her iconography, however, is far from chaotic; it reflects the richness and depth of her symbolic meaning, inviting deeper exploration and nuanced understanding.

One common depiction shows Bhuvaneshvari seated majestically on a lotus throne, her posture exuding an aura of regal serenity and absolute sovereignty. The lotus, a symbol of purity and spiritual unfolding, underscores her position as the source of all creation.

Her serene expression, often accompanied by a gentle smile, conveys a sense of profound peace and unwavering wisdom. This peaceful countenance, however, doesn't negate her inherent power; rather, it suggests a power rooted in profound stillness, a cosmic potency that flows effortlessly from the stillness of her being. This is a key element often overlooked in interpretations of the Mahavidyas; the power isn't derived from aggressive exertion, but from an inherent, intrinsic source. This serenity is not passivity; it is the stillness of the eye of a hurricane.

The colors associated with Bhuvaneshvari also contribute significantly to her iconographic significance. While interpretations may vary across different artistic traditions, gold and red are frequently featured. Gold, symbolizing the divine light and the sun's life-giving energy, reflects her supreme and radiant nature. Red, often representing energy, passion, and the vital life force, highlights the dynamic, generative aspect of her power. The combination suggests a potent synthesis of stillness and activity, of radiance and dynamic energy, mirroring the universe's constant interplay of creation and dissolution. Some depictions also include vibrant greens and blues, suggesting the vastness and multiplicity of the cosmos she embodies. The subtle variations in color palettes across different representations underscore the multifaceted nature of her energy, a spectrum of possibilities rather than a fixed entity.

Her adornments are equally significant, further enriching the layers of her symbolism. She is often depicted wearing exquisite jewelry and flowing garments, indicating her regal status and the abundance of cosmic riches she bestows. The ornaments themselves, however, often hold deeper symbolic meaning. For example, a specific type of crown, a certain kind of jewelry, or even the particular arrangement of her garments could be interpreted through the lens of specific Tantric practices or scriptures, offering clues to her deeper esoteric significance. This requires a close examination of various artistic representations across different regions and historical periods to identify recurring patterns and unique variations.

Another intriguing aspect of her iconography is the presence or absence of accompanying figures or symbols. In some representations, Bhuvaneshvari appears alone, emphasizing her self-sufficiency and independence. In others, she is accompanied by various deities or symbolic objects, signifying specific aspects of her power or her relationship with other cosmic forces. These accompanying figures can include consorts, representing the interplay of masculine and feminine energies within the cosmos, or animals that act as her vahana (vehicle), reflecting specific attributes like strength, speed, or wisdom. Detailed analysis of these accompanying elements offers a rich field for interpretation, allowing for a deeper understanding of the particular aspects of her power being emphasized in each representation.

The variation in her hand gestures (mudras) further enhances the complexity of her visual portrayal. Different mudras can convey different meanings, ranging from bestowing blessings and granting boons to expressing specific spiritual concepts or performing sacred rituals. These mudras, when interpreted within the context of her overall iconography and the specific textual traditions associating her with these forms, can illuminate a complex web of symbolic meanings connected to the performance of specific rituals, practices, and mantras. Understanding the specific significance of the mudra requires careful examination of relevant Tantric texts and traditions.

The evolution of Bhuvaneshvari's iconography across different historical periods and geographical regions also offers a valuable insight into the shifting cultural and religious contexts in which she has been venerated. For instance, early representations might differ significantly from later portrayals, reflecting changes in artistic styles, religious practices, and the evolution of Tantric thought. Comparing and contrasting these various representations allows us to trace the development of her image and how her symbolism has been interpreted and reinterpreted over centuries. Such a comparative study can provide a rich tapestry of insights into the changing dynamics of religious belief and artistic expression.

Bhuvaneshvari's attributes are as multifaceted and dynamic as her iconography. Beyond her visual representations, her character and powers are defined by a diverse range of attributes that enrich our understanding of her role within the cosmos and the human spiritual journey. Her name itself, "Bhuvaneshvari," signifies her sovereignty over all the worlds, the three worlds (Triloka) of the Hindus—Bhur, Bhuvah, and Svah, reflecting the material, astral, and causal planes. It also signifies the universe in its totality. This sovereignty, however, is not one of tyrannical control, but rather of compassionate governance, reflecting the inherent wisdom and nurturing capacity of the feminine principle.

Her association with abundance and prosperity further highlights her benevolent aspect. She is often regarded as the bestower of riches, not merely in material terms but also in spiritual fulfillment and inner peace. This abundance is not limited to material wealth but extends to a profound sense of wholeness and well-being. It represents the blossoming of one's potential and the fulfillment of one's inherent dharma. This connection to abundance reflects the generative power of the cosmos, which continually manifests life and sustains existence.

Another significant attribute is her association with time itself, the cyclical unfolding and dissolution of existence. She is often depicted as existing beyond time, as the timeless source of the cosmos' cyclical movements. This transcendence of time adds another dimension to her sovereign power, highlighting her capacity to observe and guide the ebb and flow of existence without being bound by its limitations. This aspect connects her deeply with the nature of reality, the impermanence of all things and the underlying unity that underpins the apparent diversity of experience.

Bhuvaneshvari is often linked with the concept of Shakti, the dynamic, creative energy of the universe, which is the very essence of existence. She is not merely a receptacle for Shakti; she is its embodiment, its active expression and manifestation. She exemplifies the dynamic transformative force of the cosmos. This active manifestation distinguishes her from static or passive images of divinity, emphasizing her creative potential and her transformative power. This creative energy is not limited to cosmic creation but extends to the individual's spiritual journey, empowering them to overcome obstacles, and achieve self-realization.

Her association with wisdom and knowledge is another crucial aspect of her attributes. She is not merely a repository of knowledge; she is the very source of wisdom, guiding individuals on their spiritual paths and illuminating the mysteries of existence. Her wisdom is not just intellectual; it is intuitive and experiential, born of direct communion with the divine. This intuitive wisdom is a key element in navigating the complexities of existence and achieving a deeper understanding of oneself and the world. Access to this kind of wisdom often requires dedicated spiritual practice and a conscious effort to connect with the divine, which is precisely the type of spiritual growth that Bhuvaneshvari is said to support.

Her role as a protector and defender is often emphasized in various traditions and textual accounts, highlighting her capacity to safeguard individuals and the cosmos from harm. This protection extends beyond physical safety and encompasses spiritual guidance and support. This nurturing and protective energy provides a sense of security and empowerment, fostering inner strength and resilience. This protectiveness is not a manifestation of aggression, but a compassionate response to the needs of those who seek her guidance.

Understanding Bhuvaneshvari requires going beyond mere intellectual comprehension. Her iconography and attributes, when studied together, reveal a potent synthesis of divine energy, a dynamic expression of the feminine principle's inherent wisdom, creativity, and compassionate power. Her diverse representations serve not as competing interpretations but as complementary facets of a single, multifaceted reality. The depth of her symbolism lies in the ability to connect with her energy on a personal level, allowing her to act as a guide in navigating the intricate complexities of the human experience and the journey of self-realization. Her enduring relevance stems from her capacity to empower individuals in their pursuit of spiritual growth and to inspire a deeper understanding of their own inherent divinity, revealing a hidden dimension of
strength and potential residing within each individual.

Bhuvaneshvaris Role in Cosmic Order

Bhuvaneshvari's role in the cosmic order transcends mere observation; she is actively involved in its maintenance and sustenance. Her association with creation, preservation, and destruction isn't a tripartite division of labor but a dynamic interplay, a continuous dance of cosmic energies that ensures the universe's cyclical renewal and stability. Unlike a detached, transcendent deity observing events from afar, Bhuvaneshvari is deeply immersed in the very fabric of existence, a vital force driving the ceaseless flux of creation and dissolution.

Hindu cosmology, with its cyclical view of time, recognizes the continuous process of creation, preservation, and destruction (srishti, sthiti, and samhara). Bhuvaneshvari embodies all three aspects, seamlessly integrating them into a harmonious whole. Her power isn't confined to a singular act of creation at the beginning of a cosmic cycle; rather, it is a continuous, ongoing process, a constant flow of energy that sustains the universe and fuels its evolution. She is the generative force behind the manifestation of the universe, the sustaining power that maintains its equilibrium, and the transformative energy that brings about its eventual dissolution, paving the way for a new cycle of creation. This continuous cycle, reflecting the dynamic nature of existence itself, is an integral aspect of Bhuvaneshvari's role in maintaining cosmic harmony.

The concept of *pralaya* , or cosmic dissolution, is often viewed as a destructive process, but within the framework of Bhuvaneshvari's power, it represents a necessary phase in the universe's cyclical evolution. It's not simply an ending but a prelude to a new beginning, a cleansing process that clears the way for a fresh manifestation of life and energy. Bhuvaneshvari's role in this process isn't one of mere demolition but of skillful transformation, skillfully guiding the universe through the transition from one phase to the next, ensuring the smooth continuation of the cosmic cycle. This perspective shifts the focus from a fearful anticipation of destruction to an understanding of the cyclical nature of reality, where destruction is not an end but a necessary step toward renewal and regeneration.

Bhuvaneshvari's association with abundance is not merely a symbolic representation of material prosperity; it reflects the universe's inherent capacity to sustain and nurture life. Her abundance is a cosmic reservoir, providing the necessary resources for the universe's continuous evolution and providing sustenance for all beings. This isn't a limited or finite resource, but a boundless wellspring of energy and potential, constantly replenishing itself through the cyclical processes of creation, preservation, and dissolution. Her capacity to bestow abundance mirrors the universe's generative power, highlighting the ongoing process of manifestation and sustenance that underpins the existence of all things. This abundance, therefore, is not just about material wealth but also encompasses spiritual richness, intellectual growth, and the overall well-being of all living beings. It signifies a state of holistic flourishing and encompasses all aspects of existence.

The concept of *shakti*, the dynamic feminine energy, is intrinsically linked to Bhuvaneshvari's role in cosmic order. She is not merely a manifestation of Shakti but its embodiment, the active force driving the universe's continuous transformation. Shakti, often described as the creative and dynamic power of the divine, is not a passive entity but a powerful force that permeates all of creation, continually shaping and reshaping the universe. Bhuvaneshvari, as the embodiment of Shakti, channels this energy into the cyclical processes of creation, preservation, and destruction, ensuring the universe's continuous evolution. Her connection with Shakti highlights the creative and transformative power that lies at the heart of the universe's dynamism.

Moreover, Bhuvaneshvari's role as a source of power and sustenance extends beyond the cosmic realm into the individual human experience. Just as she maintains the cosmic order, she also provides the energy and support needed for individual spiritual growth and self-realization. This is reflected in the various practices and rituals associated with her worship, which often aim to tap into her boundless power for personal transformation and empowerment. The individual's journey toward self-realization mirrors the universe's cyclical journey, and Bhuvaneshvari acts as a guide and facilitator, providing the necessary energy and support for this inner evolution.

Her association with time further emphasizes her role as a regulator and sustainer of cosmic order. Bhuvaneshvari transcends linear time, existing outside the confines of past, present, and future. She observes and orchestrates the cyclical unfolding of time, ensuring the harmonious interplay of creation and destruction. This timeless perspective allows her to maintain balance and equilibrium within the ever-changing cosmos. Her transcendence of linear time grants her the ability to perceive the interconnectedness of all events within the cosmic cycle, allowing for skillful intervention and guidance as needed.

The diverse iconographic representations of Bhuvaneshvari reflect the multifaceted nature of her cosmic role. Different images emphasize various aspects of her power, highlighting different facets of her involvement in the universe's intricate workings. The variations in her appearance, attributes, and accompanying symbols serve not to contradict but to complement each other, presenting a holistic view of her involvement in the cosmic dance of creation, preservation, and destruction. These variations demonstrate the richness and complexity of her role, highlighting the many ways in which she sustains and guides the universe's ongoing evolution.

Her role in maintaining cosmic order also extends to the realm of dharma, the righteous order of the universe. Bhuvaneshvari's actions ensure the smooth functioning of the cosmic order, upholding the principles of dharma and preventing chaos from disrupting the balance. This is not a static maintenance but a dynamic process, constantly adapting to the ever-changing circumstances of the universe. She ensures that the cycles of creation and destruction continue harmoniously, allowing for the perpetuation of life and the evolution of consciousness.

The concept of *riti*, or cosmic rhythm, is intimately connected with Bhuvaneshvari's function. She is the embodiment of the rhythm of the universe, the steady beat that underpins all of creation. This rhythm encompasses all aspects of cosmic existence, from the smallest particle to the largest galaxy, ensuring the harmonious interaction of all things. Bhuvaneshvari's role is to maintain this rhythm, ensuring the universe's continued existence and evolution within a harmonious framework. The maintenance of this rhythm is crucial for the flourishing of life and the continued unfolding of cosmic evolution.

Furthermore, Bhuvaneshvari's role extends beyond the purely cosmic. She is deeply connected to the human world, providing guidance and support to those seeking spiritual growth. Her energy can be accessed through various forms of devotion, meditation, and ritual, helping individuals to connect with their inner selves and overcome the challenges of life. This connection emphasizes the interconnectedness between the microcosm (the individual) and the macrocosm (the universe), highlighting the fact that individual growth and spiritual evolution contribute to the maintenance of the greater cosmic order. Her power is available to all who seek it, empowering individuals to participate actively in the cosmic dance of existence.

In conclusion, Bhuvaneshvari's role in the cosmic order is not merely that of a passive observer or a distant, detached deity. She is an active participant, a dynamic force shaping and sustaining the universe's existence. Her association with creation, preservation, and destruction, her embodiment of Shakti, her mastery of time, and her profound connection with dharma and riti all contribute to her vital role in maintaining cosmic balance and equilibrium. Her influence extends beyond the cosmic realm, deeply impacting the individual human experience, offering guidance and support for spiritual growth and self-realization. Understanding Bhuvaneshvari's multifaceted role offers a profound insight into the dynamic and interconnected nature of the universe and its relationship with humanity. Her presence is not simply a theoretical construct but a living reality, actively shaping the world around us and offering a pathway for individual and collective transformation. The constant interplay of her energies ensures the continuous cycle of creation, highlighting the eternal and dynamic nature of the universe.

Bhuvaneshvari and the Concept of Sovereignty

Bhuvaneshvari, as the sovereign goddess, doesn't rule through force or domination; rather, her sovereignty manifests as the inherent power that sustains and governs the universe's intricate workings. It is a sovereignty born not of conquest, but of intrinsic being, a fundamental aspect of her cosmic nature. This is subtly different from the more readily understood concepts of political or earthly sovereignty. Her reign is not imposed but inherent, a natural order stemming from her very essence as the embodiment of cosmic energy. It is a sovereignty that encompasses not only the maintenance of the cosmic order but also the nurturing and guidance of all beings within it.

The concept of sovereignty often evokes images of power wielded by a ruler over their subjects. However, Bhuvaneshvari's sovereignty transcends this limited human understanding. Her power is not wielded for personal gain or aggrandizement; instead, it is employed for the benefit of the entire universe. She is not a tyrant enforcing her will, but a benevolent sovereign ensuring the smooth functioning of cosmic processes. Her reign is one of harmonious balance, where creation, preservation, and destruction work in concert, ensuring the cyclical renewal of life. This cosmic equilibrium, maintained by her inherent sovereignty, ensures the continued flourishing of existence.

One could argue that Bhuvaneshvari's sovereignty is analogous to the self-organizing principles observed in complex systems. Just as a healthy ecosystem maintains itself through intricate interactions between its various components, the universe, under Bhuvaneshvari's sovereign rule, operates with a similar level of self-regulation and balance. Her sovereignty is not a forceful imposition but an inherent quality that arises from the interconnectedness and interdependence of all things within creation. It's a dynamic equilibrium, constantly adapting and adjusting to maintain the cosmic rhythm. This perspective removes the anthropomorphic element often associated with the idea of a ruling deity, replacing it with a more nuanced understanding of intrinsic cosmic order.

The Devi Gita, a significant text within Shaktism, offers further insight into Bhuvaneshvari's sovereign nature. While not explicitly focusing on her as a sovereign entity in the manner of a political ruler, the Gita highlights her pervasive influence and control over all aspects of the cosmos. The text reveals her ability to manifest as diverse forms, each embodying a specific aspect of her cosmic power. This ability to manifest in countless forms reflects the multifaceted nature of her sovereignty, demonstrating her complete and thorough influence across all planes of existence. The multiplicity of her manifestations underscores her pervasive presence, ensuring that her influence permeates every corner of the universe.

Analyzing her sovereignty through the lens of different philosophical interpretations within Hinduism yields further insights. From a Vedantic perspective, Bhuvaneshvari's sovereignty might be seen as an expression of Brahman, the ultimate reality, manifesting in its dynamic cosmic form. In this view, her sovereignty is not separate from the divine but an integral part of it, an emanation of the supreme power that sustains and governs all.

Her actions are not independent choices but reflect the inherent dynamics of Brahman itself, revealing the workings of cosmic reality through her actions. This suggests that understanding her sovereignty is tantamount to understanding the fundamental principles of the universe.

From a Tantra perspective, her sovereignty takes on a different, yet complementary, meaning. Here, her power is viewed as a manifestation of Shakti, the dynamic feminine energy that fuels the universe's constant evolution and transformation. Her sovereignty is then the active, generative force driving creation, preservation, and destruction. This dynamic force ensures that the cosmic rhythm is maintained, ensuring continuous cycles of birth, growth, decay and renewal. The fluidity and dynamic nature of Shakti, as represented by Bhuvaneshvari, reveals her sovereignty not as static control, but as continuous creative action.

The interplay between her cosmic sovereignty and the human experience is particularly significant. While Bhuvaneshvari governs the universe on a macrocosmic scale, her sovereignty also manifests in the microcosm of individual lives. Her power is not just a distant, inaccessible force but can be accessed and harnessed for personal growth and spiritual development. Through devotion, meditation, and ritual, individuals can connect with her energy, receiving guidance and empowerment on their spiritual journeys. This connection implies that her sovereignty is not just about cosmic governance but also about enabling individual self-realization.

The concept of *adhikar*, or authority, within the context of Bhuvaneshvari's sovereignty, is critical. Her authority isn't based on force or coercion but on inherent cosmic authority, the natural right to govern and sustain the universe. It is a righteous authority, underpinned by Dharma, the cosmic order, and operating in harmony with the principles of Rita, the cosmic rhythm. It's not a tyrannical rule but a compassionate guidance that facilitates the evolution of both the universe and its inhabitants. This authority is not to be feared but respected and revered, offering a pathway to spiritual and personal growth.

Furthermore, her sovereignty is not static or unchanging; it adapts and evolves along with the universe. This dynamic aspect is crucial to understanding her role. Her sovereignty is not a rigid, inflexible control but a flexible and responsive force constantly adjusting to the ebb and flow of cosmic events. This ensures that the universe maintains balance and harmony throughout its continuous cycles of change. This responsiveness is not weakness, but a demonstration of wisdom and adaptability, crucial to maintaining the intricate balance of existence.

Another critical aspect is her sovereignty's connection with abundance. Bhuvaneshvari isn't just a provider of material prosperity; she embodies cosmic abundance, a limitless wellspring of energy and resources. Her sovereignty ensures the sustenance and flourishing of all life forms, highlighting the concept of abundance as not just material wealth but as encompassing spiritual, intellectual, and emotional well-being. It emphasizes the holistic nature of her dominion, extending beyond material provision to encompass the entire spectrum of human existence.

In conclusion, Bhuvaneshvari's sovereignty is a complex and

multifaceted concept that transcends simple notions of earthly rulership. It is a dynamic, responsive, and compassionate power that sustains and guides the universe's intricate workings, while simultaneously offering pathways for individual spiritual growth. Her sovereignty is not an imposition of will but an intrinsic aspect of her being, reflecting the inherent order and balance of the cosmos. Understanding her sovereignty provides profound insights into the workings of the universe and the relationship between the cosmic order and the individual human experience. Her reign is a continuous act of creation, preservation, and transformation, ensuring the ongoing evolution and harmonious functioning of the universe. It is a sovereignty not of control, but of nurturing,
guidance, and the ultimately benevolent governance of the cosmos.

Bhuvaneshvari in Different Textual Sources

The multifaceted nature of Bhuvaneshvari, as previously discussed, extends to her representation across various textual sources. A thorough examination reveals both striking similarities and intriguing discrepancies in her depiction, underscoring the dynamic and evolving nature of her symbolism within the broader Hindu and Tantric traditions. The Devi Gita, while not explicitly dedicating a chapter to Bhuvaneshvari, alludes to her pervasive influence through the goddess's inherent sovereignty and her capacity to manifest in diverse forms. This inherent sovereignty, as described in the Gita, is not a forceful dominance but a subtle, all-pervasive energy shaping the cosmic order. This inherent power, rather than being a result of conquest, is a fundamental attribute of her cosmic being, an intrinsic aspect of the divine feminine.

The Devi Mahatmya, another significant text within Shaktism, doesn't feature Bhuvaneshvari as prominently as some other Mahavidyas. However, her presence is implied through the overarching theme of the Devi's ever-changing forms and manifestations. The numerous battles fought by the Devi, and her ultimate victory over the demons, can be interpreted as symbolic representations of Bhuvaneshvari's ability to overcome chaos and maintain cosmic harmony. Her absence in a focused narrative does not diminish her importance; rather, it highlights her omnipresence, her influence subtly woven into the tapestry of the narrative's larger cosmic themes. Her power is not limited to specific episodes but is implicitly present in the overall narrative arc, a silent force upholding the cosmic equilibrium.

Moving beyond the overtly Shaktic texts, we find Bhuvaneshvari mentioned, albeit less frequently, in certain Puranas and Agamas. These texts often focus on specific aspects of her being, highlighting particular attributes or functions. For instance, some Puranas might emphasize her role as the sustainer of the universe, highlighting her nurturing aspect, while others may focus on her destructive power, emphasizing her ability to bring about necessary change and renewal. This variation in emphasis reflects the diverse interpretations and understandings of her nature within different schools of thought. The Puranas, often narrative-driven, present Bhuvaneshvari's influence through episodic manifestations, highlighting specific acts of creation, preservation, or destruction. These narratives showcase her adaptability, showcasing different facets of her cosmic power depending on the narrative context.

The Agamas, which are primarily ritualistic and esoteric texts, provide a deeper insight into the practices associated with Bhuvaneshvari worship. These texts often detail specific mantras, yantras, and rituals designed to invoke her blessings and connect with her energy. The details contained within these texts provide practical applications of her symbolic power, showing how her energy can be channeled through ritual and devotion. By offering guidance on ritualistic practice, the Agamas provide a means of direct interaction with Bhuvaneshvari's energy, giving her symbolic representations tangible form and spiritual purpose.

Different schools of Tantra, with their varying approaches to spirituality and ritual, also portray Bhuvaneshvari in unique ways. Some traditions emphasize her role as a source of transformative power, capable of guiding practitioners towards spiritual enlightenment, while others focus on her ability to grant material prosperity and worldly success. This diversity of interpretation stems from the inherently flexible and adaptable nature of Tantric thought, which allows for multiple interpretations and practices based on individual needs and inclinations. This diversity of understanding doesn't diminish the reverence for Bhuvaneshvari, rather it highlights the richness and versatility of her symbolic potential.

The evolution of Bhuvaneshvari's symbolism over time is also worthy of note. Her iconography, for instance, has evolved, reflecting changing cultural and religious contexts. While early depictions may have been simpler, later representations incorporated more elaborate details and symbolic attributes, reflecting the deeper understanding and interpretations of her multifaceted nature. This evolution also includes the blending of her symbolism with other deities or concepts, leading to hybrid forms that reflect the syncretic nature of religious practice in certain regions.

The variations in textual portrayals are not necessarily contradictory; rather, they represent different facets of a single, multifaceted deity. Each text illuminates a specific aspect of Bhuvaneshvari's cosmic nature, offering a glimpse into her vast and complex powers. Her depiction as a benevolent sovereign in some texts doesn't negate her capacity for fierce protection in others. These differing representations highlight the dynamic and flexible nature of the divine feminine, constantly adapting and evolving to meet the changing needs of her devotees and the world around her. The seemingly disparate narratives, therefore, contribute to a richer and more complete understanding of Bhuvaneshvari, rather than undermining her overall significance.

Furthermore, the geographical variations in her worship and depiction are also significant. Regional traditions might emphasize specific aspects of her character or powers, resulting in localized variations in iconography, rituals, and stories associated with her.

This diversity highlights the adaptability of Hindu religious traditions, allowing for the integration of local customs and beliefs into the broader framework of the larger faith. The localized interpretations, though diverse, rarely contradict the core beliefs associated with her as a Mahavidya, underscoring the unity within the diversity of her worship.

Considering Bhuvaneshvari's symbolism within the context of Kali Yuga adds further depth to our understanding. In this age, often characterized by challenges and complexities, her role as a sovereign maintaining cosmic balance becomes even more significant. Her ability to adapt and respond to changing circumstances, as reflected in the diverse textual portrayals, offers hope and guidance for navigating the complexities of the present time. Her symbolism provides reassurance that even amidst chaos, the inherent order of the cosmos persists, guided by her unwavering sovereignty.

The continuing relevance of Bhuvaneshvari in contemporary society lies in her ability to offer a framework for understanding and navigating the complexities of the modern world. Her sovereignty, viewed not as political dominance, but as the inherent cosmic order, provides a sense of stability and meaning in an ever-changing world. Her capacity for both nurturing and destruction reminds us of the constant interplay of creation and destruction, highlighting the cyclical nature of life and the importance of accepting both growth and decay. This resonates deeply with individuals seeking meaning and purpose in a world often characterized by uncertainty and instability.

In conclusion, the varying depictions of Bhuvaneshvari across different textual sources enrich our understanding of her multifaceted nature. These variations highlight the flexibility and dynamism of her symbolism, reflecting the evolving interpretations and practices within the broader Hindu and Tantric traditions. Far from being contradictions, these diverse portrayals complement each other, providing a comprehensive view of this powerful and significant Mahavidya, whose sovereignty continues to inspire and guide devotees across centuries and across diverse cultural contexts, even in the complex context of Kali Yuga. Her continued relevance underscores her enduring significance as a symbol of cosmic balance, transformative power, and the inherent order within the seemingly chaotic universe. The rich tapestry of her depictions across various texts offers a dynamic and evolving portrait of a goddess whose influence permeates the cosmos and offers spiritual guidance for all who seek her grace.

Bhuvaneshvari and Contemporary Challenges

Bhuvaneshvari's relevance extends far beyond the pages of ancient texts; her symbolism offers a potent framework for navigating the complexities of the 21st century. While traditional interpretations focus on her cosmic sovereignty and role in maintaining universal balance, her energy can be understood as a powerful tool for fostering social harmony and addressing contemporary challenges. The inherent order she represents, not as a rigid structure but as a dynamic equilibrium, provides a crucial lens through which to view the often chaotic aspects of modern life.

One of the most pressing contemporary issues is the escalating social fragmentation fueled by rapid technological advancement, globalization, and socio-political polarization. The information age, while empowering, has also created echo chambers and filter bubbles, reinforcing existing biases and hindering meaningful dialogue. This fragmentation challenges the very fabric of social cohesion, leading to conflict and instability. Bhuvaneshvari's energy, understood as the principle of cosmic order, can be seen as a counterforce to this fragmentation. Her capacity to maintain balance amidst diversity suggests a path towards fostering inclusivity and understanding across differing viewpoints. This doesn't necessitate a suppression of individuality or a homogenization of beliefs, but rather a conscious effort to cultivate mutual respect and tolerance within a framework of shared values.

The concept of "Vasudhaiva Kutumbakam," often translated as "the world is one family," resonates deeply with Bhuvaneshvari's symbolism. Her sovereignty isn't a hierarchical dominance, but a recognition of interconnectedness. Each individual, like each element in the cosmos, plays a role in maintaining the overall balance. This understanding encourages a move away from adversarial approaches to conflict resolution and towards cooperative strategies that prioritize mutual benefit and sustained harmony. In this context, Bhuvaneshvari's energy can be harnessed to promote empathy, compassion, and a sense of shared responsibility for the well-being of the community and the planet as a whole.

Another significant challenge of our time is the environmental crisis. The unsustainable practices of modern society are leading to widespread ecological damage, threatening the delicate balance of the natural world. Bhuvaneshvari's association with the earth and its sustenance provides a powerful framework for addressing these issues. Her capacity for both creation and destruction serves as a reminder of the interconnectedness of human actions and their impact on the environment. The destructive aspects of her power, often misinterpreted as solely negative, symbolize the necessity of acknowledging and addressing the consequences of unsustainable practices. Conversely, her creative energy represents the potential for regeneration and healing, offering hope for a more sustainable future. This holistic understanding encourages a responsible approach towards environmental stewardship, emphasizing the importance of maintaining ecological balance for the collective good.

Furthermore, the rise of social injustice and inequality poses a significant threat to social harmony. Disparities in wealth, opportunity, and access to resources contribute to widespread discontent and instability. Bhuvaneshvari's energy can be viewed as a catalyst for social justice, encouraging a more equitable distribution of resources and opportunities. Her sovereignty, interpreted as a just and impartial cosmic order, demands a commitment to fairness and equality. This aligns with the core principles of Dharma, emphasizing the importance of righteous action and the pursuit of justice. By embracing Bhuvaneshvari's energy, individuals can be empowered to work towards creating a more just and equitable society, reducing the imbalances that fuel conflict and instability.

The application of Bhuvaneshvari's symbolism in addressing contemporary challenges requires a deeper understanding of her multifaceted nature. While her association with sovereignty and cosmic balance provides a crucial framework, her connection with specific mantras, yantras, and rituals, as detailed in the Agamas, offers practical tools for harnessing her energy. These practices, often involving meditation, visualization, and chanting, can facilitate a deeper connection with her energy, fostering inner peace and promoting a sense of harmony within oneself, which then extends to one's interactions with the world.

The practice of mindful engagement with the world, guided by Bhuvaneshvari's principles, becomes essential. This involves cultivating a keen awareness of the interconnectedness of all beings and actions, recognizing the ripple effect of one's actions on the broader social and environmental landscape. It encourages a conscious effort to choose actions that promote balance, harmony, and justice, fostering a sense of shared responsibility for the collective well-being. This mindful approach allows individuals to become active participants in creating a more peaceful and equitable world, aligning their actions with the underlying principles of Bhuvaneshvari's energy.

The modern world, characterized by rapid change and uncertainty, often leaves individuals feeling disconnected and lost.

Bhuvaneshvari's unwavering sovereignty offers a sense of stability and grounding in the midst of chaos. Her energy, understood as the principle of cosmic order, provides a framework for understanding the inherent interconnectedness of all things, fostering a sense of belonging and purpose. This understanding helps individuals navigate the challenges of modern life with greater resilience and clarity. The inherent order she represents is not static but dynamic, constantly adapting to change while maintaining its essential structure. This adaptability provides a model for navigating the uncertainties of life, finding strength and resilience in the face of adversity.

Furthermore, the understanding of Bhuvaneshvari's energy as both creative and destructive provides a crucial perspective on the cyclical nature of life and the world. This acceptance of both growth and decay, creation and destruction, is essential for a healthy and balanced approach to life. The ability to acknowledge and embrace the impermanent nature of things allows for greater adaptability and resilience in the face of inevitable change. This acceptance allows for a more balanced engagement with life's challenges, fostering a sense of peace and acceptance.

Finally, the diverse interpretations and representations of

Bhuvaneshvari throughout history highlight the adaptive and inclusive nature of her energy. Her symbolism resonates with individuals from various backgrounds and belief systems, offering a unifying framework for understanding and addressing universal challenges. This adaptability makes her a particularly relevant figure in the modern world, where diversity and inclusivity are paramount. Her inclusive nature emphasizes the importance of embracing differences while recognizing the fundamental interconnectedness of all humanity. This fosters a sense of unity and shared purpose, even amidst the diversity of human experience. Bhuvaneshvari's energy, therefore, offers a powerful and enduring path toward creating a more just, equitable, and harmonious world, providing a framework for navigating the complexities of the modern era with grace, wisdom, and resilience.

Bhairavis Iconography and Attributes

Bhairavi, the sixth Mahavidya, presents a fascinating study in visual representation, her iconography reflecting the multifaceted nature of her power. Unlike some Mahavidyas whose depictions remain relatively consistent across various artistic traditions, Bhairavi's visual representations demonstrate a significant degree of variation, each offering a unique lens through which to interpret her essence.

This diversity, however, is not chaotic; rather, it reflects the rich tapestry of Tantric thought and the adaptability of her symbolism to different cultural and historical contexts.

One common representation depicts Bhairavi as a beautiful, youthful woman, often adorned with elaborate jewelry and fine garments. This portrayal emphasizes her inherent power and captivating allure, reflecting her association with both grace and fierce strength. Her complexion is frequently described as golden or reddish, symbolizing energy, vitality, and the warmth of creation. The jewelry she wears is not merely ornamental; it holds symbolic significance, often including necklaces representing the flow of cosmic energy, bangles denoting cyclical time, and earrings symbolizing the balance between opposing forces. The intricate details of her attire, often including scarves and flowing garments, represent the fluidity and dynamism of her energy.

The variations begin to appear in the specifics of these details. In some depictions, her garments are opulent and regal, reflecting her sovereignty and cosmic power. In others, they are simpler, suggesting a focus on inner strength and spiritual attainment rather than worldly possessions. This variation underscores the different interpretations of her power – some emphasizing her dominion over the cosmos, others highlighting her potential as a guide on the spiritual path. The choice of colors and fabrics also contributes to the overall impression, with some artists favoring rich, vibrant hues to emphasize her dynamism, while others utilize more subdued tones to suggest a more introspective and contemplative nature.

The weapons she wields also contribute significantly to the visual narrative. While some depictions show her unarmed, emphasizing her inherent power and the control she exercises without external tools, others equip her with a range of instruments, including a sword, a trident, or a skull-topped staff. These weapons are not merely symbols of destruction, but rather representations of her ability to sever karmic bonds, overcome obstacles, and transcend limitations. The sword symbolizes the cutting through of illusion, the trident represents the three gunas (sattva, rajas, and tamas), and the skull-topped staff signifies her mastery over death and the limitations of the physical form. The selection and arrangement of weapons can indicate a specific aspect of her energy that the artist wishes to emphasize.

Another striking element in Bhairavi's iconography is the presence or absence of specific animals. She is sometimes depicted riding a lion or a tiger, signifying courage, strength, and untamed power. In other instances, she might be accompanied by a peacock, representing beauty, grace, and the unfolding of spiritual potential. The choice of animal companion reflects the artist's interpretation of her energy and the aspects they seek to highlight. For instance, the lion emphasizes her dominance and power, while the peacock focuses on her refined beauty and spiritual expression. These animal companions are not mere accessories; they are integral to the overall message conveyed by the image.

Her posture and mudras (hand gestures) also contribute to the complex visual language of Bhairavi's iconography. She may be depicted in a standing posture, radiating strength and confidence, or in a seated posture, suggesting contemplation and inner peace.

The mudras she performs, such as the abhaya mudra (gesture of fearlessness) or the varada mudra (gesture of bestowing boons), add another layer of meaning to the image, indicating specific aspects of her power and blessings. These postures and mudras are not arbitrary; they are carefully chosen to communicate a precise message about her nature and the effect she has on her devotees.

Beyond the individual elements, the overall composition of the artwork plays a crucial role in conveying the essence of Bhairavi. The background, the setting, and the interplay of light and shadow all contribute to the overall mood and message of the image. A dark background might emphasize her association with the night, mystery, and the unknown, while a bright background could highlight her connection with the sun, light, and creation. The details of the environment – whether a forest, a battlefield, or a celestial realm – can also reflect different aspects of her energy and power.

The variations in Bhairavi's iconography reflect the diverse philosophical interpretations of her nature and power. Some traditions highlight her as a fierce goddess of destruction, while others emphasize her nurturing and creative aspects. Some focus on her association with time and the cycle of birth, death, and rebirth, while others see her as a guide on the spiritual path. These diverse interpretations are not necessarily contradictory; rather, they represent different facets of her multifaceted personality, all contributing to the richness and complexity of her symbolism.

The influence of different schools of thought is also apparent in the variations of Bhairavi's depictions. The Kashmiri Shaivism tradition, for instance, may portray her with a different emphasis than the Bengal school, reflecting the unique spiritual and cultural contexts in which these traditions developed. This interplay between artistic style and philosophical interpretation enriches the overall understanding of Bhairavi's iconography. Each depiction offers a unique window into the complex and multifaceted nature of this powerful Mahavidya.

Furthermore, the evolution of Bhairavi's iconography over time reflects changes in religious and cultural landscapes. Earlier representations may differ significantly from later ones, not only in artistic style but also in the emphasis on certain attributes and aspects of her power. These changes highlight the adaptability of Tantric symbolism and the ability of Bhairavi's image to resonate with different generations and communities.

The study of Bhairavi's iconography is therefore not simply an aesthetic exercise; it is a rich exploration into the depths of Tantric thought and the evolving understanding of the Divine Feminine.

Her varied representations offer a compelling case study in the dynamism of religious symbolism and the multi-layered meanings embedded within visual art. The multitude of interpretations, far from diminishing her significance, enhances her richness and allows for a deeper engagement with her multifaceted nature and potent energy. The seemingly endless variations in her depiction underscore her adaptability and enduring power to inspire and transform across diverse cultural and historical contexts. Analyzing these variations provides valuable insight into the ongoing dialogue between religious thought, artistic expression, and cultural evolution. It is a testament to the enduring power of the Divine Feminine, constantly adapting and renewing itself while retaining its core essence. The continued study and appreciation of these diverse representations is essential for a complete and nuanced understanding of Bhairavi's profound significance within the Tantric tradition.

Bhairavis Association with Power and Transformation

Bhairavi's association with power is multifaceted, extending far beyond the simple categorization of "destructive" or "creative." She embodies a dynamic interplay of these seemingly opposing forces, reflecting the inherent duality present within the cosmos itself. Her power isn't merely a force of annihilation; it's a transformative energy that dismantles old structures to pave the way for new beginnings. This process of destruction and regeneration is fundamental to the cosmic cycle, mirroring the cyclical nature of time itself, a concept deeply interwoven with Bhairavi's essence.

She represents not only the end of a cycle, but also the fertile ground from which new life springs forth.

The Devi Gita, a pivotal text within Shaktism, offers valuable insights into Bhairavi's transformative power. While she may be depicted wielding weapons symbolizing destruction, such as a sword or a trident, these instruments are not employed for random violence. Instead, they serve as tools for dismantling illusion, severing karmic bonds, and clearing away obstacles that impede spiritual growth. This "destruction" is not an act of malice but a necessary prelude to purification and transformation. It is the clearing away of the dross, the impurities that obscure the true self, allowing the divine light within to shine forth. This is a crucial aspect of her role as a guide on the spiritual path; she helps the devotee shed their limiting beliefs, ingrained habits, and attachments that hinder their spiritual evolution.

Bhairavi's capacity to inspire both fear and awe speaks to the complex nature of her power. The fear she evokes is not simply the fear of physical harm, but rather the fear of confronting one's own shadow self, the aspects of oneself that one might prefer to ignore or deny. This confrontation is essential for spiritual growth, as it is only by acknowledging and integrating these "shadow" aspects that true wholeness can be achieved. The awe she inspires, on the other hand, stems from her immense power and her ability to facilitate profound transformation. She is revered not merely for her strength but for her capacity to guide devotees through the darkest depths of their being towards enlightenment.

The association of Bhairavi with time further underscores her transformative power. Time, in the Tantric worldview, is not linear but cyclical, a continuous process of creation, preservation, and destruction. Bhairavi is intimately linked to this cycle, representing both the ending of one phase and the beginning of another. She is the goddess of change, of transition, and of the inevitable flow of time itself. Her association with time allows her to act as a catalyst for transformation, propelling the devotee through the various stages of spiritual growth, from initial ignorance to ultimate liberation.

The visual representations of Bhairavi consistently reinforce this theme of transformation. The variations in her iconography—from the youthful, radiant goddess to the more fierce and terrifying aspects—reflect the multifaceted nature of her power and its ability to inspire both comfort and terror. This isn't a contradiction; rather, it points to the complex journey of spiritual growth, which often involves confronting difficult emotions and experiences. The fearsome aspects represent the challenges and trials that must be overcome, while the more benevolent representations symbolize the ultimate rewards of spiritual practice.

The fluidity of Bhairavi's iconography also signifies her adaptable nature. Her symbolism isn't fixed or static; it evolves and adapts to different cultural and historical contexts. This reflects the adaptability of the Tantric tradition itself, its capacity to integrate and transform itself in response to changing circumstances. The various depictions of Bhairavi across different regions and time periods showcase this remarkable flexibility, illustrating the richness and complexity of the Tantric worldview.

Moreover, the association of Bhairavi with specific animals further emphasizes her transformative power. Animals often act as symbolic representations of various qualities or energies. The lion, for example, signifies courage, strength, and untamed power. The tiger, similarly, represents fierceness and untamed energy, while the peacock represents beauty, grace, and the unfolding of spiritual potential. Each animal companion underscores a specific aspect of Bhairavi's power and its potential for transformation within the devotee.

The study of Bhairavi's iconography reveals a deeper understanding of her transformative potential. The careful analysis of her visual attributes—her attire, jewelry, weapons, animal companions, postures, and mudras—unveils the various dimensions of her power and the subtle ways in which she guides her devotees on the path to spiritual liberation. Each detail serves as a symbolic key to unlocking the deeper layers of meaning embedded within her representation.

Furthermore, the varying depictions of Bhairavi across different schools of Tantric thought highlight the richness and diversity of the tradition. Each school offers its own unique interpretation of her essence, reflecting the diverse philosophical perspectives and cultural contexts within which these traditions developed. These variations, rather than diminishing Bhairavi's importance, actually enrich our understanding of her multifaceted nature.

Bhairavi's association with power, then, is not merely about dominion or control, but about the transformative potential of both destruction and creation. She is a catalyst for change, a guide on the spiritual path, and a powerful symbol of the cyclical nature of time itself. Her capacity to inspire both fear and awe reflects the complex and challenging yet ultimately rewarding journey of self-discovery and spiritual growth. By understanding the multifaceted nature of her power, we gain a deeper appreciation for the depth and richness of the Tantric tradition and its profound relevance in the contemporary world.

The continued study of Bhairavi, through her iconography, her textual representations within the Devi Gita and other scriptures, and her role within the wider context of the ten Mahavidyas, allows for an ever-evolving understanding of her significance. Her influence extends beyond mere theological discussion; her energy inspires artists, poets, and spiritual seekers across centuries. The enduring power of Bhairavi lies not only in her ability to inspire awe and fear but in her capacity to act as a transformative force, guiding devotees on a journey of self-discovery and spiritual liberation. She stands as a potent symbol of the dynamic interplay between destruction and creation, the constant flux of the universe, and the boundless potential for transformation inherent within every individual. Her legacy continues to resonate, offering a powerful and enduring message of hope, empowerment, and the potential for profound inner change in the face of seemingly insurmountable obstacles. She is not merely a deity; she is an archetype, a mirror reflecting the potential for transformation inherent within us all. This transformative power, capable of both dismantling old structures and creating new possibilities, is perhaps the most defining characteristic of Bhairavi, the sixth Mahavidya. Her enduring appeal lies in her ability to embody the paradoxical nature of reality – the simultaneous existence of destruction and creation, darkness and light, fear and awe – ultimately leading the devotee toward a deeper understanding of the self and the divine.

Her continuing relevance in the modern world stems from her capacity to resonate with the constant state of flux and transformation that characterizes our contemporary experience. She offers a potent reminder that even amidst chaos and change, the potential for profound transformation always exists

Bhairavis Role in Tantric Rituals

Bhairavi's presence in Tantric rituals is not merely symbolic; she is an active participant, a powerful force invoked to facilitate profound spiritual transformation. Her role extends beyond passive observation; she is actively engaged in the process, guiding the practitioner through the complexities of the ritual and fostering a direct connection with the divine feminine energy she embodies. Understanding her function requires exploring the specific practices, mantras, and yantras associated with her worship.

The most crucial aspect of Bhairavi's role in Tantric rituals is the invocation of her energy. This isn't a simple act of calling upon her name; it's a profound engagement with her essence, a process of aligning oneself with her transformative power. This often involves intricate preparatory practices, including purification rituals, meditation, and the recitation of specific mantras. The goal is to create a sacred space, a purified environment where the practitioner can connect with Bhairavi's energy without interference from external distractions. This purification, however, extends beyond the physical realm. It involves a purification of the mind, a silencing of the internal chatter that often hinders spiritual progress. Only through this internal cleansing can the practitioner truly connect with the profound energy of Bhairavi.

The mantras associated with Bhairavi are powerful tools for invoking her presence and aligning oneself with her energy. These are not merely sounds; they are vibrational keys, unlocking specific aspects of her essence. Different mantras might focus on different qualities of Bhairavi, for example, one mantra might emphasize her power of destruction and transformation, while another might focus on her ability to bestow wisdom and insight. The careful selection and recitation of these mantras are essential to the success of the ritual, as they act as conduits for her energy, allowing it to flow into the practitioner. The precise pronunciation and intonation are crucial, as even slight variations can affect the quality and potency of the mantra's effect. Experienced practitioners often devote years to mastering the proper pronunciation and understanding the subtle nuances of these mantras. The rhythmic recitation, often accompanied by specific mudras (hand gestures), can induce altered states of consciousness, facilitating deeper connection with the divine feminine.

Yantras, geometric diagrams representing specific deities or energies, play a crucial role in Bhairavi's Tantric rituals. The Bhairavi Yantra is a complex geometric design that acts as a focal point for meditation and visualization. Through the contemplation of the yantra, the practitioner can access and experience the energy of Bhairavi directly. The yantra serves not only as a visual representation but also as a tool for focusing the mind, aligning the energy of the practitioner with the divine energy represented by the yantra. The intricate details of the yantra, its symbolic elements, and their arrangement all contribute to the overall potency and significance of the practice. The process of creating the yantra itself is considered sacred, with specific rules and rituals guiding the construction, ensuring the correct alignment of energies and the successful invocation of Bhairavi's presence. The act of creating the yantra is meditative and transformative in its own right, serving as a pathway to deeper connection.

Beyond mantras and yantras, various offerings are integral to Bhairavi's Tantric rituals. These are not simply gifts; they are symbolic expressions of devotion and an acknowledgment of her power. The types of offerings vary depending on the specific tradition and the practitioner's intentions. They might include flowers, incense, food, and other precious items, each chosen with care and intention. These offerings are not merely material; they symbolize the practitioner's surrender to Bhairavi's power and their willingness to submit to her transformative influence. The offering is a tangible act reflecting the inner devotion and a commitment to the process of transformation. The offering itself becomes a conduit for energy, strengthening the connection between the practitioner and the deity.

The spiritual significance of these rituals extends far beyond mere outward performance. They are pathways to inner transformation, tools for accessing and harnessing Bhairavi's transformative power. By engaging in these practices, the practitioner moves beyond intellectual understanding and enters into a direct experience of the divine feminine energy, leading to profound changes in consciousness and a deeper understanding of the self. The rituals are not simply about achieving specific goals or desires; they are about undergoing a process of purification, growth, and ultimately, liberation.

The specific rituals involving Bhairavi may vary across different Tantric traditions and lineages. Some might emphasize certain aspects of Bhairavi's nature more than others, while others may incorporate unique practices or variations in the mantras and yantras used. However, the underlying principle remains consistent: these rituals are aimed at facilitating a direct encounter with the divine feminine energy of Bhairavi and utilizing her transformative power for personal growth and spiritual evolution.

The efficacy of these rituals depends greatly on the practitioner's devotion, sincerity, and commitment to the process. It is not merely a mechanical undertaking but a profound spiritual practice demanding dedication and self-discipline. The transformation achieved is not merely intellectual or theoretical but deeply personal and transformative, affecting all aspects of the practitioner's life. It's a journey of self-discovery and self-transformation, guided by the potent energy of Bhairavi.

The use of specific mudras, hand gestures imbued with symbolic meaning, further enhances the efficacy of Bhairavi's rituals. Each mudra represents a particular energy or aspect of the divine feminine, allowing the practitioner to channel and focus that energy during the practice. The skillful manipulation of these mudras helps to align the practitioner's energy with Bhairavi's, facilitating a more profound and direct connection. The use of mudras isn't merely a physical act; it's a subtle manipulation of energy flow within the body, helping to amplify the effects of the ritual.

Furthermore, the setting and environment for Bhairavi's Tantric rituals are equally important. The ideal setting would be a secluded and sacred space, carefully prepared to enhance the practitioner's connection with the divine. This might involve the use of specific scents, colours, and objects designed to create a conducive atmosphere for meditation and spiritual communion. Creating a sacred space is crucial, as it helps to create a barrier between the external world and the inner spiritual experience. It facilitates a deeper immersion into the ritual and enhances the practitioner's connection with Bhairavi's energy. The carefully chosen environment acts as a catalyst, amplifying the transformative power of the ritual.

The interpretation and application of Bhairavi's Tantric rituals have evolved over centuries, adapting to various cultural and historical contexts. This evolution reflects the dynamic and adaptable nature of the Tantric tradition itself, demonstrating its capacity to integrate and transform itself in response to changing circumstances. The core principles remain constant; however, the specific practices and expressions might vary based on regional variations and the specific lineages within which the rituals are performed. Studying these variations provides a richer and more nuanced understanding of Bhairavi's multifaceted nature and the rich tapestry of Tantric traditions.

The study of Bhairavi's role within Tantric rituals offers a profound glimpse into the heart of Shaktism and the power of the divine feminine. It underscores the active engagement of the deity in the process of spiritual transformation, emphasizing the importance of dedicated practice and sincere devotion. By understanding and engaging in these rituals, practitioners can access a potent source of transformative energy, leading to personal growth, spiritual evolution, and a deeper connection with the divine. The rituals are not merely symbolic representations but are powerful tools facilitating a direct experience of the divine. Through the careful and respectful execution of these rituals, one can harness Bhairavi's immense power for positive transformation and spiritual liberation.

The enduring relevance of these rituals lies in their capacity to provide a pathway to inner transformation, a journey of self-discovery, and ultimately, a deeper connection with the divine feminine energy that permeates the universe.

Bhairavi in Different Literary and Artistic Traditions

Bhairavi's multifaceted nature is vividly reflected in the diverse literary and artistic traditions that have sought to capture her essence. Her image, attributes, and symbolism have evolved and adapted across different schools of thought and geographical regions, revealing a complex and dynamic deity whose meaning transcends temporal and spatial boundaries. Understanding these variations provides crucial insight into the rich tapestry of Hindu and Tantric thought.

In early Sanskrit texts, Bhairavi's presence is often intertwined with that of Bhairava, her consort. She is frequently portrayed as his fierce and powerful Shakti, his dynamic energy. These depictions emphasize her role as a destroyer of illusion and ignorance, a force capable of shattering limiting beliefs and paving the way for spiritual liberation. Her association with Bhairava, a manifestation of Shiva, highlights her connection to the transformative power of the divine masculine, underscoring the interplay between feminine and masculine energies in the cosmos. The early texts often focus on her terrifying aspects, reflecting her capacity to dissolve the ego and confront the darkness within. These depictions, while initially daunting, point to the transformative power inherent in facing one's deepest fears and insecurities. The fearsome aspects, however, are not presented as purely negative, rather as essential catalysts for spiritual growth.

Later Tantric texts, particularly those focused on Shaktism, offer a more nuanced and multifaceted representation of Bhairavi. While retaining her fierce and powerful aspects, these texts also emphasize her nurturing and compassionate qualities. She is depicted as a goddess who guides and protects her devotees, offering solace and wisdom to those who seek her grace. This shift reflects the evolving understanding of the divine feminine within Tantric traditions, acknowledging both its destructive and creative potential. The goddess is no longer simply a destroyer of ignorance but also a nurturer of wisdom and compassion, highlighting the dual nature of existence and the interplay between destruction and creation in the cosmic dance.

The Devi Gita, a crucial text within Shaktism, provides profound insight into Bhairavi's nature and attributes. While she might not be explicitly named throughout, her essence pervades the text. Many of the qualities attributed to the Devi within the Gita—her power, wisdom, compassion, and transformative ability—directly resonate with Bhairavi's essence. The Devi's ability to destroy ignorance and illusion, her capacity to bestow liberation, and her role as both a fierce protector and a compassionate guide—all these attributes find a powerful reflection in Bhairavi's image and symbolism. A careful study of the Devi Gita allows for a deeper understanding of Bhairavi's role within the larger framework of Shaktic thought.

Moving beyond textual representations, the artistic depictions of Bhairavi offer further insight into her evolving image and symbolism. In early sculptures and paintings, she is often portrayed in a fearsome form, with multiple arms wielding various weapons and adorned with skulls and ornaments associated with death and destruction. These depictions effectively capture her ability to dismantle illusions and overcome obstacles on the path to spiritual liberation. The imagery employed – skulls, weapons, garland of severed heads – are not merely gruesome; they symbolize the transcendence of earthly attachments, the shedding of the ego, and the courage needed to confront the darkness within. They symbolize the shattering of limitations and the fearless embrace of transformative change.

Over time, artistic representations of Bhairavi evolved to reflect the more nuanced understanding of her nature. While the fierce aspects remained, there is a gradual incorporation of more benevolent and compassionate features. Sculptures and paintings began to depict her with softer features, more graceful postures, and a greater emphasis on her wisdom and nurturing qualities. This transition is evident in the development of her iconography—the weapons might be replaced or supplemented with symbols of knowledge and
prosperity, and the grim adornments might be softened by more delicate jewelry or floral arrangements. The evolution of her artistic portrayal reflects the broadening spectrum of her significance and the evolving understanding of the divine feminine within the
Tantric tradition.

Regional variations in Bhairavi's artistic representation further illustrate her adaptability and diverse interpretations. Her iconography, attributes, and associated rituals differ slightly from one region to another, reflecting the interplay between local customs and the broader Tantric traditions. For instance, in some regions, she might be depicted riding a buffalo, symbolizing her association with the earth and its powerful, untamed energy. In others, she might be shown with a specific set of weapons or ornaments reflecting regional variations in iconographic conventions. These variations do not diminish her central essence; rather they enrich our understanding of her multifaceted nature and her capacity to integrate with diverse cultural contexts.

The artistic representations also provide visual parallels to the descriptions in texts. The fierce aspects often correspond to her role as a destroyer of illusion, while the benevolent aspects highlight her role as a guide and protector. The use of color, symbolism, and specific hand gestures (mudras) in artistic depictions further enhance the understanding of Bhairavi's complex attributes and their associated meanings. By carefully examining the artistic representations alongside textual descriptions, a richer and more comprehensive understanding of Bhairavi's symbolism and significance emerges.

The evolution of Bhairavi's image across different literary and artistic traditions underscores the dynamism of the Tantric tradition itself. Her representation is not static; it adapts and evolves in response to changing cultural contexts and evolving spiritual understandings. This adaptability highlights the living nature of the tradition, its capacity to integrate new ideas and perspectives while retaining its core principles. The ongoing interpretations and reinterpretations of Bhairavi's image reflect the enduring relevance of her symbolism and the continued search for meaning within the context of ever-changing human experiences. Bhairavi's story is not merely a historical account; it's a living testament to the transformative power of the divine feminine, eternally adapting to resonate with the spiritual seekers of each era. The study of her varied depictions therefore offers not only a historical perspective but also a crucial lens through which to understand the continuing evolution of Tantric thought and its relevance in contemporary times. Her adaptability ensures that her message remains potent and relevant, offering guidance and inspiration to spiritual seekers across cultures and generations.

Bhairavi and the Power of Transformation

The preceding exploration of Bhairavi's multifaceted nature, as reflected in historical texts and artistic representations, lays a foundation for understanding her enduring relevance in the contemporary world. While her iconography might seem rooted in a distant past, the potent energies she embodies resonate deeply with the challenges and opportunities of the twenty-first century.

Bhairavi's power isn't confined to the pages of ancient scriptures or the surfaces of antique sculptures; it offers a potent framework for personal transformation and the navigation of life's complexities.

One of the most significant aspects of Bhairavi's symbolism is her association with radical transformation. Her terrifying visage, often depicted with skulls and severed heads, is not simply a display of violence but a potent metaphor for the dismantling of limiting beliefs and outdated patterns of behavior. In a world characterized by rapid change and constant adaptation, Bhairavi's energy can be invoked to courageously confront ingrained fears, self-limiting beliefs, and destructive habits that hinder personal growth. This isn't a passive process; it demands active engagement with the shadows within, a willingness to confront the darkness that holds us back. Bhairavi acts as a catalyst, empowering individuals to sever the ties that bind them to outdated identities and embrace the potential for profound metamorphosis. The skulls and severed heads are not merely macabre imagery; they are potent symbols of letting go – releasing the past, discarding that which no longer serves, and creating space for a renewed sense of self.

This process of self-deconstruction, however, is not solely about destruction. Bhairavi's transformative power is inherently creative.

Just as the act of demolition clears the way for new construction, the dismantling of old patterns creates space for the emergence of a more authentic and empowered self. This creation is not imposed; it emerges organically from the process of confronting and transcending limitations. It's a process of self-discovery, unveiling hidden strengths and capabilities that lay dormant beneath layers of ingrained conditioning. The courage to confront one's deepest fears, the resilience to weather setbacks, and the capacity to embrace change – these are the gifts offered by Bhairavi, paving the way for personal growth, self-acceptance, and spiritual awakening.

The contemporary relevance of Bhairavi's energy is particularly potent in the context of overcoming obstacles. Life inevitably presents challenges, setbacks, and periods of intense difficulty. Bhairavi's fierce energy offers a powerful counterpoint to feelings of helplessness and despair. Her image, as a powerful, transformative force, can serve as a source of inspiration, reminding individuals of their own inner strength and resilience. Her ability to confront and overcome obstacles on a cosmic scale mirrors the individual's capacity to navigate their own personal challenges. By invoking her energy, individuals can tap into a deep wellspring of courage, allowing them to approach difficulties with greater clarity, resolve, and a willingness to confront whatever stands in their path.

The application of Bhairavi's energy in the modern context extends beyond personal transformation and obstacle overcoming. Her symbolism resonates powerfully with the challenges of social transformation and the creation of a more just and equitable world. Her capacity to dismantle outdated systems and structures mirrors the ongoing struggle for social justice and the dismantling of oppressive systems. Bhairavi's energy can be invoked as a source of strength and inspiration for those working towards positive social change, providing the courage to challenge injustice, to dismantle oppressive systems, and to build a better future. Her symbolism provides a potent metaphor for the societal need for radical transformation, highlighting the necessity of confronting ingrained prejudices, systemic inequalities, and harmful social norms.

The understanding of Bhairavi's power is not confined to a purely individual or solely social level. Her influence extends to the spiritual realm, offering a powerful framework for deepening one's spiritual practice and fostering a connection with the divine feminine. In many tantric traditions, Bhairavi represents a powerful embodiment of Shakti, the divine feminine energy. Through devotion and practice, individuals can tap into this energy, strengthening their connection to the divine and deepening their spiritual understanding. This connection can manifest in various ways: increased intuition, enhanced creativity, greater compassion, and a deeper sense of purpose and meaning in life. The practices associated with Bhairavi, such as mantra recitation, visualization, and devotional offerings, can facilitate this deeper connection.

Bhairavi's symbolic representation often involves a vibrant tapestry of colors, and these colors themselves hold symbolic significance. The deep reds and blacks often associated with her represent both the transformative power of destruction and the fertile darkness from which new creation arises. Other colors, such as gold or vibrant hues, might be incorporated depending on regional interpretations, all contributing to the multifaceted nature of her visual representation and offering a rich source of contemplation and spiritual practice. The careful study of these colors and their symbolism further enhances the understanding of Bhairavi's multifaceted energy and can serve as a powerful tool for personal reflection and spiritual growth.

The application of Bhairavi's energy necessitates a balanced approach. While her transformative power involves a necessary destruction of limiting beliefs and outdated patterns, this process should not be viewed as purely negative. The destruction is always in service of creation. It is a process of clearing away the old to make way for the new, a necessary step toward growth and evolution. This balance highlights the dual nature of existence, the constant interplay between destruction and creation inherent in the cosmos and within the human experience. The cultivation of this balance is crucial for a successful engagement with Bhairavi's energy, ensuring that the transformative process is one of empowerment and growth rather than mere demolition.

Furthermore, the invocation of Bhairavi's energy necessitates an understanding of responsibility and ethical considerations. Her power is immense, and it must be wielded with wisdom and discernment. The transformative process requires self-awareness, discipline, and a commitment to personal responsibility. The ability to distinguish between necessary destruction and unnecessary harm is paramount. The goal is not to engage in destructive actions or cause harm to others; rather it is to utilize Bhairavi's energy for personal growth, social justice, and spiritual awakening. This necessitates a deep understanding of the ethical implications and a commitment to harnessing her power for the greater good.

In conclusion, the contemporary relevance of Bhairavi lies in her capacity to inspire courage, resilience, and the capacity to embrace change. Her symbolism provides a powerful framework for personal transformation, overcoming obstacles, and fostering social justice. Her energy can be invoked to dismantle limiting beliefs, outdated patterns, and oppressive systems, creating space for the emergence of a more authentic, empowered, and compassionate self and a more just and equitable world. The study of Bhairavi, therefore, is not merely a historical or academic exercise; it is a living practice, a potent tool for personal growth and societal transformation,
relevant and empowering in the complexities of the modern world.

The invocation of her power is a journey of self-discovery, a testament to the enduring potential for transformation within each individual and within society at large.

Chhinnamastas Unique Iconography

The transition from Bhairavi's transformative power to the even more striking iconography of Chhinnamasta requires a shift in perspective, from the controlled demolition of the self to a radical act of self-sacrifice. Bhairavi dismantles limiting beliefs; Chhinnamasta transcends them entirely through a symbolic self-severing. This seemingly violent image, however, is far from a depiction of mere destruction. It is a potent representation of supreme self-mastery, a complete surrender to the divine will, and an embodiment of the ultimate sacrifice necessary for spiritual liberation.

Chhinnamasta's iconography is perhaps the most immediately arresting of all the Mahavidyas. Her image, often depicted as a three-eyed goddess, stands in stark contrast to the more conventional representations of other goddesses. The most striking element is her self-decapitated head, held aloft in her left hand, from which streams of blood gush forth. This blood, however, is not a symbol of death and destruction, but of life-giving energy. Two attendants, often depicted as Dakinis (female spirits associated with empowerment and liberation), eagerly drink this blood, signifying the nourishment and sustenance provided by the supreme sacrifice. The image is not one of morbidity, but of radical liberation and the ultimate offering of the self to the divine.

The symbolism of Chhinnamasta's self-decapitation is multifaceted and open to varied interpretations within Tantric traditions. One prominent interpretation views the severed head as representing the ego, the limited and illusory self that stands between the individual and ultimate realization. By severing this head, Chhinnamasta symbolically transcends the limitations of the ego, demonstrating the path to liberation from the cycle of birth and death (samsara). This act is not one of self-destruction, but of self-transcendence – a complete surrender of the individual will to the divine.

The act of self-decapitation can also be understood as a metaphor for the severing of attachment to worldly possessions and desires. In the pursuit of spiritual liberation, letting go of these attachments is crucial. Chhinnamasta's self-sacrifice, therefore, symbolizes the complete detachment necessary for spiritual awakening. The streams of blood represent the life force that is released when these attachments are relinquished, a life force that nourishes and sustains the spiritual journey. The act is not one of negation but a powerful affirmation of the divine, a total emptying of the self to make space for the divine to fully manifest.

The two Dakinis who drink Chhinnamasta's blood represent the inherent duality within the universe – the dynamic interplay of creation and destruction, preservation and transformation. They symbolize the complementary forces that are essential to the process of spiritual evolution. Their eager consumption of the life-giving blood represents the sustenance and nourishment that comes from surrendering to the divine will. They embody the acceptance of the cycle of death and rebirth, a cycle that is transcended through complete surrender. The act of drinking the blood underscores the symbiotic relationship between the goddess and her followers, a relationship built on selfless devotion and the acceptance of sacrifice as the path to liberation.

The positioning of Chhinnamasta is also significant. Often she is depicted standing on a copulating couple, representing the transcendence of worldly desires and the limitations of the physical realm. The act of standing on this couple signifies her elevation above the realm of physical pleasure and attachment. She has moved beyond the dualities of the material world and stands as a representation of pure spiritual energy. The couple, in this context, symbolizes the base desires and attachments that need to be
overcome on the path to liberation. Chhinnamasta's position above them highlights the attainment of a state of spiritual freedom.

Furthermore, Chhinnamasta is often shown wielding various weapons and symbols, adding layers to her already complex iconography. The Kamadhenu (the wish-fulfilling cow) and the mṛga (deer) sometimes appear in her iconography, representing abundance and the divine grace bestowed upon the truly devoted. These additions reinforce the notion of Chhinnamasta as a provider, a nourisher, not merely of spiritual sustenance, but also of material blessings for those who have surrendered completely to the divine.

The symbolic representation of abundance highlights the paradoxical nature of sacrifice, which leads to greater abundance.

Artistic representations of Chhinnamasta vary considerably across different schools of thought and geographical regions. Some depictions emphasize her fierce and terrifying aspects, reflecting the radical nature of her self-sacrifice. Other portrayals focus on her compassionate side, highlighting her role as a provider and nurturer. These variations, far from contradicting each other, reflect the multifaceted nature of the goddess and the many paths to spiritual realization. The diversity underscores that the path to liberation is not singular, but rather adapts to the spiritual maturity and understanding of the individual.

The variations in iconography also highlight the dynamism of Tantric traditions. Different schools of thought, over time, have adapted and interpreted the symbolism of Chhinnamasta to suit their particular philosophical perspectives and practices. This dynamism is a key characteristic of Tantrism, its ability to adapt and evolve while remaining rooted in its fundamental principles. The continuous evolution in her iconographic representations is a testament to the living tradition that encompasses her.

The understanding of Chhinnamasta's iconography requires a shift in perspective, a willingness to move beyond conventional understandings of sacrifice and self-destruction. Her image, while initially startling, is a powerful reminder of the necessity of transcending the limitations of the ego and surrendering completely to the divine will. Her self-sacrifice is not an act of negativity, but a radical affirmation of the divine, a complete emptying of the self to make space for the transcendent.

The diverse artistic representations of Chhinnamasta serve as a powerful testament to the dynamism and adaptability of Tantric traditions. The varying interpretations and stylistic choices, far from being contradictions, offer a rich tapestry of understanding, allowing individuals to connect with the goddess on multiple levels, according to their own spiritual development and understanding.

The iconography is not static; it is a living tradition, constantly evolving and adapting to the needs and understanding of different devotees and practitioners throughout history.

The blood flowing from her severed neck is not a sign of gruesome violence, but a life-giving stream of energy. It represents the energy released when we let go of attachments, ego, and limitations. This energy, consumed by the Dakinis, is a source of spiritual nourishment and empowerment, propelling the devotee towards liberation. This act of nourishing oneself through the divine sacrifice of the Goddess is integral to the understanding of Chhinnamasta and her transformative power.

The symbolism of Chhinnamasta extends beyond the purely visual. The study of her iconography is a spiritual practice in itself, prompting contemplation and self-reflection. The process of engaging with her image, of contemplating the meaning of her various attributes, can lead to deeper understanding of the self and the path to spiritual liberation. This contemplative process is crucial to the full appreciation of Chhinnamasta's power and her message of radical surrender.

In conclusion, Chhinnamasta's unique iconography, while seemingly violent and shocking at first glance, represents a profound spiritual truth: the necessity of self-transcendence and the radical surrender to the divine will. Her self-decapitation symbolizes the transcendence of the ego, the severance of attachments, and the ultimate sacrifice necessary for liberation. The diverse artistic representations across different schools of thought reflect the multifaceted nature of the goddess and the many paths to spiritual realization. The careful study of her iconography provides a powerful tool for self-reflection, enabling devotees to connect deeply with her transformative power and to embark on their own journey of spiritual liberation. The message remains a potent one for contemporary practitioners seeking true self-realization, highlighting the path of radical selflessness as a means to profound spiritual transformation. The image, once understood, becomes not a symbol of horror but of empowerment and a potent metaphor for the profound transformation inherent in the spiritual journey.

Chhinnamasta and the Concept of SelfSacrifice

The radical iconography of Chhinnamasta, with her self-severed head and the life-giving blood flowing from her neck, demands a deep exploration beyond the initial shock value. This image, central to her understanding, is not a representation of self-destruction, but rather a profound and powerful metaphor for the ultimate act of self-sacrifice necessary for spiritual liberation. The self-decapitation is not a physical act but a symbolic one, representing the transcendence of the ego, the illusory self that obscures our true nature and binds us to the cycle of samsara. In Tantric philosophy, the ego is often seen as the primary obstacle to spiritual enlightenment. It is the source of our attachments, desires, and illusions, keeping us trapped in the cycle of birth, death, and rebirth. Chhinnamasta's act of self-decapitation, therefore, represents a decisive severing of this ego-centric perspective, a complete renunciation of the limited self in favor of embracing the infinite divine.

This act of self-sacrifice, however, should not be misinterpreted as self-harm or nihilism. Quite the contrary, it represents a radical act of self-mastery and surrender to the divine will. By severing the head, Chhinnamasta symbolizes the complete relinquishing of individual control, a surrender to a higher power that transcends the limitations of the human mind. This is not a passive surrender, but an active choice, a conscious decision to embrace a reality beyond the confines of the ego. It is an act of profound courage and faith, requiring a complete trust in the divine plan and an
unwavering belief in the power of self-transcendence.

The blood that flows from Chhinnamasta's severed neck is not a symbol of death, but of life-giving energy. It represents the life force that is liberated when we relinquish our attachments and surrender to the divine. This energy is not lost or wasted; it nourishes and sustains the spiritual journey. The two Dakinis, who eagerly drink this blood, represent the duality inherent within the universe – the interplay of creation and destruction, preservation and
transformation. They embody the acceptance of the cycle of death and rebirth, a cycle that is ultimately transcended through complete

surrender to the divine. Their consumption of the blood signifies the sustenance and empowerment that comes from embracing this cycle, not as a trap, but as a necessary stage in the process of spiritual evolution. The act is not one of morbid fascination, but a celebration of life, transformation and the acceptance of cycles in the cosmos.

The symbolism of Chhinnamasta's self-decapitation can also be interpreted within the context of renunciation. In many Tantric traditions, renunciation plays a crucial role in the path to spiritual liberation. This does not necessarily mean abandoning all worldly possessions and relationships, but rather detaching from the attachments and desires that bind us to the material world.

Chhinnamasta's self-sacrifice represents the ultimate form of renunciation, a complete letting go of the ego and its attachments.

It is a radical embrace of emptiness, a willingness to surrender everything in order to achieve ultimate liberation. This act is not one of negation but of affirmation, a potent declaration of faith and trust in the divine.

The position of Chhinnamasta, often depicted standing on a copulating couple, further underscores the theme of renunciation.

This image represents her transcendence of worldly desires and attachments, her elevation above the realm of physical pleasure and sensual gratification. The couple symbolizes the base desires and attachments that need to be overcome on the path to liberation. Chhinnamasta's position above them highlights her attainment of a state of spiritual freedom, a state where she is no longer bound by the limitations of the material world. She demonstrates that true liberation is achieved not through the suppression of desires, but through transcending them completely.

The diverse artistic representations of Chhinnamasta across different schools of thought and geographical regions highlight the multifaceted nature of this goddess and the various paths to spiritual realization. Some depictions emphasize her fierce and terrifying aspects, reflecting the radical nature of her self-sacrifice. Others focus on her compassionate side, highlighting her role as a provider and nurturer. These variations, far from being contradictions, reflect the adaptability of Tantric traditions and their ability to accommodate diverse perspectives and practices.

The varying representations serve to remind us that the path to liberation is not singular, but rather a personalized journey, shaped by individual experiences and spiritual development.

The weapons and symbols often associated with Chhinnamasta also contribute to her complex iconography. The presence of the Kamadhenu (the wish-fulfilling cow) and the mṛga (deer) sometimes featured in her depictions, represents abundance and the divine grace bestowed upon the truly devoted. These elements reinforce the notion of Chhinnamasta not merely as a symbol of self-sacrifice, but also as a provider and nurturer, offering spiritual and material blessings to those who have surrendered completely to the divine. This highlights the paradoxical nature of sacrifice, demonstrating that true renunciation often leads to greater abundance and fulfillment. It is a testament to the transformative power of selflessness, showing that by emptying the self, we make space for the divine to fill us with unimaginable grace and abundance.

The study of Chhinnamasta's iconography is itself a spiritual practice. Contemplating the meaning of her various attributes, the symbolism of her self-decapitation, and the significance of the blood and the Dakinis, can lead to profound self-reflection and deeper understanding of the self and the path to liberation. This process is crucial for appreciating Chhinnamasta's transformative power and connecting with her energy. It's not merely a passive observation, but an active engagement, a spiritual journey in itself, leading to profound self-awareness.

The blood flowing from Chhinnamasta's severed neck should not be viewed with aversion or disgust, but as a life-giving stream of energy, the very essence of spiritual nourishment and empowerment. It is the energy released when we let go of attachments, ego, and limitations. It is the force that fuels our spiritual journey, pushing us towards liberation and self-realization.

The consumption of this blood by the Dakinis underscores the cyclical nature of existence, the continuous interplay of death and rebirth, and the ultimate transcendence of this cycle through complete surrender. It emphasizes the symbiotic relationship between the goddess and her devotees, highlighting the profound nourishment that comes from selfless devotion and acceptance of the divine will.

The message of Chhinnamasta, though expressed through shocking iconography, remains deeply relevant in the contemporary world. In an age characterized by ego-driven pursuits, consumerism, and relentless striving, Chhinnamasta's message of self-sacrifice, renunciation, and surrender offers a powerful antidote. Her image serves as a potent reminder that true fulfillment is not found in external acquisitions or the pursuit of worldly desires, but in the liberation of the self and the embrace of the divine. The path she embodies is one of radical selflessness, a journey that demands courage, faith, and a profound willingness to let go of the limitations of the ego in order to embrace the infinite possibilities of the divine within. The shocking beauty of her image ultimately serves as a profound and enduring symbol of transformation and liberation.

Chhinnamastas Role in Tantric Practices

Chhinnamasta's potent iconography extends far beyond its visual impact; it forms the bedrock of a rich tapestry of Tantric practices. Her presence in ritual and devotional life is not merely symbolic; it's an active engagement with the transformative energy she embodies.

Understanding her role in these practices requires exploring the interwoven threads of mantra, yantra, and specific ritualistic actions, each contributing to a profound spiritual experience.

Central to Chhinnamasta's Tantric practices is the use of mantra. Mantras, sacred syllables or sounds, are believed to possess potent vibrational energy capable of transforming consciousness.

Chhinnamasta's mantra, often chanted during her worship, acts as a conduit to connect with her energy and access her transformative power. The precise mantras vary across different lineages and traditions, often guarded within the guru-shishya parampara (the teacher-student lineage). These mantras are not mere incantations; they are keys that unlock deeper levels of awareness and spiritual understanding. Through repeated chanting, the practitioner aligns their consciousness with Chhinnamasta's energy, gradually dissolving the ego and fostering a sense of unity with the divine.

The rhythmic repetition of the mantra is not merely a vocal exercise, but a meditation in itself, a journey towards self-transcendence guided by the resonant energy of the sacred syllables. The power of these mantras lies not in the act of chanting itself, but in the practitioner's devotion, faith, and intention.

The yantra, a geometric diagram, serves as another crucial element in Chhinnamasta's Tantric practices. These complex designs are not simply aesthetic creations; they are considered sacred tools imbued with potent spiritual energy. The yantra associated with Chhinnamasta often incorporates intricate patterns and symbols that reflect her essence and attributes. The visual contemplation of the yantra, during meditation or ritual, is a way to focus the mind and connect with the goddess's energy. Each line, shape, and symbol within the yantra holds deep spiritual meaning, acting as a focal point for concentration and a guide towards deeper levels of consciousness. The process of creating the yantra itself is also a significant act of devotion, requiring precision and focus. The construction of the yantra acts as a meditative act in itself, imbuing the practitioner with the goddess's energy as they carefully create the sacred geometry. The act of creating or contemplating the yantra serves as a powerful tool for achieving meditative states, accessing Chhinnamasta's power, and fostering self-transformation.

Beyond mantras and yantras, specific rituals form the cornerstone of Chhinnamasta worship. These rituals vary across different Tantric traditions, but generally involve offerings, visualizations, and the recitation of mantras. Offerings to Chhinnamasta often include flowers, fruits, incense, and sometimes even blood, symbolically representing the surrender of the ego and the acceptance of the cyclical nature of life and death. While the use of blood should be approached with deep respect and understanding, it doesn't represent self-harm or violence, but rather signifies the ultimate sacrifice – the surrender of the ego. The symbolic act represents a complete relinquishing of attachment, allowing for spiritual growth and liberation. The visualization techniques employed during Chhinnamasta's worship involve focusing on her image and contemplating her symbolism, which fosters a connection with the goddess and her energy. Such visualizations are not merely visual exercises; they serve as active pathways to access the deeper spiritual essence of the goddess and foster self-transformation.

The rituals surrounding Chhinnamasta often involve advanced Tantric practices, reserved for those with proper training and guidance from a qualified guru. These practices are not to be undertaken lightly, requiring significant spiritual maturity and a deep understanding of the principles of Tantra. It's crucial to emphasize that these practices should never be approached without proper guidance. Improper understanding or execution can lead to negative consequences. The rituals are designed to facilitate a profound transformation within the practitioner, leading to the dissolution of the ego and the realization of the divine within.

These advanced practices demand dedicated practice and self-discipline, requiring a high level of commitment and personal responsibility.

The significance of Chhinnamasta's presence in Tantric practices lies not in mere ritualistic performance, but in the transformative potential it unlocks. The practices are meant to foster a radical shift in perspective, encouraging the practitioner to confront their deepest fears and attachments. This confrontation is not designed to be punishing but rather to catalyze profound personal growth and liberation. The process encourages the practitioner to release the self's limitations, thereby making space for a deeper understanding of the divine reality.

The association of Chhinnamasta with specific deities and concepts further enriches her Tantric role. Her connection with other Mahavidyas, particularly Kali, highlights the multifaceted nature of the divine feminine. The two goddesses, despite their contrasting iconography, share a common thread – the transcendence of limitations. Kali, often associated with destruction and transformation, shares Chhinnamasta's power to break down the ego. This shared characteristic indicates that the path to liberation, though expressed through diverse paths, leads towards the same destination: self-realization. Her relationship with other Shaktic deities further underscores the interconnectedness within the larger cosmic framework. It reveals the various manifestations of divine energy, each offering different paths to understanding and realization.

In conclusion, Chhinnamasta's role in Tantric practices is multifaceted and powerful. Her association with mantras, yantras, and specific rituals provides pathways to connect with her potent transformative energy. These practices are not mere symbolic actions; they are potent tools for self-transformation and spiritual liberation. The journey involves confronting limitations, surrendering the ego, and ultimately embracing the divine within. It is a path that necessitates proper guidance, dedication, and a profound understanding of the principles of Tantra. The ultimate goal is not simply to perform the rituals, but to undergo the transformation they are designed to facilitate – a journey towards self-realization and liberation from the cycle of samsara. The power of these practices lies in their ability to catalyze a profound inner shift, leading to a deeper understanding of oneself and the divine reality. The path is challenging, but the potential rewards – self-realization and liberation – are beyond measure. Understanding

Chhinnamasta within the context of these practices offers a profound insight into the transformative power of Tantric traditions and the dynamic nature of the divine feminine. The seemingly paradoxical nature of her iconography reflects the complex journey of spiritual growth, emphasizing the need for both radical surrender and unwavering faith.

Chhinnamasta in Various Textual Sources

Chhinnamasta's presence in textual sources offers a fascinating glimpse into the evolution of her symbolism and the diverse interpretations that have emerged across different traditions and time periods. While her most striking iconography – self-decapitation and the consumption of her own blood – remains a constant, the nuances surrounding this central image vary considerably. Understanding these variations requires examining the different textual traditions that depict her, acknowledging that interpretations often reflect the specific theological and philosophical framework of each source.

The earliest textual references to Chhinnamasta are often shrouded in ambiguity, making it challenging to pinpoint the precise origin of her iconography. Some scholars suggest that her roots may lie in pre-Tantric traditions, possibly connected to ancient goddesses associated with blood sacrifice and life force. However, the most significant textual accounts of Chhinnamasta emerge within the context of the various Tantric traditions, particularly those within Shaktism. These texts, often composed in Sanskrit and other regional languages, provide detailed descriptions of her appearance, attributes, and the spiritual significance she embodies. However, it's vital to remember that these texts are not always consistent or unified in their depictions. Variations exist across different lineages, schools of thought, and geographical regions, reflecting the fluid and dynamic nature of Tantric traditions.

Within the various Tantric texts, Chhinnamasta's iconography is typically detailed, though the interpretations can differ. Many texts depict her as a three-eyed goddess, adorned with ornaments and celestial attributes. Her severed head is often shown held aloft by one of her hands, while she consumes her own blood, which flows into the mouths of her two attendants, typically identified as her shaktis or energies. The symbolism of self-decapitation is a central point of interpretation. Some scholars see it as a representation of the ultimate sacrifice, a complete renunciation of ego and attachment. The self-consumption of her blood signifies the cyclical nature of existence, the constant regeneration and transformation inherent in the cosmos. The act isn't interpreted as self-mutilation or violence but as a profound symbolic gesture of self-offering to the divine. The blood, interpreted as life force or creative energy, is then shared with her attendants, highlighting the interconnectedness of all beings and the shared participation in the divine energy.

The variations in textual descriptions extend to the interpretation of her attendants. While frequently depicted as her shaktis, the identities of these attendants sometimes vary across different texts, suggesting a degree of fluidity in their symbolic role. Some texts provide specific names for the attendants, associating them with particular aspects of Chhinnamasta's power or energy. These variations don't necessarily indicate contradictions but rather highlight the adaptability of her symbolism within diverse Tantric lineages. Each lineage or tradition might emphasize particular aspects of Chhinnamasta's personality or powers, resulting in slightly different depictions and interpretations.

The textual accounts also differ in their descriptions of the specific contexts in which Chhinnamasta appears. Some texts place her within larger mythological narratives, linking her to other deities and events. These narratives provide further context for her symbolism, offering insights into her wider role within the cosmic order. Other texts focus primarily on her iconography and her mantras, emphasizing the practical aspects of her worship and the ritualistic practices associated with her. The emphasis on ritual and practice underlines the practical application of Tantric knowledge, highlighting the importance of experiential understanding. The texts offer a rich tapestry of symbolic layers, ranging from the cosmological to the highly personal.

Another crucial aspect of understanding Chhinnamasta in different textual sources is the context of Kali Yuga. Many Tantric texts emphasize the significance of the Mahavidyas in the current age, associating their emergence and power with the specific challenges and characteristics of Kali Yuga. These texts often portray Chhinnamasta as a potent force for overcoming the obstacles and negative energies prevalent in this age. The radical nature of her iconography – the self-sacrifice, the consumption of her own blood

– is interpreted as a powerful metaphor for confronting and transcending the limitations of the ego, which is often seen as a central obstacle to spiritual growth in Kali Yuga. In this context, her blood isn't merely a symbolic representation but a dynamic force capable of purification and transformation.

Furthermore, certain texts associate Chhinnamasta with specific mantras and yantras, offering practical instructions for ritual worship. These mantras, considered powerful vibrational tools, are believed to activate Chhinnamasta's energy and facilitate a connection with her power. The yantras, geometrical diagrams, provide a visual focus for meditation and concentration, serving as sacred tools to channel the goddess's energy. The precise mantras and yantras vary across different textual traditions, reflecting the diversity of Tantric practices. However, their common purpose is to guide the practitioner towards deeper states of consciousness and spiritual transformation.

The textual descriptions of Chhinnamasta's worship practices also vary, with some texts emphasizing specific offerings, visualizations, and rituals. While many practices remain esoteric and accessible only through the guru-shishya parampara (teacher-student lineage), certain common themes emerge. The importance of devotion, surrender, and a sincere intention to transcend egoistic limitations repeatedly appears. The symbolic acts of offering and sacrifice are not merely outward expressions but inner transformations. The emphasis is on inner purification, leading to a deeper understanding of oneself and the divine.

Beyond the specific Tantric traditions, Chhinnamasta also appears in some non-Tantric texts, albeit less prominently. These appearances often offer a different perspective on her symbolism, sometimes integrating her into a broader mythological or philosophical context. These instances highlight the adaptability and inclusivity of Hindu mythology, allowing for multiple interpretations and integrations of various goddesses within the wider pantheon. Analyzing these non-Tantric references can illuminate the evolution of her image and meaning across broader religious and cultural landscapes.

In conclusion, Chhinnamasta's representation in various textual sources offers a rich and complex tapestry of interpretations. While her core iconography remains consistent, the nuances in her depiction vary according to the specific theological and philosophical framework of each source. Understanding these variations allows us to appreciate the dynamic and fluid nature of Tantric traditions and the multifaceted symbolism of this powerful goddess. Her enduring appeal lies in her capacity to inspire both profound awe and intense contemplation, prompting devotees to grapple with existential questions and strive for spiritual transformation. The ongoing scholarly exploration of these textual sources continues to shed light on the enduring power and evolving meaning of Chhinnamasta. Her image, though striking and sometimes unsettling, ultimately serves as a potent symbol of the transformative power of the divine feminine, challenging conventional notions of sacrifice, liberation, and the cyclical nature of existence. Her presence in these diverse textual sources underlines her enduring significance in the Hindu pantheon and her continuing relevance in the spiritual landscape of the present day.

The ongoing study and interpretation of these sources provide a continually unfolding appreciation of this complex and powerful goddess.

Chhinnamasta and the Path of SelfRealization

Chhinnamasta's self-decapitation, a potent image that initially strikes many as shocking, is, upon closer examination, a profound metaphor for the process of self-realization. It signifies the necessary dismantling of the ego, that false sense of self that prevents us from experiencing the true, unbounded nature of consciousness. The ego, with its clinging to attachments, desires, and fears, acts as a veil obscuring the divine within. Chhinnamasta's radical act symbolizes the courageous severing of this veil, a decisive break from the limitations imposed by the ego's constructs. This is not a literal act of self-harm, but a symbolic representation of the inner work required on the path of spiritual growth. It is a call to action, urging us to confront our deepest fears and insecurities, and to transcend the boundaries of our perceived limitations.

The consumption of her own blood further illuminates this process. The blood, often interpreted as *prana* , the life force or vital energy, represents the essential energy that sustains us. By consuming her own blood, Chhinnamasta demonstrates the cyclical nature of existence, the constant interplay of creation and destruction, life and death. It's not an act of self-destruction, but a powerful symbol of transformation and regeneration. The life force is not annihilated; it is transmuted, channeled, and ultimately shared. This act highlights the interconnectedness of all things, the inherent unity underlying the apparent diversity of existence. Just as Chhinnamasta nourishes her attendants with her life force, so too do we, through self-realization, contribute to the collective well-being and the sustenance of the cosmic order.

This act of self-sacrifice is not a passive surrender but a dynamic act of empowerment. It requires immense courage, determination, and self-awareness. The path of self-realization is rarely easy; it necessitates confronting our shadow selves, acknowledging our imperfections, and accepting the full spectrum of our being, including the aspects we may find unpleasant or challenging.

Chhinnamasta's example inspires us to embrace this process, to confront our fears with unflinching honesty, and to release the attachments that bind us to the illusion of separation. Her image serves as a reminder that true freedom lies not in clinging to the ego's desires, but in the courageous act of letting go.

The two attendants who receive Chhinnamasta's blood represent the integration of the opposing forces within us. They signify the harmonious blending of seemingly contradictory aspects of our nature. They represent the unification of Shiva and Shakti, the masculine and feminine principles within the cosmos, reflecting the need for balance and integration within ourselves. By nourishing her attendants, Chhinnamasta demonstrates the importance of nurturing and sustaining the different aspects of our being, recognizing that even seemingly opposing forces can coexist in harmony, contributing to a holistic and integrated sense of self. The path of self-realization often necessitates reconciling these polarities within us—the conscious and unconscious, the light and shadow, the rational and intuitive.

Chhinnamasta's iconography also speaks to the importance of overcoming self-limiting beliefs. These beliefs, often rooted in fear and insecurity, act as constraints, hindering our ability to realize our full potential. The act of self-decapitation can be interpreted as a symbolic dismantling of these limiting beliefs, a courageous challenge to the narratives we tell ourselves about our capabilities and limitations. By confronting and transcending these beliefs, we open ourselves to new possibilities, expanding our capacity for growth and transformation. Chhinnamasta's unwavering gaze emphasizes the importance of self-belief, the conviction that we are capable of achieving our spiritual goals, despite the challenges that may lie ahead.

In the context of Kali Yuga, Chhinnamasta's message becomes even more potent. This age, often characterized by materialism, egotism, and spiritual confusion, demands a radical approach to self-transformation. Chhinnamasta's iconography serves as a potent antidote to the negative energies of this era, urging us to confront the pervasive illusion of separation and embrace the interconnectedness of all things. Her radical self-sacrifice mirrors the need for a complete surrender to the divine, a willingness to relinquish the ego's grasp on control. In the chaos and uncertainty of Kali Yuga, Chhinnamasta provides a powerful example of unwavering resolve, guiding us towards inner peace and spiritual liberation despite the external turmoil.

The application of Chhinnamasta's energy in contemporary life extends beyond mere contemplation of her iconography. Her power can be invoked through various practices, including mantra recitation, yantra meditation, and visualization. Chanting her mantras, often found within Tantric texts, can create a powerful vibrational resonance, activating her energy within the practitioner. Yantra meditation, focusing on the geometrical patterns associated with her, can facilitate deeper states of consciousness and enhance concentration. Visualization practices, where the devotee imagines themselves embodying Chhinnamasta's qualities, can cultivate courage, determination, and the capacity to overcome self-limiting beliefs.

The path of self-realization, however, is not a solitary journey. The guidance of a qualified guru or spiritual teacher is often crucial in navigating the complexities of Tantric practices and understanding the nuances of Chhinnamasta's symbolism. The guru-shishya parampara, the teacher-student lineage, provides a framework for safe and effective spiritual development, offering support and guidance during times of challenge and doubt. This traditional lineage ensures the integrity and responsible application of these powerful spiritual tools, avoiding potential pitfalls that can arise from misinterpretations or inappropriate applications of Tantric practices.

Furthermore, Chhinnamasta's message resonates deeply with the contemporary emphasis on self-care and mindful living. Her self-sacrifice is not self-destructive, but rather a profound act of self-compassion. It highlights the importance of listening to our inner voice, recognizing our limitations, and being willing to make necessary changes for our own well-being. The radical act of self-decapitation can be understood as a metaphorical severing of unhealthy patterns and relationships that no longer serve our highest good. This necessitates self-honesty and a willingness to confront difficult truths about ourselves. The path of self-realization, therefore, requires both courage and compassion, a willingness to confront our shadows while nurturing our inner light.

Moreover, Chhinnamasta's energy can be profoundly empowering for women, particularly in addressing societal challenges related to gender inequality and discrimination. Her defiant self-assertion and radical act of self-mastery can inspire women to challenge patriarchal structures and reclaim their power. Her image stands as a symbol of strength, resilience, and self-determination, reminding women of their inherent divinity and their capacity for self-transformation. In a world often defined by external pressures, Chhinnamasta encourages self-empowerment and encourages women to take ownership of their lives and destinies.

In conclusion, Chhinnamasta's symbolic power extends far beyond the striking image of self-decapitation. She embodies a profound path of self-realization, demanding courage, determination, and a willingness to confront our deepest fears and insecurities. Her message resonates deeply with the challenges of Kali Yuga, urging us to transcend the limitations of the ego and embrace the interconnectedness of all beings. Through various practices, including mantra recitation, yantra meditation, and visualization, devotees can tap into her transformative energy, fostering inner peace, self-empowerment, and spiritual liberation. Her iconography serves as a potent reminder that true freedom lies not in clinging to the illusion of separation, but in the courageous act of letting go, embracing the cyclical nature of existence, and recognizing the divine within. Understanding her symbolic language opens a path to a deeper understanding of self and the transformative power inherent within each of us. The journey may be challenging, but the reward—the realization of our true nature—is immeasurable.

Dhumavatis Iconography and Attributes

Dhumavati, the Mahavidya associated with widowhood and the acceptance of aging and decay, presents a unique challenge to conventional interpretations of feminine divinity. Unlike the youthful, vibrant goddesses often depicted in Hindu iconography, Dhumavati embodies a different kind of power—the power of resilience, acceptance, and wisdom gained through experience. Her iconography, therefore, is far from conventionally attractive; rather, it is deliberately unsettling, forcing the viewer to confront uncomfortable truths about the cyclical nature of life and the inevitability of loss.

Her visual representation frequently depicts her as an elderly woman, her features often accentuated to emphasize age and possibly even decay. This deliberate aging is not a sign of diminished power, but a reflection of the wisdom accumulated over a lifetime of experiences. The wrinkles etched on her face, the graying hair, and the possibly hunched posture all speak to the passage of time, reminding us of the impermanence inherent in all things. This defiance of conventional beauty standards reflects the Tantric understanding that true beauty lies not in physical perfection but in spiritual maturity and acceptance of one's true self, regardless of societal expectations. The aging aspect of Dhumavati's iconography is a powerful antidote to the obsession with youth and the fear of aging prevalent in many modern societies.

Further contributing to her unconventional portrayal is her association with crows. Often depicted with or surrounded by crows, these birds are symbols of inauspiciousness in many cultural contexts. However, within the context of Dhumavati's iconography, they are not mere omens of bad luck, but rather companions that represent her acceptance of the shadow aspects of life—the undesirable, the unwanted, the overlooked. Crows, scavengers of the battlefield and the discarded, mirror Dhumavati's embrace of the seemingly undesirable, illustrating her ability to find power and wisdom even in places of apparent loss and desolation. They highlight her ability to transform negativity into understanding and the power she derives from her unconventional status.

Her vehicle, a broken-down chariot, often depicted as dilapidated and rickety, further reinforces her association with decay and impermanence. This is not a symbol of weakness or defeat, however, but rather a powerful statement about the impermanence of material possessions and the need to detach from worldly attachments. The broken chariot serves as a metaphor for the relinquishment of the ego's desire for control and the acceptance of the unpredictable nature of life's journey. This contrasts sharply with the chariots of other goddesses, often adorned with grandeur and representing power and control, highlighting Dhumavati's unique approach to power and her rejection of material opulence. The broken chariot also serves as a powerful reminder that even the most powerful structures eventually crumble, and that true strength lies not in outward displays of power but in inner resilience and spiritual fortitude.

The portrayal of Dhumavati often includes a range of attributes, further enriching the complexity of her symbolism. She is often depicted holding a skull-cup or a kapala, symbolizing the acceptance of mortality and the ultimate transience of the physical form. This skull-cup is not a gruesome symbol of death but rather a vessel representing the cyclical nature of life and death, highlighting the interconnectedness between the two. It acts as a reminder of the preciousness of life and the need to appreciate the fleeting nature of each moment. It can also be interpreted as a metaphor for the ability to consume negativity and transform it into wisdom, a crucial ability in navigating life's challenges. The skull-cup represents the vessel of her wisdom, gained through experience and acceptance of life's harsher realities.

Another common attribute is a winnowing basket, known as a sura-patra. This symbolizes the sifting and separating of the essential from the inessential, reflecting Dhumavati's ability to discern truth from illusion, wisdom from ignorance. Just as the winnowing basket separates chaff from grain, so does Dhumavati help us separate our true selves from the illusions and attachments that obscure our path to spiritual liberation. The sura-patra, therefore, acts as a potent symbol of discernment, enabling us to sift through the complexities of life and identify that which is truly valuable and meaningful.

Her staff or danda often accompanies her, representing her authority and her ability to navigate the challenges of life. The staff is not simply a tool of dominance, but a symbol of support and guidance, representing her ability to help others navigate their own difficult times. This also ties into the Tantric concept of a guru, a spiritual teacher who provides guidance and support on the path to self-realization. Dhumavati, in her form as a wise and compassionate guide, offers spiritual aid to those who seek it, leading them through darkness towards inner light.

The iconography of Dhumavati varies across different regional schools and artistic traditions. While the core elements—the elderly woman, the crows, the broken chariot, and the skull-cup—remain relatively consistent, there are subtle variations in attire, posture, and accompanying attributes. These variations highlight the fluid and dynamic nature of religious interpretations and the inherent multiplicity of meaning within Tantric traditions. These artistic differences reflect different cultural interpretations and emphasizations of Dhumavati's multifaceted nature. Some representations might highlight her compassionate side, emphasizing her role as a guide and protector, while others may portray her more austere and intimidating aspects, emphasizing her association with the challenging realities of life.

Despite these variations, the core message remains consistent. Dhumavati is not a goddess to be feared or avoided, but rather a powerful symbol of resilience, acceptance, and the wisdom that comes from facing life's inevitable challenges. Her unconventional iconography serves as a reminder that true power lies not in avoiding suffering but in facing it head-on, learning from it, and transforming it into wisdom. She is a guide for those navigating the difficult passages of life, offering solace, strength, and wisdom to those who embrace her unique, unconventional path. She represents the acceptance of the entirety of life's experiences—joy and sorrow, growth and decay—and offers a profound message of strength and resilience in the face of adversity.

Understanding Dhumavati's iconography necessitates moving beyond superficial judgments and embracing a deeper understanding of the Tantric perspective. Her unsettling appearance is not intended to repel, but to challenge our conventional notions of beauty, power, and divinity. She invites us to confront our own fears of aging, loss, and decay, urging us to accept these aspects of life as integral components of the larger cosmic dance. Her iconography is, in its own way, a form of empowerment, reminding us that true strength lies not in avoiding life's challenges but in embracing them with courage and wisdom. She is a powerful reminder of the impermanence of all things and the importance of cultivating inner strength and resilience in the face of change.

In the context of Kali Yuga, Dhumavati's message takes on a particular significance. The current era, often characterized by rapid technological advancement, societal upheaval, and a pervasive sense of uncertainty, reflects many of the themes associated with Dhumavati. Her ability to navigate the darkness and find wisdom within chaos provides a powerful archetype for navigating the complexities of modern life. Her acceptance of the imperfect and broken reflects the need to embrace the imperfections of the current age and to find strength in the face of uncertainty. Her message of resilience and acceptance serves as a powerful antidote to the pervasive anxieties and fears that characterize our times, offering a path towards inner peace and spiritual fulfillment amidst external turmoil. In a world obsessed with material success and outward appearances, Dhumavati's iconography stands as a powerful reminder of the importance of inner strength, spiritual wisdom, and the acceptance of life's inevitable challenges. The wisdom she represents becomes particularly relevant in navigating the complexities and uncertainties of Kali Yuga, highlighting the importance of inner peace and spiritual resilience in the face of unprecedented change. Her unconventional power is one that is increasingly relevant in a world grappling with its own complexities and uncertainties.

The study of Dhumavati's iconography is, therefore, not merely an academic exercise but a profound spiritual journey. It invites us to confront our own fears and insecurities, to embrace the full spectrum of human experience, and to discover the hidden wisdom

within the seemingly unsettling aspects of life. By understanding her symbolism, we open ourselves to a deeper appreciation of the Tantric worldview and discover a profound path towards self-realization and spiritual liberation, a journey that is particularly crucial in navigating the challenges and uncertainties of the present era. Her image remains a potent reminder that true power resides not in external displays but in the unwavering strength of the inner spirit, capable of transforming even the most challenging
experiences into sources of wisdom and growth. Dhumavati's iconography, therefore, serves as a potent guide for self-discovery and spiritual transformation in the 21st century.

Dhumavati and the Embracing of Solitude

Dhumavati's embrace of solitude extends beyond a simple preference for seclusion; it represents a profound spiritual practice, a deliberate withdrawal from the clamor of the external world to cultivate inner peace and wisdom. This solitude is not born of rejection or bitterness, but rather from a conscious choice to prioritize inner growth and spiritual development. It is a deliberate turning inward, away from the distractions and attachments that often obscure our true nature. Her solitary existence is not an indication of isolation, but rather a testament to the power of self-reliance and the ability to find fulfillment within oneself. This resonates deeply with the Tantric emphasis on self-realization, highlighting the importance of introspection and self-discovery as pathways to spiritual liberation.

The association of Dhumavati with widowhood adds another layer to her complex symbolism. In many societies, widowhood is often associated with loss, social isolation, and a diminished status. However, Dhumavati transcends these societal perceptions. Her widowhood is not a state of deprivation, but rather a metaphor for the relinquishment of worldly attachments and the acceptance of impermanence. It symbolizes the shedding of the ego's clinging to transient experiences and possessions, a crucial step on the path to spiritual liberation. Her solitary state mirrors the inner journey of self-discovery, a process often marked by letting go of past identities and expectations, embracing a new understanding of oneself, unbound by societal constructs. This renunciation isn't a rejection of life, but a profound acceptance of its cyclical nature. It is an understanding that life's transient nature is not inherently negative, but a necessary part of a larger, cosmic process.

The acceptance of challenging circumstances is central to Dhumavati's essence. Her iconography deliberately depicts her in a manner that challenges conventional notions of beauty and power. This deliberate unsettling nature reflects the Tantric principle of embracing the totality of existence, including its darker and more challenging aspects. The aged appearance, the association with crows, and the broken chariot all symbolize the acceptance of decay, loss, and imperfection. These are not signs of weakness or defeat but rather indicators of a profound understanding of life's cyclical nature, an acceptance of the inevitable processes of aging and death. This acceptance is not passive resignation, but rather a powerful act of empowerment, a conscious choice to find strength and wisdom in the face of adversity.

This acceptance extends beyond the personal realm. Dhumavati's embrace of solitude also involves accepting the solitude and suffering of others. She is often seen as a compassionate guide for those who have experienced loss, sorrow, and hardship. Her solitude is not an isolated existence but a position from which she offers solace and support to others navigating similar challenges.

She serves as a reminder that hardship is a shared human experience and that strength can be found in mutual understanding and compassion. This aspect of Dhumavati highlights the importance of empathy and compassion in a world often characterized by isolation and indifference.

The spiritual lessons associated with Dhumavati's form are multifaceted and profound. Her embrace of solitude teaches the importance of introspection, self-reliance, and the cultivation of inner peace. Her association with widowhood emphasizes the acceptance of impermanence, the relinquishment of attachments, and the transformative power of loss. Her acceptance of challenging circumstances underscores the significance of resilience, inner strength, and the ability to find wisdom in adversity. These lessons are not merely theoretical concepts; they are practical guides for navigating the complexities of life, offering tools for overcoming challenges and finding fulfillment amidst hardship. Her wisdom is not confined to those who have experienced widowhood, but it is a universal message of acceptance, resilience, and the power of inner transformation.

Her symbolism resonates with many practices within Tantric traditions. Her solitude can be interpreted as a form of yogic practice, mirroring the withdrawal from sensory stimulation and the cultivation of inner awareness. Her acceptance of impermanence mirrors the detachment from material possessions and ego-centric desires which are crucial aspects of many Tantric paths. Her ability to find strength in difficult situations reflects the Tantric capacity to transform negativity into spiritual growth. The crows, often associated with bad omens, become in Dhumavati's context, symbols of acceptance of the shadow self, the parts of ourselves we often try to deny or repress.

The broken chariot, her vehicle, is particularly significant. While seemingly a symbol of defeat or misfortune, it also represents the relinquishing of attachment to material possessions and the illusion of control. The brokenness itself signifies the inherent impermanence of all things, a reminder that even the most steadfast structures eventually crumble. This highlights the importance of inner strength and resilience over external displays of power. It encourages us to let go of the desire to control every aspect of our lives and instead embrace the unpredictable flow of existence. This is a powerful message in our current era defined by a relentless pursuit of control and an aversion to uncertainty.

Dhumavati's association with solitude also implies a deep connection to the inner world. Her withdrawal from societal norms is a journey of self-discovery, a deepening of one's spiritual practice. This inner journey often involves confronting one's own shadow aspects, confronting fears, and accepting imperfections. This process, far from being negative, is essential for achieving spiritual maturity. It is a process of purification, an unveiling of one's true self, free from the constraints of societal expectations and personal illusions. This solitary journey demands courage, self-discipline, and a willingness to face difficult truths about oneself and the world.

The spiritual growth fostered by embracing solitude is central to Dhumavati's essence. It is a journey of self-discovery, of confronting inner demons, and of developing inner strength and resilience. This inner strength is not a denial of pain or suffering, but rather an ability to navigate such experiences with clarity, compassion, and wisdom. It is the ability to find meaning and purpose even in the face of adversity, a crucial skill for navigating life's inevitable challenges. This inner transformation, cultivated through solitude and acceptance, is the ultimate empowerment, a journey of self-realization that transcends societal expectations and worldly attachments. It is the essence of Dhumavati's message, a potent reminder of the power of inner transformation in a world often consumed by external distractions.

Furthermore, the embrace of solitude should not be interpreted as a rejection of human connection. While Dhumavati's path emphasizes inner reflection, her compassion extends to others. Her solitary existence allows her to offer guidance and support to those who have lost their way or are grappling with difficult circumstances.

Her wisdom, gained through her own experiences of loss and solitude, becomes a beacon of hope for others navigating similar challenges. This highlights the paradoxical nature of her symbolism– the power found in solitude, utilized to enhance connection and compassion with others.

Finally, understanding Dhumavati's embrace of solitude requires a shift in perspective. It is not a retreat from life, but a transformation of one's relationship with life. It is a recognition of the impermanence of all things, an acceptance of the challenges and difficulties inherent in the human experience, and a deep commitment to inner growth and spiritual development. Her journey invites us to explore the rich inner landscape of our own being, cultivating the strength and resilience needed to navigate the complexities of life, finding wisdom and compassion even in the face of loss and suffering. This is the ultimate message of Dhumavati—the transformative power of embracing solitude as a pathway to self-realization and spiritual liberation. It is a message profoundly relevant in our modern world, often characterized by overwhelming connectivity, yet frequently marked by a profound sense of isolation and disconnection.

Dhumavatis Role in Tantric Practices

Dhumavati's role in Tantric practices extends far beyond her symbolic representation; she is an active participant in various rituals and spiritual exercises. Her invocation is not merely a recitation of mantras, but a profound engagement with the energies she embodies – the energies of solitude, acceptance, and wisdom born from facing life's harsh realities. The Tantric practitioner, seeking to integrate these powerful energies into their own being, employs a variety of methods to connect with Dhumavati's essence.

One of the primary ways to engage with Dhumavati is through the use of specific mantras. These are not merely sounds, but vibrational tools that resonate with the frequency of her energy. Different mantras are associated with different aspects of Dhumavati's being, each capable of accessing a specific dimension of her power. Some mantras are focused on invoking her wisdom and guidance, others on accessing her strength and resilience, and still others on overcoming obstacles and achieving desired outcomes. The precise mantras employed vary across different Tantric lineages and traditions, often passed down orally within specific guru-shishya parampara (teacher-disciple lineage). The effectiveness of the mantras depends greatly on the practitioner's devotion, sincere intention, and the purity of their practice. The recitation itself is typically accompanied by specific visualization techniques and yogic postures to enhance the meditative experience.

Beyond mantras, Dhumavati is also associated with specific yantras– geometric diagrams that are believed to be imbued with her energy. These yantras serve as focal points for meditation and are often used in conjunction with mantras. The intricate designs of the yantras are not merely aesthetic; each line, symbol, and geometric pattern is carefully chosen to represent a particular aspect of Dhumavati's power and influence. The meditative practice involving the yantra usually involves gazing upon the yantra and focusing one's mind on the energy it represents. The visualization of Dhumavati's form within the yantra is often incorporated into the practice to intensify the connection. The use of the yantra is believed to help the practitioner channel Dhumavati's energy for spiritual growth, overcoming obstacles, and achieving specific goals.

The rituals dedicated to Dhumavati are generally performed during periods of solitude and introspection. This aligns with her symbolism of detachment and renunciation. These rituals may include offerings of food, flowers, incense, and other symbolic items, tailored to appease and honor the goddess. The offerings are not merely material gifts but symbolic gestures of devotion and surrender. These offerings represent the practitioner's willingness to relinquish ego-driven attachments and embrace the lessons of impermanence that Dhumavati embodies. The environment for these rituals often reflects her essence – a quiet, secluded space devoid of distractions, facilitating a deeper connection with her energy. The rituals frequently involve specific mudras (hand
gestures), which are believed to channel particular energies and intensify the meditative experience.

The specific offerings and rituals vary greatly depending on the particular Tantric tradition and the practitioner's lineage. Some rituals might involve invoking her blessings for gaining knowledge, insight, overcoming obstacles in academic pursuits, or receiving help in challenging life situations. Others focus on spiritual
purification, removing negative energies, or strengthening one's capacity for resilience. The efficacy of these practices depends greatly on the practitioner's devotion, understanding of Dhumavati's essence, and the purity of their intentions. The rituals serve as a conduit for connecting with her energy, drawing upon her strength, wisdom, and compassion.

The use of specific tools in Dhumavati's worship is also significant. The crow, her vahana (vehicle), is often symbolically represented in rituals. While often considered an ill omen in conventional Hindu symbolism, within Tantric practices, it signifies the acceptance of the shadow self – the parts of ourselves we often try to deny or repress. Working with Dhumavati helps integrate these aspects, transforming perceived negativity into spiritual strength. The practitioner might meditate on the image of a crow, reflecting on the attributes of resilience, adaptability, and survival. Similarly, the broken chariot, her vehicle, represents the acceptance of impermanence and the relinquishment of the need for control. The focus isn't on fixing the chariot but understanding the wisdom that comes from embracing the transient nature of existence.

Furthermore, Dhumavati's Tantric practices often involve a focus on overcoming psychological and emotional obstacles. Her energy can be tapped into to confront and overcome feelings of isolation, loneliness, and despair. This is especially relevant in today's world, characterized by rampant isolation despite widespread connectivity.

The practitioner, by engaging with Dhumavati's energy through mantras, yantras, and rituals, can find solace and strength in confronting these inner struggles. This isn't a simple matter of positive thinking; it is about acknowledging and accepting the difficult emotions, transforming them, and gaining wisdom from them – a crucial aspect of Tantric spiritual development.

Moreover, Dhumavati's association with wisdom extends to the realm of knowledge and learning. She is invoked for gaining deeper understanding, clarifying insights, and overcoming mental blocks.

Students, scholars, and researchers might invoke her blessings to enhance their focus, improve their understanding, and overcome challenges in their intellectual pursuits. This is not limited to formal academic studies; it extends to the pursuit of self-knowledge and spiritual understanding, reflecting her overall role as a guide in the path of self-realization.

Her invocation in Tantric practices isn't simply about obtaining specific results or material benefits; it's a profound journey of self-discovery and transformation. The practitioner, through dedicated practice, learns to embrace the lessons of solitude, acceptance, and resilience. They learn to navigate the challenges of life with greater strength, compassion, and wisdom, mirroring Dhumavati's unwavering journey through the adversities she embodies. The spiritual growth achieved through these practices is not merely intellectual; it's a deep-seated transformation that impacts every aspect of the practitioner's life.

> The practices involving Dhumavati are powerful but require careful approach. The practitioner needs to possess a deep understanding of

Tantric principles and a strong spiritual foundation. Improper use of mantras, yantras, or rituals can lead to unintended consequences.

Therefore, guidance from a qualified and experienced guru is essential. The guru's role is not only to impart knowledge but also to provide appropriate guidance and protection during these potentially transformative spiritual exercises. The practitioner's sincerity, devotion, and commitment are also paramount in ensuring the efficacy and safety of the practice.

The significance of Dhumavati in Tantric practices lies in her ability to empower individuals to confront and transcend their limitations. She is not a goddess who offers easy solutions or quick fixes, but a guide who helps navigate life's complexities with strength and resilience. By engaging with her energy through various methods, the practitioner cultivates a deeper understanding of themselves and the world around them, ultimately achieving a profound sense of inner peace and liberation. Her potent symbolism, combined with the carefully crafted rituals and practices, offers a powerful pathway for spiritual growth and transformation within the Tantric framework. This transformative process moves beyond the simple recitation of mantras and visualization of yantras. It involves a deep engagement with one's inner self, a confrontation with inner shadows, and a journey of self-discovery that leads to a profound and lasting spiritual transformation. The challenges inherent in her symbolism—the widowhood, the solitude, the broken chariot—are not to be avoided, but embraced as essential steps in a transformative journey towards inner strength, wisdom, and ultimate spiritual freedom.

Dhumavati in Different Textual Sources

The multifaceted nature of Dhumavati, the tenth Mahavidya, is further illuminated by examining her portrayal across diverse textual sources. While a singular, universally accepted depiction is lacking, the variations in her portrayal offer a richer, more nuanced understanding of her symbolism and the evolving interpretations across different eras and traditions. Her appearances aren't always consistent; rather, they reflect the interpretative lenses of the various authors and the cultural contexts in which the texts were created. This divergence, rather than a contradiction, enhances the depth and complexity of her character.

The Devi Gita, a key text within the Shaktist tradition, doesn't provide a detailed description of Dhumavati in the same manner as some other Mahavidyas. Her presence is implied rather than explicitly stated. This absence, however, is significant. It suggests that her essence—that of solitude, acceptance of impermanence, and wisdom gained through adversity—is woven into the fabric of the Devi's very being, subtly influencing the overall message of the text. Her characteristics, therefore, are not presented as a separate narrative but are integrated within the broader understanding of the Divine Feminine's multifaceted nature. The silence surrounding her direct depiction in the Devi Gita compels a deeper contemplation of her hidden power and profound implications. Her absence becomes a presence, prompting a more introspective engagement with her symbolism.

In contrast to the implicit presence in the Devi Gita, other Tantric texts offer more direct, though often varied, descriptions of Dhumavati. Some texts depict her as a gaunt, emaciated figure, often depicted as a widow, riding a broken chariot pulled by crows.

This imagery vividly symbolizes desolation, decay, and the acceptance of life's inevitable decline. The crows, often perceived negatively in broader Hindu symbolism, represent the acceptance of the shadow self—the parts of ourselves we tend to suppress or ignore. Here, they transform into symbols of resilience and adaptability, embodying the capacity to find sustenance even in the bleakest environments. The broken chariot signifies the impermanence of all things material and the relinquishing of the need for control, a crucial aspect of spiritual growth within the Tantric framework. The renunciation implied by her widowhood is not a sign of despair, but rather a symbolic detachment from worldly attachments that can hinder spiritual progress.

The selection of particular attributes—her gaunt frame, the broken chariot, the crows—is not arbitrary. Each detail contributes to a powerful symbolic narrative highlighting the importance of accepting life's vicissitudes and finding wisdom within suffering. The imagery is meant to provoke introspection, not to instill fear or despair. It is through the confrontation of these seemingly negative aspects that the spiritual aspirant finds strength and gains a deeper understanding of themselves and the ephemeral nature of existence.

The seemingly harsh portrayal in these texts serves as a stark reminder of the impermanence inherent in the world and the need to embrace the cycle of birth, decay, and renewal.

Certain texts emphasize Dhumavati's association with knowledge and wisdom. Her wisdom is not the conventional type easily acquired through books or formal education. It stems from profound introspection, understanding the intricacies of the human psyche, and facing life's challenges with unwavering resilience. This wisdom is a product of her journey through sorrow and solitude, a testament to the transformative potential of adversity. This perspective elevates Dhumavati beyond a mere goddess of widowhood; she becomes a guide who imparts the wisdom gained through a life lived at the edge of conventional comfort.

The variations in Dhumavati's depiction across different textual sources highlight the fluidity and interpretive nature of Hindu mythology. Her form isn't static, frozen in time; it reflects the evolving understanding and cultural contexts within which her symbolism was interpreted. This malleability is not a weakness but a strength, allowing her to remain relevant and resonate with individuals across diverse spiritual paths and time periods. Each interpretation enriches the understanding of her essence, offering multiple avenues for spiritual exploration and self-discovery.

Furthermore, the textual descriptions of Dhumavati's practices and rituals vary across different Tantric traditions. The mantras, yantras, and specific offerings used in her worship may differ based on the lineage and specific guru-shishya parampara. This diversity reflects the richness and complexity of the Tantric tradition, which adapts and evolves across diverse communities and cultural landscapes. However, certain common themes persist: the emphasis on solitude, the focus on introspection, the acceptance of impermanence, and the cultivation of wisdom gained through adversity. These recurring themes underscore the core essence of Dhumavati, irrespective of variations in the specifics of ritual practice.

The discrepancies in her portrayal also highlight the subjective nature of spiritual experience. The understanding of Dhumavati, and the resulting practices associated with her, are not static, objective realities, but are rather products of individual and collective interpretations, shaped by personal experiences and cultural contexts. One practitioner might find resonance with one specific depiction, while another might find meaning in a different one. This diversity underscores the personal and evolving nature of the spiritual journey, reflecting the multifaceted nature of the Divine Feminine itself.

Another crucial aspect lies in understanding Dhumavati within the broader context of the ten Mahavidyas. Each Mahavidya embodies a specific aspect of the Divine Feminine, representing diverse energies and potentials. Dhumavati's role in this pantheon is vital; she offers a counterpoint to the more outwardly dynamic and often celebrated Mahavidyas. She reminds us of the transformative power inherent in solitude, acceptance, and wisdom born of adversity. Her position in the collective narrative of the ten Mahavidyas underscores the necessity of acknowledging and integrating all facets of existence –the bright and the dark, the joyful and the sorrowful – in order to achieve wholeness.

In conclusion, the diverse portrayal of Dhumavati across various textual sources, rather than detracting from her significance, strengthens her multi-layered symbolism. The inconsistencies offer a dynamic spectrum of interpretations, allowing each practitioner to engage with her energy based on their personal understanding and spiritual journey. Her representation remains potent, challenging the practitioner to confront their inner shadows and embrace the wisdom gained through life's inevitable hardships. Her journey, fraught with challenges, ultimately highlights the transformative power of acceptance and resilience, making her a deeply relevant and powerful figure in the Tantric landscape. The ongoing exploration and interpretation of her symbolism reflect the ever-evolving nature of spiritual understanding and the enduring allure of the mysterious and powerful Dhumavati.

Dhumavati and the Acceptance of Impermanence

The preceding discussion established Dhumavati's multifaceted portrayal across various texts, highlighting the dynamic and evolving nature of her symbolism within the Tantric tradition. However, the true power of Dhumavati lies not merely in her historical representation, but in her contemporary relevance—her ability to offer solace and guidance amidst the complexities of modern life. Her energy resonates deeply with the inherent impermanence of existence, a truth particularly salient in the fast-paced, ever-changing world of today. The challenges we face – from personal loss and illness to societal upheaval and global uncertainty–demand a resilience and acceptance that Dhumavati's essence embodies.

Dhumavati, often depicted as a gaunt widow residing in desolate surroundings, isn't a symbol of despair but rather a powerful representation of acceptance. Her solitary existence, far from being a state of misery, is a deliberate choice, a conscious detachment from the ephemeral nature of worldly possessions and attachments.

This detachment isn't a rejection of life, but rather a profound understanding of its fleeting nature. This understanding allows for a deeper appreciation of the present moment, a detachment from the anxieties of the future and the regrets of the past. In the modern context, where we are constantly bombarded by demands for productivity and achievement, Dhumavati's message of embracing solitude offers a crucial antidote to the relentless pressure to constantly strive and achieve. It encourages a deliberate withdrawal from the external noise to foster inner peace and self-reflection. It is through this intentional solitude that we gain clarity and perspective, enabling us to navigate life's complexities with greater equanimity.

The broken chariot she rides symbolizes the impermanence of material possessions and the illusory nature of control. In our materialistic world, we often equate happiness with acquiring possessions and achieving certain milestones. Dhumavati's broken chariot serves as a stark reminder that our attachments to material things are inherently transient, destined to break and decay. This realization is not intended to induce despair, but rather to liberate us from the anxieties associated with acquiring and maintaining these possessions. By embracing impermanence, we free ourselves from the fear of loss and the relentless pursuit of fleeting satisfaction. This acceptance allows for a shift in perspective, valuing experiences and relationships over material wealth and accomplishments.

The crows accompanying Dhumavati, often perceived negatively in Hindu iconography, represent the shadow self – the aspects of ourselves that we often repress or ignore. These aspects, however unwelcome, are integral parts of our being. Dhumavati's association with the crows suggests that true wisdom and self-acceptance necessitate acknowledging and integrating even our darkest and most uncomfortable aspects. In contemporary psychology, this aligns with concepts like shadow work and the importance of self-acceptance, both crucial elements for emotional well-being. The crows, therefore, are not symbols of ill omen but rather symbolic guides to confronting and integrating our inner complexities. By embracing these aspects of ourselves, we foster a more authentic sense of self and develop a deeper understanding of our human condition.

Dhumavati's wisdom, however, is not solely derived from contemplation and solitude; it's forged in the crucible of adversity.

Her gaunt appearance, often interpreted as a consequence of hardship, symbolizes the transformative power of suffering. It highlights the truth that growth and profound wisdom often emerge from life's challenging experiences. This perspective offers comfort and perspective during times of personal loss, hardship, or illness. It suggests that even the most difficult experiences hold transformative potential, paving the way for personal growth and a deeper understanding of oneself and the world. This is not a passive acceptance of suffering but an active engagement with it, a recognition of its capacity to cultivate resilience and wisdom.

Furthermore, Dhumavati's association with knowledge emphasizes the intrinsic value of experiential learning. Her wisdom is not acquired through rote memorization or intellectual pursuits alone; it is born from lived experience and the integration of personal struggles. This experiential wisdom is often far more profound and valuable than any academic knowledge, as it is deeply rooted in personal understanding and transformation. In our data-driven world, where information is abundant but true wisdom often elusive, Dhumavati's energy offers a crucial counterpoint, emphasizing the significance of personal experience and introspection in the acquisition of true wisdom.

In the context of Kali Yuga, the current age in the Hindu calendar, characterized by materialism, conflict, and uncertainty, Dhumavati's message holds particular significance. Her energy resonates with the anxieties and challenges inherent in this age, offering a pathway towards resilience, inner peace, and acceptance. Her message encourages a conscious detachment from the chaotic external world, emphasizing the importance of inner strength and self-reliance. In a world increasingly characterized by instability and uncertainty, Dhumavati's unwavering acceptance of impermanence offers a path toward navigating life's complexities with greater equanimity and resilience.

Applying Dhumavati's energy in contemporary life involves cultivating practices that promote introspection and acceptance. Meditation, mindfulness practices, and spending time in nature can facilitate this process. These practices help us connect with our inner selves, fostering self-awareness and acceptance of our own vulnerabilities. Furthermore, engaging with art, journaling, and creative expression can serve as powerful tools for processing emotions and integrating challenging experiences. These are not mere escapist activities; they are pathways for engaging with the shadow self and transforming personal struggles into wisdom.

The practice of gratitude, focusing on the positive aspects of life, can also be a powerful tool in aligning with Dhumavati's energy. By acknowledging the blessings in our lives, even during challenging times, we shift our focus from lack to abundance, fostering resilience and inner peace. This isn't about ignoring difficulties but about recognizing and appreciating what remains positive, strengthening our ability to navigate hardship with grace and acceptance. The cultivation of compassion, both for oneself and for others, is another crucial element in embodying Dhumavati's essence. This involves acknowledging and accepting our imperfections and extending kindness and understanding to those around us, particularly during times of conflict or disagreement.

In conclusion, Dhumavati's relevance extends far beyond historical interpretations. Her symbolism provides a potent framework for navigating the inherent impermanence of life, fostering inner strength, resilience, and the ability to find peace amidst challenging circumstances. Her message resonates deeply with the complexities of modern life, offering a valuable counterpoint to the relentless pursuit of material success and external validation. By embracing Dhumavati's energy, we can cultivate a profound sense of self-acceptance, fostering wisdom and equanimity in the face of life's inevitable challenges. Her enduring power lies in her ability to guide us towards a deeper understanding of ourselves and the ephemeral nature of existence, empowering us to navigate life's vicissitudes with grace, resilience, and profound acceptance. Her wisdom, born of solitude and adversity, offers a beacon of hope and guidance in the ever-changing landscape of the modern world.

Bagalamukhis Iconography and Attributes

Bagalamukhi, the tenth Mahavidya, presents a captivating study in iconography, her visual representations offering a rich tapestry of symbolic meaning that evolves across different artistic traditions and interpretive lenses. Unlike some Mahavidyas whose forms are relatively consistent across various depictions, Bagalamukhi's iconography exhibits a degree of fluidity, reflecting the multifaceted nature of her power and the diverse contexts in which she is invoked.

One prevalent depiction portrays Bagalamukhi as a radiant, youthful goddess, often seated on a lotus throne, radiating serenity and power. Her complexion is usually golden or yellowish, signifying her association with knowledge, wisdom, and spiritual illumination. Her eyes, often depicted as large and expressive, are imbued with a penetrating gaze that reflects her ability to pierce through illusions and unveil truth. This penetrating gaze, often described as hypnotic, represents her capacity to subdue enemies and overcome obstacles. This isn't a malevolent gaze, but one of focused intention and unwavering resolve. The serene expression on her face, despite her formidable power, suggests a mastery over the mind and a state of unshakeable equanimity.

A crucial element of Bagalamukhi's iconography is the *vajra* she often holds. The vajra, a ritualistic thunderbolt-shaped weapon, symbolizes indestructible power and spiritual strength. In Bagalamukhi's hands, the vajra transcends its purely martial connotation, becoming a symbol of her ability to shatter illusions, break through mental barriers, and conquer negativity. It represents her capacity to transform destructive energies and utilize them for positive ends. The vajra's multifaceted nature, capable of both destruction and creation, mirrors the duality inherent in Bagalamukhi's power – the capacity to both subdue negativity and nurture positive growth.

Another significant attribute frequently depicted is the *sakti* or ritual dagger, often seen alongside or in place of the vajra. The sakti represents feminine power, both creative and destructive. While the vajra represents the power of destruction to clear obstacles, the sakti is often associated with a more nuanced power – the power to cut through attachments, delusions, and the bonds of ignorance.

The combination of vajra and sakti, when both are present, underscores the balanced nature of Bagalamukhi's influence, capable of both forceful removal of obstacles and delicate disentanglement from binding situations.

The posture of Bagalamukhi in various depictions is equally telling. Sometimes she's shown in a sitting posture, emanating an aura of peace and wisdom. Other representations depict her in a more dynamic pose, suggesting movement and action, further emphasizing her ability to swiftly intervene and subdue enemies. This dynamic portrayal underscores her responsiveness to the needs of her devotees, and her readiness to act swiftly and decisively when required. The variation in her posture reflects the versatility of her energy, adaptable to diverse situations and contexts.

The color yellow or gold, repeatedly mentioned in association with Bagalamukhi, holds profound significance. In Hindu symbolism, yellow represents spiritual illumination, knowledge, and mental clarity. The goddess's association with this color reinforces her role as a dispeller of ignorance and confusion. It suggests that through her grace, the devotee can attain a higher level of awareness and understanding, transcending the limitations of the mundane.

The variations in Bagalamukhi's iconography are not merely aesthetic differences. They reflect the diverse schools of Tantric thought and the varied interpretations of her power. Some representations may show her with additional attributes or in slightly altered postures, showcasing subtle differences in emphasis or interpretation. These variations, however, do not contradict her core essence but rather enrich the understanding of her multifaceted nature. They highlight the adaptability of her symbolic power, allowing for a greater range of interpretations and applications depending on the individual and the context.

The context in which Bagalamukhi is invoked also significantly shapes her iconographic portrayal. In certain Tantric practices, she might be depicted with specific mudras (hand gestures) or mantras, further intensifying her energetic manifestation. These variations underscore the dynamic interaction between the deity and the devotee, emphasizing the personalized nature of the divine-human relationship within the Tantric framework.

The significance of Bagalamukhi's iconography extends beyond mere visual representation. It serves as a powerful tool for meditation and visualization, allowing the devotee to connect with her energy and experience her power directly. By focusing on the various attributes and symbolism embedded in her image, the devotee can cultivate a deeper understanding of her essence and invoke her blessings more effectively.

Furthermore, the consistent presence of specific attributes, such as the vajra and sakti, across diverse depictions underscores the core essence of her power. Despite stylistic variations, the underlying message remains consistent: Bagalamukhi is a goddess of irresistible power, able to subdue enemies, overcome obstacles, and dispel negativity.

The study of Bagalamukhi's iconography thus transcends a mere analysis of artistic styles. It's a profound journey into the heart of Tantric symbolism, offering insights into the dynamic interplay between the divine and the human, the subtle nuances of power, and the transformative potential of spiritual practice. Her images, whether serene or dynamic, peaceful or powerful, serve as a visual key to unlock a wealth of spiritual insight and empowerment. The careful observation and interpretation of her various forms allows the practitioner to access the deeper layers of her divine energy, engaging with her powerful presence on a deeper level.

The evolution of Bagalamukhi's iconography reflects the dynamic and evolving nature of Tantric thought itself. Different schools of Tantra, through the ages, have subtly adapted her visual representation, reflecting changing societal and spiritual contexts.

This evolution does not diminish the core essence of the goddess but rather enriches our understanding of her multifaceted nature, highlighting her adaptability and resilience as a potent force within the Hindu pantheon.

The study of Bagalamukhi's iconography is not a static exercise in art history but a living, dynamic process of interpreting and engaging with her powerful energy. Her image serves as a doorway to deeper spiritual understanding, allowing the practitioner to connect with her power and draw upon her blessings in overcoming challenges and achieving spiritual progress. The consistent reinterpretation and re-presentation of Bagalamukhi across centuries reveals the enduring relevance and transformative potential of this powerful goddess.

In conclusion, the rich tapestry of Bagalamukhi's iconography offers a fascinating and multifaceted exploration of Tantric symbolism.

The variations in her depictions, far from being contradictions, contribute to a more complete understanding of her diverse powers and attributes. Through careful observation and contemplation of these artistic representations, we gain a deeper appreciation for the enduring power and enduring relevance of this compelling Mahavidya, her image serving as a potent catalyst for spiritual growth and transformation in the modern world. The subtle shifts and continuities in her depiction across various artistic traditions highlight the fluid and evolving nature of Tantric practice and underscore the adaptable nature of her energy, forever relevant and responsive to the needs of her devotees. This dynamic interplay between visual representation and spiritual practice makes the study of Bagalamukhi's iconography a continuously enriching and rewarding endeavor.

Bagalamukhi and the Power of Speech

Bagalamukhi's influence extends far beyond the battlefield of physical conflict; she is deeply connected to the power of speech, the subtle battlefield of words and narratives. Her dominion isn't merely about silencing opponents; it's about harnessing the transformative potential of communication, ensuring that truth prevails and falsehood is exposed. This aspect of her power is often overlooked, yet it reveals a crucial dimension of her multifaceted nature, offering a profound understanding of her relevance in the modern world, dominated by the flow of information and the constant struggle for control of narratives.

The Devi Gita, while not explicitly focusing on Bagalamukhi, provides a framework for understanding the profound significance of speech within the broader context of Shaktism. The goddess, in her various manifestations, represents the supreme power of creation and destruction, and this power extends to the creation and destruction of narratives. The ability to speak truthfully, to articulate one's thoughts and feelings clearly and effectively, is a powerful tool for positive change. Conversely, the misuse of speech, the propagation of falsehoods, and the manipulation of narratives can cause immense harm. Bagalamukhi's association with speech, therefore, highlights the ethical dimension inherent in the exercise of power.

Her capacity to silence enemies is not merely a display of brute force; it represents the silencing of negativity, falsehood, and harmful rhetoric. In a world increasingly saturated with misinformation and divisive language, Bagalamukhi's ability to cut through the noise and expose the truth is particularly relevant. This silencing isn't about suppression of free speech but rather about neutralizing harmful speech that undermines truth, justice, and harmony. It's about creating space for authentic communication to flourish, where genuine dialogue can take place.

This nuanced perspective on Bagalamukhi's power is crucial in understanding her role as a protector and empowerer. She doesn't merely protect her devotees from external enemies; she equips them with the tools to defend themselves against the insidious attacks of manipulation and deceit. The mastery of speech, the ability to communicate effectively and honestly, is a potent weapon against falsehood and injustice. Bagalamukhi empowers her devotees to use this weapon wisely, to speak truth to power, and to stand up for what is right.

The Tantric practices associated with Bagalamukhi often involve the recitation of specific mantras and the performance of specific rituals aimed at enhancing communication skills and sharpening the clarity of expression. These practices are not merely about achieving rhetorical prowess but are designed to foster genuine authenticity in communication, ensuring that the words spoken align with the intention of the heart. The focus is on cultivating clear and truthful communication, promoting harmony and understanding.

Consider the contemporary context of social media and the spread of misinformation. The ease with which false narratives can proliferate presents a significant challenge to truth and justice.

Bagalamukhi's power to control speech and narratives becomes even more pertinent in this environment. Her invocation can be seen as a call for clarity, for the exposure of falsehoods, and for the empowerment of individuals to discern truth from deception. Her energy can aid in strengthening one's ability to filter the noise, to identify and resist manipulation, and to effectively communicate one's own perspective honestly and effectively.

The empowerment of truthful speech is intrinsically linked to the concept of *satya* , truth, a cornerstone of Hindu dharma.

Bagalamukhi assists in the establishment of *satya* , not through suppression, but through the illumination of truth and the dissipation of illusion. This is not a passive process; it requires active engagement, the courage to speak truth even when it's unpopular, and the wisdom to discern between genuine dialogue and manipulative rhetoric. Bagalamukhi's energy empowers devotees to navigate the complex world of communication with clarity, integrity, and confidence.

The concept of controlling narratives is not about manipulating others or forcing one's viewpoint on others, but rather about shaping one's own narrative and communicating it effectively. This involves self-awareness, understanding one's strengths and weaknesses, and the ability to articulate one's perspective clearly and concisely. It's about building authentic connections based on trust and mutual understanding. This aspect of Bagalamukhi's power is particularly relevant in leadership and interpersonal relationships.

In the context of legal disputes and conflicts, Bagalamukhi's association with justice and the triumph of truth is particularly significant. She is often invoked in situations where the truth is obscured, where falsehoods prevail, and where justice is delayed or denied. Her intervention is seen as a means of bringing truth to light, ensuring that justice is served, and that the right prevails. Her power is not about winning at all costs, but about ensuring that the truth is revealed and that justice is done.

Furthermore, the ability to control the narrative extends to the personal realm. Bagalamukhi can assist in managing one's own internal dialogue, silencing self-doubt and negative self-talk, and promoting a positive self-image. This inner work is essential for personal growth and well-being, paving the way for more authentic and fulfilling relationships with oneself and others. The ability to control one's internal narrative is a crucial step towards achieving emotional equilibrium and a sense of inner peace.

The interplay between the inner and outer realms of communication highlights the multifaceted nature of Bagalamukhi's power. She doesn't simply address external conflicts; she facilitates inner transformation, empowering individuals to communicate truthfully and authentically from a place of strength and self-awareness. This integration of inner and outer transformation is a hallmark of Tantric practices, emphasizing the interconnectedness of the individual and the cosmos.

The study of Bagalamukhi's influence on speech and communication provides a unique perspective on the power of language and its capacity to shape our reality. Her association with truth and justice underscores the ethical dimension inherent in the use of language, highlighting the importance of responsible communication in creating a harmonious and just world. In a world increasingly shaped by information and narratives, Bagalamukhi's power becomes a crucial tool for navigating the complexities of human interaction and promoting the triumph of truth. Her energy serves as a beacon of clarity, guiding us towards authentic expression and fostering a deeper understanding of the power of words. Through the study of her iconography and the practices associated with her worship, we gain access to a powerful tool for personal and societal transformation. Bagalamukhi reminds us that the power of speech is not merely about influence, but about responsibility, truth, and the creation of a world where authentic communication can flourish.

Her continued relevance in the 21st century is a testament to the enduring wisdom of the Tantric tradition and its capacity to address the challenges of the modern age. The careful exploration of her association with speech unlocks a further layer of understanding of this complex and compelling goddess. Her power is not simply destructive, but also deeply constructive, facilitating not just the silencing of falsehood, but the empowerment of genuine and truthful expression. This empowers her devotees to not only navigate the complexities of the modern world, but also to actively contribute to a more just and harmonious society. The effective harnessing of speech, as guided by Bagalamukhi's energy, becomes a powerful tool for positive transformation both within oneself and in the world at large.

Bagalamukhis Role in Tantric Practices

Bagalamukhi's role in Tantric practices is multifaceted and deeply intertwined with her essence as the goddess of speech and the vanquisher of obstacles. While her iconography often depicts her in a fierce, almost aggressive posture, her Tantric applications focus on harnessing her power for constructive purposes, primarily the purification and empowerment of speech and the skillful navigation of conflict. The practices aren't about silencing opponents in a malicious sense, but rather about strategically neutralizing negativity and falsehood, creating space for truth and clarity to prevail.

Central to these practices are specific mantras, carefully crafted phonetic sequences believed to resonate with Bagalamukhi's energy. These mantras aren't merely incantations; they are tools for inner transformation, subtly altering the practitioner's mental and emotional state, fostering focus, clarity, and a sense of inner strength. The repeated recitation of these mantras is considered a form of meditation, allowing the devotee to connect with Bagalamukhi's energy and align their intentions with her power.

The most commonly used mantra, often accompanied by visualizations and specific hand gestures (mudras), is a powerful invocation of her ability to bind and subdue negativity.

Beyond the mantras, yantras – geometric diagrams imbued with spiritual energy – play a significant role. The Bagalamukhi Yantra is a complex geometric design, often incorporating symbols related to her attributes, such as the vajra (thunderbolt), representing her power to break obstacles, and various other sacred symbols associated with speech, truth, and victory. The yantra is a focus for meditation, acting as a conduit for Bagalamukhi's energy, assisting the practitioner in accessing her power and aligning their energy with hers. Regular contemplation on the yantra is believed to strengthen the practitioner's resolve, enhance their ability to focus, and instill a greater sense of clarity in their thoughts and actions.

The rituals associated with Bagalamukhi are varied and often depend on the specific aim and the practitioner's level of experience. Some rituals are simple, involving the offering of flowers, incense, and prayers, while others are more complex, involving the creation of intricate mandalas, the recitation of extensive mantras, and the performance of specific mudras. These rituals are not merely outward displays of devotion; they are carefully designed practices aimed at invoking Bagalamukhi's energy and aligning the practitioner with her power. The precision and intention behind these rituals are critical; they are not arbitrary acts but are rooted in the understanding of subtle energies and their manipulation.

One important aspect of Bagalamukhi's Tantric practices is the use of her energy to overcome obstacles in communication. This isn't just about public speaking or persuasive rhetoric; it is about fostering authentic and effective communication in all aspects of life. This can involve clearing misunderstandings, resolving conflicts, and promoting harmony in relationships. The practice involves not just the recitation of mantras but also the cultivation of inner qualities such as patience, empathy, and clarity of thought.

These practices aim to empower the practitioner to communicate their thoughts and feelings effectively, to articulate their needs and desires clearly, and to foster genuine understanding with others.

In legal and professional contexts, the invocation of Bagalamukhi can be particularly relevant. In situations where truth is obscured or justice is delayed, the practitioner can call upon her power to help illuminate the truth and facilitate a just resolution. This doesn't imply a magical solution to every legal problem, but rather an assistance in bringing clarity, focus, and skillful communication to the situation. It's about equipping the practitioner with the inner strength and clarity to navigate complex situations effectively.

Moreover, Bagalamukhi's influence extends to the personal realm. Many practitioners utilize her energy to combat negative self-talk, to overcome self-doubt, and to cultivate a more positive self-image. This involves a conscious effort to identify and neutralize negative internal narratives, replacing them with more empowering and realistic thoughts. The mantra recitation and meditation on the yantra become tools for inner transformation, enabling the practitioner to cultivate a stronger sense of self-worth and self-confidence. This inner strength then translates into improved communication skills and a greater ability to navigate interpersonal relationships effectively.

The Tantric practices associated with Bagalamukhi are not merely esoteric rituals; they are practical tools for self-transformation and empowerment. They involve a deep engagement with the practitioner's inner world, a conscious effort to cultivate inner qualities such as clarity, focus, and self-awareness. This self-awareness is critical, as it allows the practitioner to understand their own emotional state and to communicate their needs and feelings effectively. The practices aren't about controlling others; rather they are about mastering one's own internal dialogue and enhancing one's ability to communicate authentically and powerfully.

The efficacy of these practices relies heavily on the practitioner's intention, discipline, and understanding of the underlying spiritual principles. It's not a matter of simply performing the rituals mechanically; it requires genuine devotion, a clear understanding of the goddess's attributes, and a commitment to personal growth. This commitment is vital, as the transformative potential of these practices extends beyond the immediate application; they cultivate lasting changes in the practitioner's character and behavior.

The use of Bagalamukhi's energy in Tantric practices extends beyond the individual. In some traditions, her power is invoked to promote harmony and understanding within communities, to resolve conflicts, and to promote social justice. This highlights the expansive nature of her influence – her power transcends the personal realm, extending to the social and political spheres. This demonstrates a deeper understanding of her role as not just a personal protector but also a force for social harmony and positive change. The ethical implications of harnessing her power are paramount, emphasizing the responsibility that comes with wielding such potent energy.

In summary, Bagalamukhi's role within Tantric practices goes beyond simple ritualistic actions. It's a journey of self-discovery, a path of inner transformation leading to greater self-awareness, clearer communication, and a more effective navigation of life's challenges. The mantras, yantras, and rituals serve as tools to connect with her energy, empowering the practitioner to utilize the power of speech for positive change – both within themselves and within the world around them. The practices are not about dominating others, but about mastering oneself, fostering authentic communication, and striving for justice and truth. This nuanced understanding is crucial for appreciating the profound and far-reaching implications of Bagalamukhi's presence within the Tantric tradition. Her continued relevance in modern times underscores the timeless wisdom embedded in these practices and their capacity to address contemporary challenges related to communication, conflict, and the pursuit of truth in a world saturated with information and misinformation. The judicious application of these practices, guided by ethical considerations and spiritual understanding, can prove to be transformative, leading to personal growth, societal harmony, and a greater understanding of the power of truthful and effective communication. The careful study of these practices reveals the intricate interplay between the inner and outer worlds, the subtle energies that shape our reality, and the potent potential inherent in aligning oneself with the power of a goddess like Bagalamukhi. The journey is not merely about mastering techniques but about cultivating inner wisdom and harnessing the power of truth and authentic expression.

Bagalamukhi in Different Textual Sources

The multifaceted nature of Bagalamukhi, the tenth Mahavidya, is further illuminated by exploring her representation across diverse textual sources. While the Devi Gita offers a potent glimpse into her essence, a comprehensive understanding necessitates examining her portrayal in other scriptures and traditions. This exploration reveals both fascinating variations in her iconography and attributes and remarkable continuities that underline her core significance as the goddess of speech and the vanquisher of obstacles.

The *Devi Bhagavata Purana*, a significant text in Shaktism, provides a detailed narrative surrounding Bagalamukhi. Here, her emergence is often linked to the cosmic struggle between good and evil, portraying her as a fierce warrior goddess who actively intervenes to restore dharma. The Purana elaborates on her weapons – the vajra (thunderbolt) and her powerful gaze – and describes her as possessing the ability to bind and subdue her enemies, not through physical violence alone, but through the strategic manipulation of speech and the subtle control of energy. This aspect highlights a more nuanced understanding of her power, moving beyond a simplistic interpretation of brute force to incorporate a sophisticated understanding of subtle energies and their influence.

The *Devi Bhagavata Purana* offers detailed descriptions of her appearance, emphasizing the vibrancy of her colors and the intensity of her gaze, further solidifying her image as a powerful and compelling deity. The specific mantras and rituals associated with her worship, as depicted in this Purana, often emphasize the use of specific syllables and visualizations to connect with her energy, aligning the practitioner's intention with her power for the resolution of specific conflicts.

The *Brahmanda Purana*, another significant Purana, also devotes sections to Bagalamukhi. However, the emphasis may shift slightly, with some versions highlighting her role as a protector of truth and righteousness rather than solely a warrior goddess. This variation in emphasis underscores the fluidity of her symbolism and the multiple interpretations possible within the broader Shaktic framework. The descriptions of her iconography may vary slightly across different versions of the *Brahmanda Purana*, reflecting the diverse artistic and regional interpretations that emerged over time.

This textual diversity is not a sign of inconsistency, but rather reflects the evolving understanding and adaptation of the goddess's symbolism within different cultural contexts and temporal periods.

The mantras mentioned in the *Brahmanda Purana* may also differ slightly from those found in the *Devi Bhagavata Purana*, reflecting the diversity of Tantric practices and the adaptation of these practices to specific lineages and traditions.

In contrast to the Puranas, which often embed Bagalamukhi within larger narratives, some Tantric texts provide more concise but potent descriptions of her attributes and powers. These texts, often focusing on specific rituals and practices, highlight her role as a crucial energy source for achieving specific goals. Here, the emphasis is less on narrative and more on practical application, emphasizing the use of her energy to overcome obstacles and achieve desired results. These texts frequently provide detailed instructions on the creation and use of the Bagalamukhi Yantra, the specific mantras to be recited, and the mudras (hand gestures) to be employed during the ritual. They often highlight the importance of intention and concentration, emphasizing the practitioner's active role in harnessing the goddess's energy.

The differences in descriptions across these texts are not contradictory; rather, they reflect the multifaceted nature of Bagalamukhi and the varying perspectives of different traditions and authors. Some texts emphasize her fierce warrior aspect, highlighting her ability to vanquish enemies and overcome obstacles. Others underscore her role as a protector of truth and righteousness, emphasizing her power to restore dharma and bring justice. Still others focus on her potential for personal empowerment, showcasing her ability to enhance clarity, focus, and effective communication. These diverse portrayals enrich our understanding of Bagalamukhi, revealing the complex and dynamic nature of her symbolism and the adaptability of her worship across various cultural and temporal contexts.

Furthermore, the evolution of Bagalamukhi's symbolism can be traced across different periods. Early representations might focus primarily on her ability to subdue enemies, emphasizing her martial aspects. However, later depictions often incorporate a more nuanced understanding of her power, highlighting her role in restoring balance, promoting truth, and fostering effective communication. This shift reflects a gradual evolution in the understanding of her attributes and the ways in which her energy can be harnessed. The development of different lineages within Shaktism also contributed to this evolution, with each lineage possibly emphasizing specific aspects of her power or incorporating unique rituals and practices.

The study of these varied textual sources reveals a fascinating interplay between continuity and change in the portrayal of Bagalamukhi. While her core attributes – her association with speech, her ability to overcome obstacles, and her role in restoring dharma – remain consistent across different texts, the specific emphasis and interpretation of these attributes may vary considerably. This variation underscores the dynamic and evolving nature of religious traditions and the adaptability of religious symbols to new contexts and cultural interpretations. The differences, rather than being viewed as inconsistencies, enrich our understanding of Bagalamukhi's complexity and the multiple ways in which her power can be interpreted and harnessed.

Analyzing Bagalamukhi's depiction across the *Devi Mahatmya*, various Puranas, and Tantric texts illuminates not only the goddess herself but also the evolution of religious thought and practice. The subtle shifts in emphasis, the variations in iconography, and the diverse mantras and rituals associated with her worship reflect the ongoing dialogue within Shaktism and the diverse ways in which devotees have sought to engage with and understand her power. It highlights the richness and complexity of Hindu religious traditions and the capacity of these traditions to adapt and evolve over time while maintaining their core essence. The continued relevance of Bagalamukhi in modern times underscores the enduring power of her symbolism and the continued need for the clarity and focus she represents in a world often characterized by chaos and confusion. The study of these diverse textual sources provides a valuable lens through which to understand not only Bagalamukhi but also the broader landscape of Hindu religious thought and practice. The insights gained from this comparative analysis offer a more nuanced and holistic understanding of this powerful goddess and her enduring significance within the Tantric tradition and beyond. The continuing relevance of her symbolism in our contemporary world, marked by challenges in communication and the pursuit of truth, further underscores the timelessness of her message and the enduring power of her divine energy. The study of these diverse sources encourages a deeper engagement with the richness and complexity of the Hindu pantheon, highlighting the diverse interpretations and practices that have shaped the worship of this compelling and influential deity. The journey of understanding Bagalamukhi is a journey of exploring the diverse expressions of the divine feminine and the enduring power of faith in navigating the complexities of human existence.

Bagalamukhi and the Power of Communication

The preceding exploration of Bagalamukhi across diverse textual sources reveals a consistent thread: her profound association with speech and its power. While depicted as a fierce warrior capable of subduing enemies, her power is not merely brute force but a skillful manipulation of energy, primarily manifested through communication. This nuanced understanding of Bagalamukhi's abilities brings us to a critical contemporary application: her relevance in enhancing effective communication and conflict resolution in the modern world.

In our increasingly interconnected world, communication forms the bedrock of almost all human interaction. The ability to articulate our thoughts clearly, to listen empathetically, and to navigate complex social dynamics are crucial skills, not just for personal success but for global harmony. However, the modern age is also characterized by communication breakdowns, misunderstandings, and conflict, ranging from interpersonal disagreements to international tensions. Bagalamukhi's energy, therefore, offers a potent tool for navigating these challenges.

Her symbolism directly addresses the core issues inherent in effective communication. Her ability to "bind the tongue" of adversaries, often interpreted literally, can be understood metaphorically as the ability to silence negativity, misinformation, and manipulative rhetoric. In a world saturated with noise and disinformation, this ability to discern truth from falsehood, to filter out distracting elements and focus on essential communication, is invaluable. This doesn't imply suppressing dissenting opinions but rather cultivating the discernment to engage constructively, recognizing the intent behind the message and responding thoughtfully rather than reactively.

Furthermore, Bagalamukhi's energy can foster assertive communication. While often associated with subduing opponents, this shouldn't be interpreted as aggressive dominance. Rather, it speaks to the power of clear, confident expression of one's needs and boundaries. Assertiveness is not aggression; it is the ability to communicate your needs respectfully and firmly, without resorting to manipulation or intimidation. Bagalamukhi's energy can help cultivate this inner strength, enabling individuals to articulate their perspectives without fear or hesitation. This is particularly relevant in situations where one might feel overwhelmed or silenced by powerful figures or conflicting narratives.

The practice of invoking Bagalamukhi's energy, through meditation, mantra recitation, or yantra worship, can help individuals develop a clearer and more focused mind. This clarity of mind is fundamental to effective communication, allowing for well-articulated thoughts and a heightened awareness of both our own emotions and the emotions of others. This enhanced self-awareness reduces the likelihood of misunderstandings and misinterpretations, which often lie at the root of conflicts. By quieting the internal chatter and cultivating inner peace, we create space for more thoughtful and receptive communication.

The application of Bagalamukhi's energy in conflict resolution extends beyond personal interactions. Her influence can be seen on a broader social scale. In times of political strife or international tension, the ability to foster clear and respectful dialogue is paramount. Bagalamukhi's energy can be channeled to promote understanding, empathy, and a commitment to peaceful solutions.

By promoting truthful communication and discouraging manipulative rhetoric, she can help create an environment where genuine dialogue is possible, allowing conflicting parties to find common ground and work towards mutually beneficial solutions.

The modern emphasis on digital communication introduces new layers of complexity. The anonymity of the internet often emboldens individuals to engage in aggressive or disrespectful behavior. Bagalamukhi's energy can help counteract this negativity, promoting responsible online interactions. Her symbolism reminds us of the power of our words, both spoken and written, and the responsibility we have to use them constructively. Invoking her energy can help us cultivate mindful online engagement, promoting respectful discourse and discouraging cyberbullying or the spread of misinformation.

The practical application of Bagalamukhi's energy for improved communication involves a multifaceted approach. This involves not only invoking her mantras and visualizing her energy but also cultivating inner qualities such as self-awareness, empathy, and assertiveness. These qualities are not simply inherent; they are skills that can be developed and refined through conscious practice. Meditation techniques can help quiet the mind, enhancing clarity and focus. Mindfulness practices can cultivate self-awareness, allowing us to better understand our own reactions and those of others. Active listening skills are crucial in ensuring effective communication and conflict resolution.

Moreover, understanding the underlying causes of conflict is key to effective resolution. Conflicts often stem from unmet needs, misinterpretations, or differing values. By employing Bagalamukhi's energy to cultivate clarity and empathy, we can identify these underlying causes, facilitating open and honest conversations that address the root of the problem rather than just the surface symptoms. This approach fosters a more sustainable resolution, preventing future conflicts from arising.

The utilization of Bagalamukhi's energy is not about magically resolving conflicts but about enhancing our ability to communicate effectively and approach conflicts with wisdom and compassion. It's about harnessing the power of clear articulation, focused intention, and an unwavering commitment to truth and understanding. It empowers individuals to navigate complex social situations with greater grace, assertiveness, and empathy. In a world often characterized by communication breakdowns and conflict, Bagalamukhi's energy offers a pathway towards more harmonious interactions, both on a personal and global scale. Her symbolism serves as a potent reminder of the transformative power of thoughtful communication, encouraging us to harness the divine energy within to create a more peaceful and understanding world.

By embracing the principles she embodies – truth, clarity, and assertive yet compassionate communication – we can strive towards a more connected and collaborative society, where conflict is approached not as an impasse but as an opportunity for growth and mutual understanding. This approach, deeply rooted in the Tantric traditions and the symbolism of Bagalamukhi, provides a powerful framework for navigating the complexities of human interaction in the modern world, enabling individuals to find their voice, express themselves with clarity, and contribute to a more peaceful and harmonious existence. The continued study and application of Bagalamukhi's teachings offer a timeless wisdom that remains profoundly relevant in addressing the challenges of communication and conflict resolution in the contemporary age.

Matangis Iconography and Attributes

The transition from Bagalamukhi's mastery of communication to Matangi's multifaceted persona presents a fascinating shift in the Mahavidya pantheon. While Bagalamukhi focuses on the strategic manipulation of speech and the power of clear articulation, Matangi embodies a more expansive creative force, encompassing music, learning, and the arts. Her iconography reflects this multifaceted nature, often revealing a goddess simultaneously powerful and graceful, embodying both fierce determination and artistic refinement.

Understanding Matangi's iconography requires acknowledging the diverse artistic traditions that have shaped her visual representations across centuries and geographical regions. There is no single, universally accepted image of Matangi, and the variations in her depiction reflect the rich tapestry of Hindu artistic and theological interpretations. However, certain recurring themes and attributes consistently emerge, offering valuable insights into her essence.

One common representation depicts Matangi as a youthful, attractive woman, often riding a donkey or a mule, symbolic of her ability to traverse the mundane world with grace and ease. This contrasts sharply with the fiercer depictions of other Mahavidyas, suggesting a different approach to achieving liberation. Matangi's journey is not necessarily one of fierce battle against demons, but rather a more subtle yet equally powerful engagement with the world, utilizing the power of knowledge, art, and creative expression. The donkey, while not conventionally majestic, symbolizes practicality and endurance, suggesting that Matangi's path to enlightenment is grounded in the everyday world rather than detached from it.

The choice of vehicle also hints at the accessibility of Matangi's teachings. Unlike some goddesses who are only approachable through arduous spiritual practices or rigorous asceticism, Matangi's association with the humble donkey suggests that her wisdom is accessible to all, irrespective of social standing or spiritual attainment. Her path is not necessarily one of renunciation, but rather one of integration – integrating spiritual practices into the fabric of daily life, finding divinity within the ordinary.

Another prominent attribute frequently associated with Matangi is the *vina*, a lute-like stringed instrument. This instrument is not merely a prop; it profoundly symbolizes her connection to music, art, and the power of creative expression. The *vina* represents the harmonious interplay of different energies, the subtle balance between opposing forces that creates the symphony of existence.

The act of playing the *vina* is not just a performance but a meditative practice, a way of aligning oneself with the cosmic rhythm of the universe.

The sounds produced by the *vina* are not simply aesthetically pleasing; they have a transformative power, capable of elevating consciousness and dissolving the illusion of separation. In Tantric traditions, sound is considered a potent tool for spiritual transformation, a vibrational energy that can harmonize the inner and outer worlds. Matangi, as a master of sound, harnesses this power to unlock spiritual insight and foster inner peace. The *vina*, therefore, is not just an instrument; it is a symbol of spiritual awakening, a conduit for divine energy.

Furthermore, Matangi is often depicted with specific hand gestures or *mudras*. These mudras are not arbitrary postures but carefully chosen gestures that convey specific energies and intentions. The specific mudras used in Matangi's iconography vary depending on the artistic tradition and the specific interpretation of her symbolism. However, the general intention behind these mudras is to convey her power to grant knowledge, inspire creativity, and bestow spiritual wisdom. Studying these mudras offers a deeper understanding of Matangi's esoteric symbolism and her capacity to facilitate spiritual growth.

Her association with knowledge and learning is often emphasized by depictions showing her seated amidst books or scriptures. This underscores her role as a patron of education and scholarship. Matangi isn't merely a goddess of the arts; she is also a goddess of knowledge, empowering individuals to seek understanding and to use knowledge for positive transformation. This intellectual aspect of Matangi complements her artistic abilities, demonstrating that true creativity arises from a deep understanding and appreciation of the world.

The colors associated with Matangi also hold symbolic significance. Often depicted in dark blue or black, these colors are not necessarily associated with negativity but rather with the profound mysteries of the cosmos and the boundless depths of the subconscious mind. These darker shades represent the unknown, the hidden potential waiting to be unlocked through creativity and insight. These colors also signify the ability to transcend limitations and to embrace the transformative power of darkness.

The variations in Matangi's iconography are not merely stylistic choices; they reflect the diverse interpretations of her essence across different schools of Tantric thought. Some representations might emphasize her fierce warrior aspect, highlighting her power to overcome obstacles and conquer ignorance. Others might focus on her nurturing side, highlighting her ability to inspire and guide seekers on their path to enlightenment. These variations do not contradict each other but rather offer a richer, more nuanced understanding of her complex and multifaceted nature.

The study of Matangi's iconography is not simply an academic exercise; it is a path to deeper spiritual understanding. By carefully analyzing the symbolism embedded in her artistic representations, we can gain valuable insights into her essential nature and her relevance in the contemporary world. Her ability to harness the power of music, knowledge, and creative expression offers a potent model for personal transformation and social harmony. Her iconography serves as a visual reminder of the transformative potential of art, learning, and the conscious engagement with the creative forces of the universe.

Moreover, the variations in Matangi's depictions underscore the fluidity and adaptability of Hindu iconography. The goddess is not a static entity, confined to a single image or interpretation. Rather, she is a dynamic force, capable of adapting and manifesting in diverse ways, reflecting the ever-evolving spiritual landscape and the multiplicity of human experience. This fluidity challenges the limitations of rigid interpretations, encouraging a more flexible and inclusive approach to understanding the divine.

In the context of Kali Yuga, Matangi's relevance resonates profoundly. The current age is often characterized by information overload, technological advancements, and a rapid pace of change. Matangi's patronage of learning and her mastery of creative expression offer a potent antidote to the potential for disorientation and disillusionment. Her energy can help us navigate the complexities of the modern world by cultivating critical thinking, enhancing creative problem-solving, and fostering a deeper understanding of ourselves and our place in the cosmos.

Her emphasis on knowledge and artistic expression can empower individuals to find meaning and purpose in an often-chaotic world. By embracing her teachings, we can utilize our creative potential to build a more harmonious and fulfilling existence. Her presence reminds us that even amidst the challenges of Kali Yuga, the power of knowledge, art, and compassionate action can bring about positive transformation, leading to individual and collective growth. The continued study and contemplation of Matangi's iconography and attributes, therefore, offer a valuable pathway for navigating the complexities of the contemporary world and harnessing the creative energy within to create a more meaningful and fulfilling life. Her symbolism serves as a beacon of hope, reminding us of the transformative power inherent in artistic expression, intellectual curiosity, and the unwavering pursuit of knowledge. This pursuit, deeply rooted in the Tantric traditions and the profound wisdom of the Mahavidyas, offers a timeless path to self-discovery and societal harmony, fostering a world where creativity and knowledge intertwine to uplift humanity and manifest a brighter future.

Matangi and the Power of Music and Art

Matangi's association with music transcends mere aesthetic appreciation; it delves into the very essence of creation and spiritual transformation within the Tantric framework. The *vina*, her most prominent attribute, isn't simply a musical instrument; it's a symbolic representation of the cosmic symphony, the harmonious interplay of energies that underpins the universe. Each string, each note, represents a different aspect of reality, a different energy vibrating in concert with the others. The act of playing the *vina*, therefore, becomes a meditative practice, a conscious alignment with the cosmic rhythm, a pathway to understanding the interconnectedness of all things.

This understanding is crucial in appreciating Matangi's significance within the context of the Devi Gita and broader Shaktism. The Devi Gita, a pivotal text within Shaktism, emphasizes the dynamic interplay of energies, the constant dance between creation and destruction, manifestation and dissolution. Matangi, as a master of music, embodies this dynamic interplay. Her music isn't a static composition but a living, breathing entity, reflecting the ever-changing nature of reality. The notes she plays are not merely sounds but vibrational energies capable of shaping consciousness, influencing emotions, and ultimately, facilitating spiritual growth.

The sounds produced by the *vina* are described in ancient texts not merely as aesthetically pleasing but as possessing transformative power. They are considered capable of dissolving the illusion of separateness, the veil that obscures our perception of the interconnectedness of all beings. This echoes the central message of the Devi Gita, which emphasizes the unity underlying apparent diversity, the divine feminine energy that permeates and animates all of existence. Matangi's music, therefore, becomes a conduit for this divine energy, a means of experiencing the unity that lies beyond the illusion of separation.

Furthermore, the type of music Matangi plays, and the manner in which she plays it, carries symbolic meaning. Different ragas (melodic scales) and talas (rhythmic cycles) are associated with different emotional states and spiritual experiences. The choice of raga and tala in Matangi's musical performance isn't arbitrary; it's a carefully chosen tool for influencing the listener's consciousness, guiding them towards a specific spiritual state. This skillful manipulation of sound reflects Matangi's mastery not only of music but also of the subtle energies that shape human experience.

Beyond the *vina*, Matangi's association with art extends to all forms of creative expression. Painting, sculpture, dance, poetry – all these are seen as avenues for manifesting the divine energy within. The creative act itself is considered a form of spiritual practice, a way of aligning oneself with the creative force of the universe. Matangi, as the patron of the arts, inspires and empowers individuals to unlock their creative potential, to express the divine within through various mediums. This creative expression is not merely a form of self-expression; it is a pathway to self-realization, a means of connecting with the deeper layers of one's being and the divine consciousness.

This connection to creativity is further strengthened by Matangi's association with knowledge and wisdom. She is often depicted surrounded by books and scriptures, emphasizing her role as a patron of learning and scholarship. The knowledge she embodies is not merely intellectual; it is intuitive, experiential, and transformative. It's the kind of knowledge that arises from a deep understanding of the interconnectedness of all things, a knowledge that transcends the limitations of the intellect and reveals the profound truths underlying the surface of reality. This knowledge, in turn, fuels her artistic expression, creating a powerful synergy between creativity and wisdom. Her art isn't merely aesthetically pleasing; it carries a deep spiritual message, conveying profound truths about the nature of reality and our place within it.

The relationship between Matangi's mastery of music and her role as a muse is also significant. Musicians, artists, and scholars often invoke Matangi's blessings to seek inspiration and guidance. She is seen as the source of creative inspiration, the divine energy that fuels artistic creation. Her presence inspires creativity, not simply by providing a stimulus but by facilitating a deeper connection with the creative force within, enabling the artist to tap into their inner wellspring of inspiration and manifest their artistic vision. This act of channeling divine energy through art is an essential aspect of Tantric practice, a way of transforming mundane experience into a sacred act.

The integration of music and art with knowledge and wisdom within Matangi's persona underscores the holistic nature of her teachings. She isn't simply a goddess of music or art; she is a goddess of holistic development, emphasizing the interconnectedness of all aspects of human experience. Her teachings encourage a balanced approach to life, integrating spiritual practices with daily activities, cultivating both intellectual and artistic capabilities, and fostering a harmonious relationship between the inner and outer worlds. This holistic approach is consistent with the broader philosophy of Shaktism, which emphasizes the divine feminine energy as the force that animates and sustains all of existence.

Matangi's association with learning also encompasses a deeper understanding of the human condition. Her teachings are not limited to theoretical knowledge; they address practical challenges and empower individuals to overcome obstacles. This practical aspect of her teachings is evident in her ability to help individuals navigate the complexities of life, to find meaning and purpose, and to develop their full potential. She is not simply a provider of knowledge but a guide, a mentor, and a source of strength and empowerment.

In the context of Kali Yuga, Matangi's relevance is profound. The current age, often characterized by rapid technological advancements, information overload, and a sense of fragmentation, necessitates a balanced approach to life. Matangi's emphasis on holistic development, creativity, and wisdom offers an antidote to the potential for disorientation and disillusionment. Her teachings help individuals cultivate critical thinking skills, enhance creative problem-solving abilities, and develop a deeper understanding of themselves and their place in the world.

Matangi's guidance provides a framework for integrating technology and information into a meaningful life, preventing the potential for these advancements to lead to detachment and spiritual emptiness. Her emphasis on the creative process—the journey of learning, creating, and expressing—offers a potent path to self-discovery and meaning-making in a rapidly changing world.

The pursuit of knowledge and artistic expression, guided by Matangi's energy, fosters a sense of purpose and connection, countering the isolation and alienation that can accompany modern life.

In conclusion, Matangi's association with music and art goes far beyond superficial aesthetics. It represents a profound spiritual practice, a pathway to self-realization, and a means of experiencing the interconnectedness of all things. Her teachings, rooted in the wisdom of the Devi Gita and broader Shaktism, offer a potent framework for navigating the challenges of Kali Yuga and cultivating a more harmonious and fulfilling existence. By embracing her energy and integrating her teachings into our lives, we can unlock our creative potential, cultivate wisdom, and contribute to the creation of a more meaningful and compassionate world. Her enduring legacy serves as a powerful reminder of the transformative power of creativity, knowledge, and compassionate engagement with the world. The ongoing study and contemplation of Matangi's symbolism offer a timeless and essential pathway to self-discovery and societal harmony in the present age and beyond.

Matangis Role in Tantric Practices

Matangi's role within Tantric practices extends far beyond her association with music and the arts. She is deeply integrated into a rich tapestry of rituals, mantras, and yantras, each imbued with potent spiritual energy designed to facilitate spiritual growth and transformation. Her presence in these practices underscores her multifaceted nature as a goddess who empowers practitioners to unlock their inner potential and connect with the divine feminine energy that permeates the universe.

One of the most significant aspects of Matangi's involvement in Tantric rituals is the use of her specific mantras. These sacred sounds, when chanted with proper intention and focus, are believed to invoke her blessings and activate her transformative energy. The phonetic structure of these mantras is carefully crafted, each syllable resonating with specific vibrational frequencies that are believed to affect the practitioner's subtle energy bodies (chakras) and ultimately, their consciousness. The repetition of these mantras is not merely a mechanical exercise; it's a meditative practice, a process of aligning oneself with the energy of the goddess, thereby facilitating a profound shift in consciousness.

Different Matangi mantras serve different purposes, reflecting the multifaceted nature of the goddess herself. Some mantras are focused on enhancing creativity and inspiration, while others are aimed at fostering knowledge and wisdom. Still others may be used for protection, healing, or achieving specific spiritual goals. The choice of mantra depends on the practitioner's individual needs and intentions. The effectiveness of the mantra, however, depends critically on the practitioner's level of devotion, sincerity, and understanding of the underlying spiritual principles. The mantra is not a magical incantation but a powerful tool that requires dedication, discipline, and proper guidance for its effective use.

The use of yantras further enhances the efficacy of Matangi's Tantric practices. Yantras are geometric diagrams considered to be sacred symbols that represent the goddess's energy in visual form. They are intricate designs composed of various geometric patterns, colors, and symbols, each element carrying specific symbolic meanings and vibrational frequencies. The contemplation and visualization of Matangi's yantra are believed to focus the practitioner's mind and harmonize their energies, facilitating a deeper connection with the goddess.

The process of creating and using a Matangi yantra is a deeply significant ritual in itself. The preparation of the yantra often involves intricate procedures, including specific times, locations, and materials. The creation itself is considered a meditative practice, requiring precision, focus, and devotion. Once the yantra is completed, it is often consecrated through specific rituals, further imbuing it with sacred energy. The yantra then acts as a focal point for meditation and prayer, serving as a visual representation of Matangi's energy and a conduit for accessing her blessings. The placement of the yantra within a sacred space further enhances its effectiveness.

The rituals associated with Matangi are diverse and multifaceted, reflecting the various aspects of her divine personality. Some rituals focus on invoking her blessings for creative inspiration, while others are aimed at acquiring knowledge and wisdom. Some rituals center around healing, protection, or overcoming obstacles. These rituals often involve elaborate procedures, including specific mantras, offerings, and visualizations, creating a powerful and transformative experience for the practitioner.

The offerings made during Matangi rituals are also symbolically significant. These offerings can range from flowers and incense to fruits, sweets, and other sacred items. Each offering carries a symbolic meaning, representing aspects of devotion, respect, and gratitude. The act of offering itself is a form of worship, a gesture of humility and surrender to the divine. The acceptance of the offering by the goddess, whether symbolically or through inner experience, marks the practitioner's successful connection to the divine feminine energy.

The spiritual significance of Matangi's Tantric practices extends beyond individual spiritual growth. These practices are also seen as a way of connecting with the broader cosmic energy and participating in the larger cosmic dance of creation and destruction. By engaging in these practices, the practitioner is not simply interacting with a deity; they are actively participating in the creative energy of the universe.

Furthermore, the context of Kali Yuga deeply influences the understanding and application of Matangi's Tantric practices. The challenges of the current age, characterized by rapid technological advancements, information overload, and a potential disconnect from nature, make Matangi's guidance more relevant than ever. Her emphasis on holistic development, the integration of knowledge and creativity, and the cultivation of wisdom provide a crucial antidote to the potential disorientation and fragmentation of modern life.

In the context of Kali Yuga, Matangi's Tantric practices offer a powerful tool for navigating the complexities of the modern world. Her emphasis on creativity and knowledge helps individuals harness the potential of technology for positive purposes, preventing its misuse and the potential for detachment. Her teachings encourage mindful engagement with information, fostering critical thinking and wise decision-making. The rituals and practices associated with Matangi provide a framework for integrating spirituality into daily life, creating a sense of balance, purpose, and connection in a rapidly changing world.

The use of Matangi's mantras and yantras in a modern context requires a nuanced approach. It necessitates a deep understanding of the underlying spiritual principles, proper guidance from an experienced teacher, and a commitment to ethical practices. The goal is not to manipulate supernatural forces for personal gain but to cultivate inner transformation, foster creativity, and contribute to the creation of a more compassionate and harmonious world.

The study and practice of Matangi's Tantric traditions therefore offer a powerful path for self-discovery and social contribution in Kali Yuga. Her emphasis on the integration of knowledge, creativity, and spiritual practice provides a framework for navigating the challenges of the modern world and cultivating a more balanced and meaningful existence. The continued exploration of Matangi's symbolism and ritual practices reveals enduring wisdom applicable to contemporary challenges, reaffirming the timeless relevance of the Mahavidyas in the twenty-first century and beyond. Through dedicated practice and a sincere approach, Matangi's energy can empower individuals to tap into their inner potential, fostering creativity, fostering wisdom, and creating positive change in the world. Her teachings provide a pathway to integrate the spiritual and the material, the ancient and the modern, forging a future where creativity, knowledge, and compassion are not just ideals but integral aspects of daily life. The continued exploration and application of Matangi's Tantric practices offer a vibrant and evolving pathway to self-realization and societal progress in the context of Kali Yuga and beyond.

Matangi in Different Textual Sources

Matangi's presence in Hindu scriptures is not as prominently featured as some of the other Mahavidyas, yet her appearances offer valuable insights into her evolving symbolism and significance across different traditions. Unlike goddesses whose iconography and attributes are consistently detailed across multiple texts, Matangi's depiction reveals a fascinating evolution of understanding and interpretation across different periods and schools of thought. This lack of uniform representation is not an indication of lesser importance; rather, it reflects the fluidity and adaptability of Tantric traditions, where goddesses are often seen as multifaceted and capable of manifesting in diverse forms to suit specific needs and contexts.

One of the earliest mentions of Matangi appears in the *Devi Mahatmya*, a core text of Shaktism. While not a central figure in the narrative's primary battles and victories, her presence is still implicitly significant. The *Devi Mahatmya* establishes the supreme power of the Devi, whose manifestations encompass the entire cosmos. Matangi's inclusion, however subtle, underscores her position within this larger cosmic order as a manifestation of the Divine Mother. The text's focus on the Devi's triumph over demonic forces establishes a broader context for understanding Matangi's power – she is not merely an artistic muse but a participant in the cosmic drama of creation, preservation, and destruction. Her inclusion highlights the importance of even seemingly less prominent goddesses within the greater pantheon.

The *Tantras* offer more detailed portrayals of Matangi, but these descriptions often vary depending on the specific text and the particular school of Tantra involved. Some *Tantras* emphasize Matangi's association with music, dance, and the arts, portraying her as a captivating and inspiring figure. These texts often depict her as a beautiful goddess adorned with jewelry and surrounded by musicians and dancers. This emphasis aligns with her role as a patron of the arts and a source of creativity and inspiration. The visual and sensory aspects of these descriptions are significant, reinforcing the connection between the divine and the aesthetic experience. The detailed imagery found in these texts reveals an attempt to evoke a feeling of profound reverence and awe in the devotee, facilitating a deeper connection to the divine.

Other *Tantras*, however, portray Matangi in a more mystical and esoteric manner. These texts may emphasize her connection to hidden knowledge, secret wisdom, and the occult arts. They often associate her with spells, mantras, and rituals intended for specific purposes. This perspective reflects the inherent ambiguity within Tantric thought, where the divine manifests in multiple forms, some hidden and some overtly present. This duality is crucial to understanding Matangi's multifaceted nature; she is both readily accessible through her artistic representations and simultaneously elusive, requiring deeper study and devotion to reveal her full spiritual significance. This ambiguity, far from being a limitation, enhances her mystery and her capacity to serve as a guide and protector in various aspects of life.

The *Devi Gita*, a pivotal text within Shaktism, offers a more nuanced portrayal of Matangi. While not explicitly detailed as extensively as some other goddesses, her inherent presence within the broader cosmology depicted in the *Devi Gita* is implied through her association with various forms of the Divine Mother. The *Devi Gita*'s focus on spiritual realization and the journey towards liberation provides a valuable lens through which to interpret Matangi's role. Her connection to knowledge and creativity can be seen as instruments on the path towards self-knowledge and spiritual awakening. The *Devi Gita* suggests that the creative force of Matangi is not merely for aesthetic appreciation, but a powerful force in spiritual transformation.

Comparing Matangi's portrayal in the *Devi Gita* with her depiction in other Tantric texts illuminates the dynamic nature of her symbolism. While other texts might focus on specific mantras and rituals associated with her, the *Devi Gita* positions her within a larger cosmic narrative, emphasizing her role in the overarching divine plan. This perspective aligns with the overarching spiritual aims of the *Devi Gita*, which emphasizes liberation and self-realization as ultimate goals. Therefore, Matangi's representation in the *Devi Gita* transcends her association with the arts, suggesting a deeper involvement in the spiritual evolution of the devotee.

The variations in Matangi's depictions across different texts highlight the richness and complexity of the Tantric tradition. These variations are not contradictions but rather expressions of the goddess's multifaceted nature, reflecting her ability to manifest in diverse forms and serve a range of purposes. Her connection to music, arts, knowledge, and occult practices demonstrates the multifaceted nature of spiritual experience itself. The integration of these seemingly disparate elements within her persona underscores the Tantric emphasis on the interconnectedness of all aspects of reality.

Furthermore, the evolution of Matangi's symbolism over time offers valuable insights into the changing socio-cultural context. As societal priorities shifted, the emphasis on specific aspects of Matangi's persona might have changed. For instance, periods emphasizing artistic expression may have seen a heightened focus on her artistic attributes, while periods valuing occult knowledge and wisdom might have focused on her esoteric aspects. This adaptation demonstrates the dynamism of the Tantric tradition and its ability to adapt to evolving societal needs and cultural values.

The study of Matangi's portrayal across diverse textual sources reveals a goddess whose significance transcends temporal boundaries and rigid interpretations. Her multifaceted nature – encompassing artistic expression, mystical wisdom, and spiritual guidance – exemplifies the richness and depth of the Tantric tradition. Her image is not static; rather, it evolves and adapts, reflecting the ever-changing landscape of human spirituality and the enduring power of the Divine Feminine to inspire, guide, and transform. The ongoing exploration of Matangi in various texts continues to enrich our understanding of the multifaceted nature of the Divine Mother and her role in the spiritual evolution of humankind. The absence of a single, definitive description only serves to highlight her ever-evolving nature, mirroring the dynamic and evolving journey of spiritual seekers. This fluidity underscores the living, breathing nature of the Tantric tradition, where the goddess is not a fixed entity, but a source of ever-present and ever-changing inspiration. Her enduring presence in diverse textual sources testifies to the continued relevance of the Mahavidyas in the modern world and beyond. Her image is a powerful reminder of the boundless potential of the Divine Feminine, constantly adapting and evolving to meet the needs and aspirations of humanity.

Matangi and Creative Expression

Matangi, the Mahavidya associated with knowledge, music, and the arts, offers a potent lens through which to examine the intersection of spirituality and creative expression. Her symbolism transcends mere aesthetic appreciation; it speaks to the transformative power of creativity as a path to self-discovery and spiritual growth. In the context of the modern world, saturated with information and technological advancements, Matangi's energy becomes particularly relevant, urging us to cultivate innovative thinking and find meaningful ways to translate inner wisdom into tangible realities.

Unlike goddesses whose iconography remains relatively static across different texts, Matangi's visual representation is fluid, mirroring the dynamic nature of artistic expression itself. This fluidity is not a weakness but a strength, emphasizing the boundless potential of creativity and its capacity to adapt to evolving contexts. Her depictions vary, sometimes showing her as a beautiful, adorned goddess surrounded by musicians, dancers, and artistic paraphernalia, while other times she appears in more esoteric forms, emphasizing her connection to hidden knowledge and mystical wisdom. This duality underscores her role as a patroness of both the tangible and intangible aspects of creative endeavor – the visible artwork and the invisible spark of inspiration that birthed it.

The contemporary relevance of Matangi lies in her ability to inspire innovation and break down creative blockages. In today's rapidly changing world, the ability to adapt, innovate, and generate new ideas is crucial for personal and collective progress. Matangi's energy serves as a catalyst for this process, encouraging us to explore unconventional approaches, embrace experimentation, and move beyond established paradigms. This aligns with the Tantric concept of *śakti* , the dynamic feminine energy that permeates the universe and fuels creation. Matangi, as a manifestation of this *śakti* , embodies the power to transform potential into reality, to translate inner visions into concrete forms.

Her association with music offers a profound insight into the transformative power of sound and rhythm. Music, in its various forms, has been used throughout history as a tool for spiritual practice, emotional healing, and social bonding. Matangi's connection to music extends beyond mere entertainment; it signifies the potential of sound to access deeper levels of consciousness and to facilitate spiritual awakening. In modern times, sound healing therapies, music therapy, and the use of mantras and chants reflect the continued relevance of Matangi's energy in promoting well-being and spiritual growth. The rhythmic patterns of music can help to quiet the mind, allowing for a deeper connection with intuition and inner wisdom. This connection is essential for creative expression, as it allows for the emergence of original ideas and insights, unhindered by the limitations of the conscious mind.

Matangi's connection to knowledge extends beyond the acquisition of factual information; it encompasses the pursuit of deeper understanding and wisdom. She represents the ability to synthesize information, to connect seemingly disparate concepts, and to translate complex ideas into accessible and meaningful forms. In the modern age, bombarded by a deluge of information, Matangi's energy becomes crucial in navigating the complexities of knowledge and extracting meaningful insights. She encourages us to critically evaluate information, to discern truth from falsehood, and to use knowledge as a tool for personal and societal transformation. This ability to discern and synthesize information is critical for creative expression, as it allows for the creation of innovative and impactful works that reflect a deeper understanding of the world and its complexities.

The pursuit of knowledge, in the context of Matangi's symbolism, is not a passive activity but an active engagement with the world. It involves questioning assumptions, exploring different perspectives, and continually seeking new understanding. This continuous exploration and self-improvement are inherent to creative expression, urging artists to refine their skills, to experiment with different techniques, and to continually strive for excellence.

Matangi, as a patroness of knowledge and the arts, inspires this continuous evolution, reminding us that creative expression is a journey, not a destination.

Furthermore, Matangi's association with the occult arts underscores the importance of embracing the unseen and the mysterious in our creative pursuits. The occult, in this context, does not necessarily refer to the supernatural, but rather to the hidden aspects of reality– the unconscious mind, intuition, and the deeper layers of human experience. Accessing these hidden dimensions can unlock profound creative potential. Modern creative practices, such as dream work, automatic writing, and intuitive painting, reflect this ongoing exploration of the unconscious and its connection to artistic expression. Matangi's energy encourages this exploration, reminding us that the most impactful creative works often emerge from a place of deep intuition and subconscious inspiration.

The application of Matangi's energy in contemporary life extends beyond individual creative endeavors. Her symbolism can also be applied to collective creativity and collaborative projects. Her energy inspires teamwork, encourages open communication, and fosters a shared vision. In the modern world, where collaboration is becoming increasingly essential, Matangi's energy can help to facilitate innovative partnerships and generate collective solutions to complex problems. This collaborative approach to creativity mirrors the multifaceted nature of Matangi herself, highlighting the power of collective effort in achieving meaningful and lasting results.

The relevance of Matangi in the 21st century is not simply a matter of historical interpretation. It is a call to action, urging us to embrace our creative potential and use it as a tool for personal growth and societal transformation. Her energy encourages us to engage actively with the world, to explore our intuition, and to translate our inner wisdom into tangible expressions of creativity.

Whether it is through music, writing, visual arts, or any other creative endeavor, Matangi's energy can serve as a powerful catalyst for innovation, self-discovery, and spiritual growth. Her legacy transcends time and cultural boundaries, providing a timeless message of empowerment and artistic exploration. In an era characterized by rapid technological advancements and an ever-increasing flow of information, Matangi's message of discerning knowledge, embracing intuition, and channeling inner wisdom into creative expression remains profoundly relevant. She is not merely a goddess of the arts; she is a guide on the path to self-realization through creative expression, urging us to unleash our potential and leave our mark on the world. This ongoing engagement with Matangi's symbolism allows for a continuous reinterpretation of her significance, adapting her message to the ever-evolving needs and aspirations of humanity. Her enduring presence serves as a powerful reminder of the transformative potential of creative expression and the importance of tapping into our inner resources to create a more meaningful and fulfilling life.

Kamalatmikas Iconography and Attributes

Kamalatmika, the tenth Mahavidya, presents a fascinating study in iconography, where her visual representation often reflects the multifaceted nature of her essence: the embodiment of supreme consciousness and creative potential. Unlike some of the other Mahavidyas whose depictions remain relatively consistent across various artistic traditions, Kamalatmika's iconography exhibits a wider range of stylistic variations, reflecting the fluidity and adaptability of her energy. This variability, however, does not imply a lack of coherence; rather, it highlights the diverse ways in which her potent energy manifests and interacts with the world.

One common depiction shows Kamalatmika seated upon a fully blossomed lotus flower, a symbol of purity, enlightenment, and the unfolding of consciousness. The lotus, rising from the muddy waters, represents the ability to transcend the limitations of the material world and achieve spiritual liberation. Kamalatmika's association with the lotus underscores her role as a guide on the path to self-realization, a journey that requires navigating the complexities and challenges of life while maintaining inner peace and unwavering focus. The vibrant colors of the lotus—often depicted in shades of pink, white, or red—further enhance the symbolic meaning, each color carrying its own specific connotation within the rich tapestry of Hindu symbolism. Pink often signifies spiritual awakening and divine love, while white represents purity and enlightenment, and red signifies energy, passion, and transformation. The particular shade of the lotus in any given depiction of Kamalatmika might, therefore, offer further clues to the artist's specific interpretation of her essence.

The number of petals on the lotus itself can also carry significant meaning. In some representations, the lotus may have eight petals, reflecting the eightfold path of Buddhism, or it might have a hundred petals, symbolizing the totality of existence and the infinite potential of consciousness. This careful attention to detail in the artistic representation serves as a subtle reminder that each aspect of Kamalatmika's iconography is imbued with profound spiritual significance, inviting deeper contemplation and understanding.

Further enriching the visual narrative, Kamalatmika is often depicted with multiple arms, each holding a symbolic object reflecting one of her multifaceted attributes. The number of arms can vary, but the objects they hold typically represent aspects of creation, preservation, and destruction – the dynamic interplay of cosmic forces that shape the universe. These objects may include a sword, representing the power to sever attachments and overcome obstacles; a trident, symbolizing the threefold nature of time (past, present, and future); a lotus flower, representing purity and spiritual awakening; and a skull, signifying the impermanence of all things and the acceptance of mortality as a natural part of the cycle of existence. The specific objects and their arrangement provide a visual narrative, conveying a deeper understanding of Kamalatmika's multifaceted nature and her dominion over various aspects of reality. A careful study of these objects, therefore, offers a window into the artist's interpretation of Kamalatmika's role within the cosmic drama.

The color of her complexion also contributes to the symbolic richness of her iconography. While some depictions show her with a radiant golden complexion, symbolizing purity and divinity, others portray her with a darker complexion, reflecting the profound mysteries of the cosmos and the untamed power of the divine feminine. The variation in complexion is not a mere aesthetic choice; it highlights the multifaceted nature of the divine, capable of both radiant light and impenetrable darkness, embodying both creation and destruction as integral aspects of the cosmic dance.

The artist's choice of complexion, therefore, provides a valuable insight into their understanding of Kamalatmika's role in the intricate tapestry of existence.

Her ornaments and attire also speak volumes about her status and attributes. She is often adorned with exquisite jewelry and fine clothing, reflecting her regal status and her connection to the highest realms of consciousness. The types of ornaments and their arrangement can also hold symbolic weight, suggesting specific attributes or connections to particular deities or aspects of the divine. For example, specific types of necklaces might indicate her connection to particular mantra or cosmic energies, while the choice of garments might reference particular seasons or aspects of nature. Even the intricate details of her clothing and jewelry—the patterns, the gemstones, the type of fabric—are all intentional choices that contribute to the rich tapestry of her visual representation.

The presence or absence of specific features, such as a garland of flowers, a particular type of headdress, or specific hand gestures (mudras), can also subtly alter the meaning and emphasis of her portrayal. Each element within her iconography functions as a piece of a larger puzzle, contributing to a holistic understanding of her essence. In analyzing the iconography, one must not focus on individual elements in isolation, but rather consider the overall composition and the interrelationship between different elements to glean a deeper understanding of the artist's vision and their interpretation of Kamalatmika's divine qualities.

Analyzing Kamalatmika's iconography across different schools of Tantric art provides further insights into the varied interpretations of her energy and attributes. While certain elements, such as her association with the lotus and her multiple arms, remain consistent across diverse representations, variations in her appearance reflect the differing perspectives and emphases of various Tantric traditions. These variations are not contradictions, but rather expressions of the multifaceted nature of the divine feminine, emphasizing the fluidity and adaptability of her energy as it manifests in different contexts and cultural landscapes.

The study of Kamalatmika's iconography, therefore, transcends mere aesthetic appreciation; it involves a deep dive into the symbolic language of Tantric art, requiring careful observation and rigorous interpretation. Each element of her depiction – the lotus, the ornaments, the number of arms, the specific objects held in her hands, her complexion, her attire – carries a significant symbolic weight, offering clues to her essence and her connection to the cosmic energies she embodies. By studying these elements across diverse artistic representations, we gain a richer and more nuanced understanding of Kamalatmika's multifaceted nature and her enduring relevance in the contemporary world. The diversity of her representations, rather than signifying confusion, actually serves to highlight the inexhaustible depths of her divine energy and her capacity to manifest in countless forms, adapting her message to the needs and aspirations of individuals and communities across time and cultures. Her enduring presence in Tantric art underscores the continuous relevance of her message, a message that speaks to the human condition and the eternal pursuit of spiritual awakening.

Her iconography, therefore, becomes a dynamic and evolving narrative, constantly adapting to the changing context while maintaining a core message of empowerment, transformation, and the boundless potential of the divine feminine. This exploration deepens our understanding not only of Kamalatmika herself, but also the rich tapestry of Tantric thought and practice, offering a lens through which to examine the complex interplay of symbolism, art, and spiritual experience. The continued study and appreciation of her iconography allow us to engage with her message on a

profound level, fostering a deeper connection to the divine and enhancing our understanding of the intricacies of the Tantric worldview.

Kamalatmika and the Lotus Symbolism

The profound connection between Kamalatmika and the lotus flower transcends mere aesthetic representation; it delves into the heart of her symbolism, illuminating her essence as a goddess of creation, purity, and spiritual awakening. The lotus, a perennial aquatic plant, holds immense significance across various cultures, but its symbolism within the Hindu tradition is particularly rich and multifaceted. Emerging from the muddy depths of a pond or lake, the lotus flower unfurls its petals towards the sun, a breathtaking metaphor for the journey of spiritual growth. This remarkable journey mirrors the human experience, where one navigates the murky waters of earthly existence – the challenges, the disappointments, the struggles – to ultimately blossom into a state of enlightenment and self-realization.

Kamalatmika, as a Mahavidya, embodies this transformative process. Her association with the lotus signifies her ability to guide devotees through the complexities of life, helping them transcend the limitations of the material world and achieve spiritual liberation. The lotus's ability to thrive in seemingly inhospitable environments – the muddy waters – perfectly reflects Kamalatmika's power and resilience. Just as the lotus does not allow the mud to taint its purity, Kamalatmika empowers her devotees to navigate life's challenges without compromising their spiritual integrity. This resilience underscores her role as a protector and a guide, offering unwavering support and guidance on the path to self-discovery.

The color of the lotus further enhances the rich tapestry of symbolism. In depictions of Kamalatmika, the lotus is frequently portrayed in shades of pink, white, or red, each color carrying its own profound meaning. The pink lotus is often associated with spiritual awakening and divine love, symbolizing the blossoming of the heart and the opening of the soul to the divine. The white lotus, on the other hand, represents purity, enlightenment, and the transcendence of worldly attachments. Finally, the red lotus is associated with energy, passion, and transformation, signifying the dynamic force of creation and the power to overcome obstacles.

The specific shade of the lotus in a particular depiction of Kamalatmika can offer subtle insights into the artist's interpretation of her essence and the specific aspects of her energy that are being emphasized. A pink lotus might highlight her nurturing and compassionate nature, while a red lotus could emphasize her dynamic and transformative power. The artist's choice of color, therefore, functions as a subtle yet powerful element within the visual narrative, adding layers of meaning to the overall composition.

Furthermore, the number of petals on the lotus also holds symbolic weight. While some depictions show a lotus with eight petals, alluding to the eightfold path of Buddhism, others depict a lotus with numerous petals, sometimes even a hundred. This representation often signifies the totality of existence and the infinite potential of consciousness, reflecting the boundless energy and transformative power of Kamalatmika. The artist's choice of the number of petals further adds to the complexity and nuance of the symbolic representation, hinting at the artist's unique interpretation of Kamalatmika's role within the cosmic order.

The lotus's symbolism extends beyond its visual representation. In Tantric practices, the lotus is often used as a meditative device, representing the unfolding of consciousness and the expansion of awareness. The image of the lotus can serve as a focal point for meditation, helping practitioners to connect with the divine feminine energy embodied by Kamalatmika. Through the practice of visualization and mantra recitation, devotees can utilize the symbolic power of the lotus to access deeper levels of consciousness and experience a heightened sense of connection with the divine.

The association of Kamalatmika with the lotus further underscores her role as a guide in the process of spiritual unfoldment. Just as the lotus unfolds its petals gradually, revealing its beauty and magnificence, so too does the spiritual journey unfold gradually, with each stage revealing new levels of understanding and awareness. Kamalatmika serves as a compassionate guide throughout this process, offering support, encouragement, and guidance as devotees navigate the complexities of their spiritual growth.

The lotus's roots, firmly anchored in the mud, represent the grounding and stability needed during periods of spiritual upheaval. This speaks to the importance of maintaining a connection to the earth and the material world while simultaneously striving for spiritual enlightenment. Kamalatmika's connection with the lotus underscores this essential balance. She helps individuals ground themselves in the present moment, while simultaneously pointing towards the higher realms of consciousness.

The lotus's capacity to bloom even in adversity underscores Kamalatmika's resilience and ability to thrive in the face of challenges. She represents the power of the feminine principle to overcome adversity, to emerge from hardship stronger and more radiant, and to utilize obstacles as stepping stones towards greater understanding and growth. This quality makes her a particularly relevant figure in the modern world, where many face constant challenges and uncertainties. Her association with the lotus provides a comforting message of hope and resilience.

The lotus flower's cyclical nature – its daily opening and closing – also reflects the cyclical nature of life, death, and rebirth. This cyclical process is integral to Hindu cosmology, and Kamalatmika, as a Mahavidya, embodies this dynamic energy of constant transformation and renewal. Her connection to the lotus underscores her role in guiding individuals through the cyclical process of life, helping them to embrace change and to accept the impermanence of all things as a natural part of the cosmic order.

Moreover, the lotus's perfect symmetry and its exquisite beauty reflect the divine harmony and perfection that lie at the heart of existence. This beauty speaks to the inherent goodness and potential for beauty and perfection that reside within each individual,
awaiting their unfolding. Kamalatmika, by her association with the lotus, reminds us of our inherent divinity and encourages us to strive towards the realization of our full potential.

In conclusion, Kamalatmika's association with the lotus is not merely a decorative element in her iconography; it is a profound and multifaceted symbol that illuminates the essence of her divine nature and her role in guiding devotees on their spiritual path. The lotus's symbolism of purity, resilience, growth, and transformation mirrors Kamalatmika's own attributes, making the connection deeply resonant and meaningful. It is a reminder that even amidst life's challenges, the potential for beauty, growth, and spiritual awakening is always present, just as the lotus flower unfurls its beauty from the depths of the murky waters. The lotus, therefore, becomes a powerful metaphor for the journey of spiritual growth, a journey that Kamalatmika guides her devotees through with unwavering compassion and unwavering support. The deeper one delves into this symbolism, the richer and more profound the understanding of Kamalatmika's divine essence becomes.

Kamalatmikas Role in Tantric Practices

Kamalatmika's role within the framework of Tantric practices extends far beyond her symbolic representation. She is actively engaged in the ritualistic landscape, manifesting her power through specific mantras, yantras, and carefully orchestrated rituals.

Understanding these practices provides crucial insight into the dynamic interplay between the devotee and the divine, illustrating the practical application of Kamalatmika's energy for spiritual growth and transformation.

The most direct manifestation of Kamalatmika's presence in Tantric practices lies in the recitation of her specific mantra. These mantras, often consisting of Sanskrit syllables, act as vibrational keys, unlocking specific energies and facilitating a direct connection with the goddess. The precise mantras associated with Kamalatmika vary across different lineages and traditions; however, their core function remains consistent: to invoke her presence, align the devotee's energy with hers, and facilitate the desired spiritual outcome. The recitation of the mantra is not a mere mechanical repetition but a deeply meditative practice requiring focus, devotion, and a clear intention. The rhythmic repetition of the sounds creates a
vibrational resonance that resonates within the practitioner's subtle energy bodies, subtly altering their energetic state and opening them to the transformative potential of Kamalatmika's grace.

The efficacy of the mantra is significantly enhanced when combined with visualization techniques. Devotees are often instructed to visualize Kamalatmika's form, adorned with the lotus, while reciting her mantra. This visualization process bridges the gap between the mundane and the sacred, allowing the practitioner to immerse themselves more fully in the devotional experience. The clarity and intensity of this visualization directly impact the effectiveness of the mantra, strengthening the connection with the goddess and accelerating the spiritual progress. The process is not simply an act of imagination; rather, it's a refined form of focused attention that cultivates a profound sense of presence and connection with the divine.

Yantras, geometric diagrams imbued with potent spiritual energy, further enhance Kamalatmika's role in Tantric practice. These intricate designs, often containing specific symbols and arrangements of lines and shapes, act as conduits for channeling Kamalatmika's energy. The Kamalatmika yantra, like her mantra, is not simply a decorative image; it is a tool for spiritual transformation, activating and directing specific energies within the practitioner's energy field. The process of creating a yantra is itself a ritual, requiring meticulous attention to detail and a deep meditative state. This meticulous process serves to purify the practitioner's intentions and align their energy with the intended outcome.

The yantra is often used in conjunction with mantra recitation, creating a synergistic effect that amplifies the transformative power of the practice. The visualization of the yantra, during mantra recitation, enhances the meditative experience and facilitates a more profound connection with Kamalatmika. Devotees may gaze upon the yantra, focusing their attention on its intricate design, allowing the symbolic energy to permeate their consciousness. This practice strengthens the practitioner's resolve, helping them to deepen their connection with the divine feminine principle embodied by Kamalatmika. Moreover, the yantra can be used as a focal point for meditation, serving as a gateway to accessing higher states of consciousness.

Specific rituals incorporating both mantra and yantra form the core of Kamalatmika's Tantric practices. These rituals are often performed at specific times, under specific conditions, and with particular offerings to enhance their effectiveness. These rituals are not simply outward expressions of devotion; they represent a sophisticated system of energetic manipulation, designed to harness Kamalatmika's power for spiritual transformation. The meticulous preparation, precise actions, and focused intention involved in these rituals ensure the harmonious alignment of the devotee's energy with the divine, maximizing the potential for spiritual growth.

The offerings presented during these rituals are not mere symbolic gestures; they represent a tangible expression of the devotee's devotion and intention. Flowers, fruits, incense, and other sacred substances are often presented, each imbued with symbolic meaning and energetic properties. The act of offering is a form of surrender, a conscious relinquishing of the ego in favor of the divine, allowing the practitioner to open themselves to Kamalatmika's grace and guidance. The offerings also serve a practical purpose, purifying the ritual space and creating a conducive environment for spiritual transformation.

The choice of specific rituals often depends on the practitioner's goals and intentions. Some rituals are geared toward overcoming obstacles, attracting prosperity, or cultivating specific spiritual qualities. Others are aimed at fostering a deeper connection with the divine feminine principle, deepening the practitioner's understanding of their own spiritual nature, or achieving a state of enlightenment. The versatility of Kamalatmika's Tantric practices makes them relevant to a wide range of spiritual aspirations.

The use of mudras (hand gestures) and asanas (postures) further enhances the effectiveness of Tantric practices involving Kamalatmika. These practices, deeply rooted in the yoga tradition, are designed to regulate the flow of prana (life force energy) within the practitioner's body. By employing specific mudras and asanas, the devotee enhances the receptivity to Kamalatmika's energy, promoting a deeper level of integration between the divine and the earthly. The precise positions of the fingers and the body align the subtle energy channels, amplifying the practitioner's connection to the cosmic energy.

Furthermore, the location and timing of these rituals hold significant weight. Practitioners may choose specific auspicious times, such as during full moons or new moons, to amplify the effectiveness of the practice. Likewise, the environment plays a significant role, with many practitioners preferring secluded, natural settings to foster a deeper sense of connection with the divine. The careful consideration of these elements underscores the holistic and integrated nature of Tantric practices, emphasizing the importance of aligning oneself with the natural rhythms of the cosmos.

Beyond the strictly ritualistic aspects, the teachings associated with

Kamalatmika provide a profound framework for ethical living and spiritual development. Her association with purity, resilience, and spiritual awakening inspires devotees to cultivate these qualities in their own lives. The principles embedded in her symbolism and practices serve as guidelines for navigating life's challenges with grace, compassion, and unwavering faith. The deeper one delves into Kamalatmika's teachings, the more profound becomes their understanding of the interconnectedness of the inner and outer worlds.

In conclusion, Kamalatmika's role in Tantric practices is multifaceted and dynamic. She is not merely a passive symbol but an active participant in the ritualistic process, offering her grace and guidance to those who seek her blessings. Through the skillful use of mantra, yantra, ritual, mudra, and asana, devotees can harness her energy for spiritual growth, personal transformation, and a deeper understanding of the divine feminine principle. The practice is not simply a series of rituals but a holistic approach to spiritual development, integrating the physical, mental, and spiritual aspects of human existence. The meticulousness and precision involved underscore the power of intention and the importance of aligning oneself with the divine energy to achieve spiritual fulfillment. The journey with Kamalatmika, therefore, is not merely a path to spiritual attainment; it is a profound transformation of consciousness, leading to a deeper connection with the divine and a richer understanding of one's true nature.

Kamalatmika in Different Textual Sources

The diverse textual landscape of Hindu and Tantric traditions offers a fascinating tapestry of interpretations regarding Kamalatmika. While a singular, definitive description remains elusive, a careful examination of various scriptures reveals a consistent core essence, interwoven with nuanced variations reflecting the diverse cultural and philosophical contexts in which she emerged. Understanding these variations is crucial to appreciating the richness and complexity of Kamalatmika's symbolic power.

The Devi Gita, a pivotal text within Shaktism, offers one of the most significant accounts of Kamalatmika, albeit often indirectly. While she isn't explicitly named as one of the ten Mahavidyas in the Devi Gita itself, her attributes and symbolism strongly resonate with the descriptions of the divine feminine principle found within the text. The Devi Gita's emphasis on the goddess as the ultimate source of creation, preservation, and destruction aligns perfectly with Kamalatmika's role as a manifestation of the divine creative energy. The text's focus on the goddess's multifaceted nature, her capacity for both nurturing and fierce power, mirrors the dualistic representations often associated with Kamalatmika. This indirect depiction, therefore, allows for a wider interpretation, embedding Kamalatmika's essence within the broader theological framework of the Devi Gita's cosmology. The text's emphasis on self-realization through devotion and understanding of the divine feminine can be viewed as a pathway to accessing the spiritual power associated with Kamalatmika.

Moving beyond the Devi Gita, we encounter a multitude of other Tantric texts that offer glimpses into Kamalatmika's nature and power. These texts often present her within a specific Tantric lineage or tradition, leading to variations in her iconography, attributes, and associated practices. Some texts emphasize her connection to Lakshmi, the goddess of wealth and prosperity, highlighting her role in bestowing material abundance. In these traditions, rituals focused on attracting wealth, prosperity, and success are central to Kamalatmika worship. The lotus, her primary symbol, is interpreted here not only as a symbol of purity and spiritual awakening but also as a representation of unfolding potential and abundance. These texts often depict her with a more benevolent and nurturing aspect, showcasing her as a bestower of boons and a protector of her devotees.

Other textual sources, particularly those associated with more esoteric lineages of Shaktism, emphasize Kamalatmika's more powerful and transformative aspects. These texts might depict her with a more fierce or wrathful countenance, highlighting her ability to destroy obstacles and overcome negativity. The lotus, in this context, may represent the transcendence of the material world and the attainment of a higher spiritual state. Rituals associated with these interpretations often focus on overcoming internal and
external obstacles, achieving spiritual liberation, and severing ties with limiting beliefs and patterns. This aspect reveals a deeper dimension of Kamalatmika's nature, demonstrating her capacity to act as a transformative force in the spiritual journey.

The variations in textual descriptions are not necessarily contradictory but rather complementary, representing different facets of the same divine energy. The diversity of interpretations reflects the multifaceted nature of the divine feminine and the different approaches devotees might take in their spiritual practices. The choice of a particular textual interpretation often depends on the individual practitioner's spiritual path, lineage, and personal experiences. This emphasis on individual experience highlights the fluidity and adaptability of Tantric practices, allowing for diverse interpretations and approaches to the divine.

It is important to note that many of the textual sources mentioning Kamalatmika are often not widely available or accessible. Many of them are kept within specific lineages and passed down through oral tradition, resulting in a limited dissemination of this
knowledge. This adds another layer of complexity to the study of Kamalatmika, making it a continuous journey of discovery and interpretation. The scarcity of easily accessible texts underscores the need for careful scrutiny of existing materials and the importance of preserving and understanding these diverse traditions.

Further complicating the matter is the potential for syncretism and the blending of different traditions. Over centuries, the worship of Kamalatmika has undoubtedly evolved, integrating elements from various sources, leading to further variations in her iconography and attributes. This blending is not simply a matter of confusion but a testament to the dynamic and evolving nature of Hindu and Tantric traditions, demonstrating the ability of these traditions to adapt and absorb new influences while retaining their core essence.

The analysis, therefore, requires a nuanced understanding of historical context and the possibility of intercultural exchange.

Beyond written texts, the visual arts offer another significant source for understanding Kamalatmika. Sculptures, paintings, and other artistic representations provide visual interpretations of her form, attributes, and symbolism. These artistic representations offer valuable insight into the ways in which Kamalatmika has been perceived and understood throughout history. While the textual descriptions might offer abstract concepts, the visual
representations provide a tangible embodiment of these concepts, allowing for a richer and more multi-sensory engagement with the divine feminine. These visual aids often supplement the textual interpretations, offering a different perspective on the same themes and concepts.

Analyzing the evolution of Kamalatmika's iconography across different periods and regions reveals fascinating shifts in her representation. Earlier depictions might focus on her serene and nurturing aspects, emphasizing her connection to Lakshmi. Later depictions may highlight her more fierce and transformative qualities, reflecting changes in cultural attitudes and spiritual emphasis. The study of art history, therefore, provides a visual record of the evolution of Kamalatmika's symbolism and its adaptation to different social and spiritual contexts.

The study of Kamalatmika across different textual sources is not merely an academic exercise; it is a spiritual journey of its own.

Each encounter with a new textual interpretation deepens our understanding of the richness and complexity of the divine feminine principle. The inconsistencies and variations are not signs of weakness or contradictions but rather highlights of the dynamic, evolving nature of spiritual understanding. The journey through these texts allows us to appreciate the diverse pathways towards spiritual growth and the multitude of ways in which the divine feminine can manifest. The process of interpretation, comparison, and synthesis ultimately enhances our ability to connect with the essence of Kamalatmika, fostering a more profound and personal understanding of her power and grace. It is a testament to the enduring power of the goddess and the enduring relevance of her teachings for contemporary spiritual seekers. This exploration continues to illuminate the depths of the divine feminine and invites us into a deeper relationship with this powerful manifestation of the divine.

Kamalatmika and Spiritual Growth

The multifaceted symbolism of Kamalatmika extends beyond historical interpretations and into the practical application of her energy for contemporary spiritual growth. Her association with the lotus, a flower arising from mud to achieve radiant beauty, serves as a potent metaphor for the transformative journey of the self. Just as the lotus transcends its murky origins to blossom, so too can individuals overcome life's challenges and emerge stronger and more enlightened. This process of personal transformation, mirroring Kamalatmika's own symbolic journey, is central to her contemporary relevance.

Kamalatmika's resilience, embodied in the lotus's ability to flourish in seemingly inhospitable environments, offers a powerful message for navigating the complexities of modern life. In an era marked by uncertainty and rapid change, her energy encourages perseverance and the cultivation of inner strength. The challenges we face – be they personal, professional, or societal – can be viewed as the "mud" from which we can rise. By embracing the lessons learned from adversity, we can foster resilience, cultivating a strength and adaptability that mirrors the lotus's ability to thrive.

The journey to self-realization is rarely linear; it is often characterized by setbacks and obstacles. Kamalatmika's symbolic power lies in her ability to inspire us to persevere through these difficulties. Her image can be a source of strength and encouragement during times of hardship, reminding us that even in the darkest moments, the potential for growth and transformation remains. Her energy can be channeled to foster courage, determination, and the unwavering belief in our ability to overcome adversity. This is not merely a passive acceptance of hardship but an active engagement with it, viewing challenges as opportunities for spiritual growth and self-discovery.

Furthermore, Kamalatmika's connection to creativity and abundance offers valuable insights into the creative potential residing within each individual. The lotus, with its intricate and beautiful design, symbolizes the unfolding of inner potential and the manifestation of abundance in all its forms. This abundance is not limited to material wealth but encompasses all aspects of a fulfilling life, including meaningful relationships, personal fulfillment, and spiritual growth. By tapping into Kamalatmika's energy, we can unlock our creative potential and manifest a life rich in purpose and joy.

The practice of meditation on Kamalatmika's imagery can be a powerful tool for personal transformation. Visualizing her serene yet powerful form, surrounded by the radiant beauty of the lotus, can help to cultivate inner peace and a sense of connection with the divine feminine. This practice can foster a deeper understanding of our own inner strength and resilience, empowering us to navigate life's challenges with grace and determination. Regular meditation on her form can also help to cultivate a feeling of abundance and gratitude, enhancing our appreciation for the blessings in our lives.

The application of Kamalatmika's energy extends beyond personal meditation and into various aspects of daily life. In our professional endeavors, her resilience can serve as an inspiration to overcome obstacles and achieve success. In our relationships, her nurturing aspect can help to foster understanding, compassion, and empathy. Even in seemingly mundane activities, we can draw upon her energy to cultivate a sense of purpose and intention.

The contemporary world often emphasizes external validation and material success, leading to a sense of emptiness and dissatisfaction for many. Kamalatmika's message offers an alternative path, one that emphasizes inner growth and spiritual fulfillment. She reminds us that true abundance lies not in external possessions but in the richness of our inner lives. By cultivating inner peace, resilience, and creative potential, we can achieve a sense of well-being that transcends the limitations of the material world.

The symbolism of the lotus, intricately woven into Kamalatmika's essence, provides a profound metaphor for the process of spiritual awakening. The flower's journey from the muddy depths to the sunlit surface represents the arduous yet ultimately rewarding path of self-discovery. The mud signifies the challenges, obstacles, and karmic imprints that often obscure our true nature. Yet, from this seemingly inauspicious beginning, the lotus blossoms into a symbol of purity, beauty, and enlightenment. This mirrors the transformative power of spiritual practice, where we transcend our limitations and reveal our inherent divinity.

Furthermore, the multi-petaled lotus symbolizes the unfolding of consciousness. Each petal represents a layer of the self that is progressively revealed through spiritual practice. The journey is gradual, unfolding layer by layer, until the full potential of the being is realized. This gradual unfolding mirrors the process of self-realization, a journey of continuous growth and understanding. Each step brings us closer to our true nature, revealing new facets of ourselves along the way.

Kamalatmika's association with Lakshmi, the goddess of wealth and prosperity, adds another layer to her contemporary relevance. While this wealth encompasses material abundance, it extends far beyond mere possessions. It encompasses a richness of experience, fulfilling relationships, good health, and inner peace. This understanding aligns with the holistic approach to well-being that is increasingly valued in the modern world. The pursuit of this holistic wealth, encompassing both material and spiritual abundance, aligns with Kamalatmika's energy, guiding us toward a life of both prosperity and fulfillment.

The practice of invoking Kamalatmika's energy can involve various methods, including mantra recitation, meditation on her imagery, and the offering of prayers and flowers. These practices are not simply ritualistic acts but rather tools for cultivating a deeper connection with the divine feminine and accessing her transformative power. The act of devotion, whether through prayer, meditation, or offering, helps to create a space for inner transformation, fostering a sense of peace and connection with something larger than oneself.

In conclusion, Kamalatmika's relevance in the contemporary context extends beyond historical interpretations. Her symbolism provides a potent framework for personal transformation, encouraging resilience, fostering creativity, and inspiring the pursuit of a life filled with both material and spiritual abundance. Her energy can be harnessed through various practices, empowering individuals to navigate life's challenges and achieve their full potential, mirroring the lotus's journey from mud to magnificent bloom. The exploration of Kamalatmika's power offers a dynamic path towards self-realization, providing a powerful and relevant message for the spiritual seeker in the 21st century and beyond. Her enduring legacy lies not just in historical accounts, but in the transformative potential she offers to each individual who seeks to connect with her energy. The journey towards spiritual growth, facilitated by her guidance, remains a potent and enduring pathway to self-discovery and fulfillment. This journey, fueled by devotion and practice, is the key to unlocking the abundance and resilience that reside within each of us, a testament to the timeless power of the divine feminine.

Similarities and Differences in Iconography

The ten Mahavidyas, while distinct in their individual manifestations and powers, share underlying thematic connections reflected in their iconography. A comparative analysis reveals both striking similarities and fascinating divergences in their artistic representations across different schools of thought and historical periods. Understanding these nuances provides deeper insight into the complex tapestry of Shakti worship and the multifaceted nature of the Divine Feminine.

One prominent similarity lies in the consistent depiction of the Mahavidyas as powerful, independent goddesses, often defying conventional representations of feminine deities. They are not passive recipients of devotion, but active agents of cosmic energy, embodying both terrifying and benevolent aspects. This rejection of passive femininity is visually rendered through their dynamic postures, fierce expressions, and often fearsome weaponry. Whether wielding a sword, a trident, or a skull-topped staff, the Mahavidyas are portrayed as forces to be reckoned with, asserting their dominance over the material and spiritual realms. This shared defiance of patriarchal norms forms a unifying thread in their iconography, irrespective of individual variations in attributes and symbolism.

However, significant differences exist in the specific attributes and symbolism associated with each Mahavidya. Kali, for example, is often depicted as a dark, ferocious goddess, adorned with a garland of skulls and draped in a skirt of severed limbs. Her terrifying visage, symbolic of destruction and transformation, contrasts sharply with the serene beauty of Tripura Sundari, whose iconography emphasizes grace, elegance, and the aesthetic appeal of the Divine Feminine. Tripura Sundari's depictions often show her adorned with exquisite jewelry and flowers, reflecting her association with beauty, love, and spiritual bliss. This stark contrast exemplifies the diverse facets of Shakti manifested through the Mahavidyas.

Another key difference lies in the use of color in their iconography.

Kali's predominantly dark hues symbolize the primordial darkness from which creation emerges, contrasting with the vibrant reds and golds frequently associated with Tripura Sundari, reflecting her association with fire, passion, and the radiant energy of creation. Similarly, the use of specific colors, animals, and objects in each Mahavidya's iconography provides clues to their distinct attributes and powers. The blue hue often associated with Tara suggests her connection to the sky and celestial realms, while the more earthbound hues associated with Bhuvaneshvari reflect her role as the protector and nourisher of the earth.

The postures adopted by the Mahavidyas also vary significantly, reflecting their unique attributes and energies. Kali's dynamic, often dancing pose symbolizes the cosmic dance of creation and destruction, while Tara's serene, seated posture hints at her meditative nature and mastery over spiritual energies. The variations in their mudras (hand gestures) further underscore their individual functions and powers. These subtle differences in posture and gesture serve as visual cues for understanding the particular energy or power each Mahavidya embodies.

Furthermore, the presence or absence of specific weapons and ornaments contributes to the distinct visual identity of each goddess. While some Mahavidyas, like Chhinnamasta, are depicted with overtly gruesome attributes, reflecting their role in overcoming obstacles and severing karmic bonds, others, like Matangi, are presented with more subtly symbolic objects, hinting at their connection with learning, art, and music. These differences are not merely aesthetic choices but serve to highlight the complex and multifaceted nature of Shakti.

The animals associated with each Mahavidya further distinguish their iconography. Kali's association with the jackal signifies her role as a destroyer of illusion and ego, while Tara is often depicted with a lion, emphasizing her courage, strength, and regal nature. These animal companions symbolize the different aspects of Shakti's power, revealing deeper layers of meaning within the visual representations.

The symbolic use of flowers, particularly the lotus, also adds another layer of complexity. While the lotus appears in the iconography of several Mahavidyas, its meaning can vary depending on the context. In some depictions, it symbolizes purity and enlightenment, while in others it might signify the arising of consciousness from the primordial waters of existence. The understanding of these subtleties requires a nuanced approach, taking into account the specific school of thought and historical context in which the iconography was created.

Beyond the obvious visual distinctions, subtle variations in facial expressions and gaze further refine the iconographic portrayal of the Mahavidyas. The fierce, unwavering gaze of Kali contrasts sharply with the compassionate and nurturing gaze of Bhuvaneshvari, indicating the different aspects of Shakti's engagement with the world. Even slight variations in the tilt of the head or the curve of the lips can significantly alter the interpretation of the image, revealing the depth and complexity of the artist's intent.

Analyzing the variations in iconography across different regions and periods reveals further complexities. For example, regional variations in artistic styles and traditions have resulted in diverse representations of the same Mahavidya. A comparison of Kali images from Bengal with those from South India reveals distinct differences in style, attire, and symbolic attributes, while maintaining a core resemblance in her general representation as a dark, powerful goddess. These variations highlight the fluidity and adaptability of Shakti worship across different cultural landscapes.

Furthermore, the influence of different schools of thought, particularly Shaktism, Saivism, and Vaishnavism, has resulted in varied interpretations of the Mahavidyas' iconography. Each school emphasizes certain aspects of the goddesses' powers and attributes, leading to variations in their artistic representation. The integration of Vajrayana Buddhist elements into the iconography of some Mahavidyas also contributes to the diversity of their visual representation. Understanding these influences is crucial for deciphering the deeper symbolic meanings embedded within the images.

The study of the Mahavidyas' iconography offers a unique lens through which to understand the complexities of Tantric thought and the diverse ways in which the Divine Feminine is manifested and worshipped. While similarities in their representations emphasize their shared power and agency, the subtle and sometimes stark differences in their attributes, postures, and symbolic objects reflect the multifaceted nature of Shakti and her boundless capacity for expression. The variations in iconography not only enrich our understanding of each individual Mahavidya but also offer a rich tapestry of visual symbols that continue to inspire and intrigue practitioners and scholars alike. This vibrant interplay of similarities and differences serves as a testament to the enduring power and enduring relevance of these ten powerful goddesses. Their enduring presence in art, ritual, and spiritual practice underscores their continuing significance in the contemporary world, reminding us of the boundless potential inherent within the feminine divine. The continued study and analysis of these iconographic variations offer an ongoing journey of discovery into the profound mysteries of the Mahavidyas.

Comparative Analysis of Their Roles and Functions

The ten Mahavidyas, while distinct entities, are interwoven within the larger tapestry of Tantric cosmology, sharing a fundamental role in the manifestation and unfolding of the cosmos. Their shared characteristic is their embodiment of Shakti, the dynamic, creative energy of the universe, but their individual functions and specializations delineate their unique contributions to the cosmic drama. Understanding these distinctions offers a deeper appreciation of the rich complexity of Tantric thought.

A fundamental similarity lies in their capacity for both creation and destruction. This duality, often perceived as paradoxical in the West, is central to Tantric philosophy. Creation is not merely a passive act of bringing forth form; it requires the simultaneous destruction of pre-existing structures, the dismantling of limitations, and the transformation of energy. Each Mahavidya embodies this duality in varying degrees. Kali, for instance, is the ultimate embodiment of destruction, yet her destructive act is simultaneously creative, paving the way for renewal and rebirth.

Similarly, Tripura Sundari, associated with beauty and creation, also possesses the power to dissolve illusion and ignorance, thereby creating space for true spiritual understanding. This inherent duality, common to all ten Mahavidyas, underlines the dynamic interplay of opposing forces that shape the universe.

Their roles in preservation and protection also exhibit both shared aspects and individual nuances. While all the Mahavidyas can offer protection and guidance to their devotees, they achieve this through different means. Bhuvaneshvari, for instance, is explicitly associated with the earth and its nourishment, providing stability and security.

Her protection is rooted in the nurturing aspect of the Divine Feminine, offering solace and support to those who seek refuge in her embrace. Tara, on the other hand, offers protection through her strength and courage, acting as a fierce guardian against external threats. Her protection is active, dynamic, and assertive, providing a shield against adversity and enabling devotees to overcome obstacles. These examples illustrate how the concept of protection is multifaceted within the Mahavidya pantheon, reflecting the diverse ways in which the Divine Feminine provides support and guidance.

The Mahavidyas are also associated with specific spiritual practices and paths, reflecting their individual energies and attributes. Kali's association with Kundalini Shakti highlights her role in awakening dormant spiritual energies within the individual. The practice of Kali worship often involves intense rituals and meditations aimed at confronting and transcending the limitations of the ego, leading to a deeper connection with the primordial energy of the universe. In contrast, Tripura Sundari's worship is frequently linked to gentler, more aesthetic practices, emphasizing the cultivation of inner beauty and the pursuit of spiritual bliss. Her devotees might engage in practices such as mantra recitation, devotional singing, and contemplation of her iconography, nurturing a sense of inner peace and harmony. These differences highlight the diversity of spiritual paths available within the Tantric tradition, catering to the diverse needs and inclinations of practitioners.

Another significant aspect of the Mahavidyas' functions lies in their ability to address specific karmic challenges. Each Mahavidya is associated with particular obstacles or impediments that individuals might face in their spiritual journey. Chhinnamasta, for example, is invoked to overcome fear, emotional blockages and karmic entanglements. Her gruesome iconography, while shocking to some, is a powerful symbol of the need to sever ties with limiting patterns of behavior and belief. Similarly, Bagalamukhi, often depicted with a bound tongue, helps in overcoming enemies and negative influences, assisting in navigating challenges related to personal power and self-assertion. These examples showcase the practical applications of the Mahavidyas' power, demonstrating their relevance in addressing the everyday challenges faced by individuals.

The differences in their roles are not mutually exclusive. The Mahavidyas are not limited to a single function; their energies are interconnected and often overlap. For instance, while Kali is primarily associated with destruction, she also plays a role in preservation, cleansing the way for new beginnings. Tripura Sundari, while primarily associated with creation and beauty, also possesses the power to destroy illusions and ignorance, facilitating spiritual growth. This interconnectedness highlights the fluidity and multifaceted nature of Shakti, showcasing the interconnectedness of cosmic processes.

Furthermore, the context in which a particular Mahavidya is invoked significantly influences the interpretation of her function. The same goddess can manifest differently depending on the specific needs and intentions of the devotee. A practitioner facing a challenging life transition might invoke Kali for strength and guidance, while the same practitioner might invoke Tripura Sundari for solace and healing after overcoming a difficult experience. This highlights the adaptability of the Mahavidyas and their capacity to provide support and guidance throughout the various stages of life's journey.

The understanding of the Mahavidyas' roles and functions requires a nuanced approach, considering their symbolic representations, associated mantras, and prescribed practices. The study of their iconography provides valuable insights into their energetic attributes, but it is crucial to supplement this with a deep engagement with the relevant Tantric texts and traditions. Through this combined approach, we can gain a deeper understanding of the intricate workings of Shakti and the profound implications of the Mahavidyas' presence in the cosmic order.

The significance of the Mahavidyas extends beyond the purely metaphysical realm. They offer a framework for understanding the diverse facets of human experience and the challenges inherent in spiritual growth. Their ability to address specific karmic issues, provide emotional support, and empower devotees to overcome obstacles makes them relevant figures for individuals navigating the complexities of modern life. Their enduring presence in spiritual practice is a testament to the continuing power of their message, providing guidance and inspiration to those seeking spiritual awakening. The study of the Mahavidyas offers not merely an academic exercise but a path of self-discovery, guiding us towards a deeper understanding of ourselves and our connection to the divine.

Their intricate interplay and multifaceted functions continue to hold relevance and inspiration in the complexities of the contemporary era, underscoring the timeless wisdom embedded within the Tantric tradition. The continued exploration and study of the Mahavidyas promises to unlock further layers of understanding and deepen our appreciation for the profound depths of the Divine Feminine. Their enduring presence ensures their continued relevance as guides and protectors, illuminating the path towards spiritual growth and empowerment. The ongoing engagement with their teachings offers a transformative journey, fostering deeper self-awareness and a strengthened connection to the boundless energy of Shakti.

Comparing Their Associations with Different Deities

The interconnectedness of the Mahavidyas extends beyond their internal relationships; they are deeply intertwined with the broader Hindu pantheon, exhibiting a complex network of associations and influences. Understanding these relationships reveals further layers of meaning and illuminates the rich tapestry of Tantric cosmology. A key aspect of this interconnectedness is the interplay between the Mahavidyas and the fundamental divine couple, Shiva and Shakti. While each Mahavidya embodies Shakti in her unique form, their relationships with Shiva vary significantly, reflecting the diverse facets of their individual energies and functions.

Some Mahavidyas, such as Kali, are directly associated with Shiva as his consort, embodying his destructive power, often depicted as arising from his fierce and terrifying aspects. This union signifies the interplay of creation and destruction, highlighting the cyclical nature of cosmic processes. Kali's dance of destruction is not merely chaotic annihilation; it is a cosmic dance of transformation, paving the way for new creation. Her association with Shiva underscores the inherent duality within the divine, the interconnectedness of opposing forces that drive the universe's dynamism. The destructive energy of Kali, while seemingly terrifying, is essential for the cyclical renewal inherent in the cosmic process. It is a destructive force that is ultimately generative and transformative. Her unification with Shiva further underscores this powerful creative-destructive energy that underlies the very fabric of existence.

Other Mahavidyas exhibit a more nuanced relationship with Shiva. Tripura Sundari, for example, while embodying the supreme Shakti, is often depicted in a more harmonious union with Shiva, emphasizing the aesthetic and blissful aspects of their relationship.

This association highlights the gentler, more creative aspects of Shakti, focusing on beauty, grace, and the manifestation of the cosmos in its harmonious and blissful form. The iconography often portrays their union as a celebration of divine love and harmony, representing the creative power of divine unity. Unlike Kali's fierce and destructive energy, Tripura Sundari's union with Shiva represents a gentler, more nurturing aspect of Shakti, focusing on the creation and preservation of beauty and harmony. This difference underscores the diverse manifestations of Shakti and her multifaceted relationship with Shiva.

The Mahavidyas' connections with other deities extend beyond Shiva and Shakti. Their interactions with various avatars of Vishnu, the preserver, and other significant Hindu figures reveal a complex web of relationships and influences. For instance, certain Mahavidyas may be seen as manifestations of specific aspects of Vishnu's consort, Lakshmi. This further complicates and enriches our understanding of the interplay between these powerful divine beings, highlighting the fluidity and interconnectedness of the divine energies. It reveals a dynamic exchange between different religious traditions and philosophical viewpoints within the broad Hindu framework.

The variations in these relationships are not arbitrary; they reflect the specific functions and energies embodied by each Mahavidya.

The association with a particular deity highlights the context in which the Mahavidya's power is most effectively channeled. For instance, the association of Kali with Shiva emphasizes her destructive power, while the association of Tripura Sundari with Shiva in a more harmonious union underscores her creative and nurturing aspects. This nuanced interplay underscores the importance of understanding the context in which these goddesses are invoked and worshipped, reflecting the diverse needs and purposes of the devotees.

The comparative analysis of their associations reveals the intricate dynamics of the Hindu pantheon. The Mahavidyas are not isolated entities; they are integral parts of a vast, interconnected network of divine beings, their relationships reflecting the complex interplay of cosmic energies and forces. The fluidity and dynamism of these relationships highlight the multifaceted nature of divinity, showcasing the boundless creative potential of the Divine Feminine and the profound interconnectedness of all things. Studying these relationships reveals deeper layers of meaning and understanding, allowing us to appreciate the subtle nuances and complexities inherent within Tantric cosmology.

The variations in their iconography also reflect the diverse influences and relationships. The depiction of a specific Mahavidya with certain attributes or symbols can indicate her close association with a particular deity or aspect of the divine. For instance, the presence of specific weapons, animals, or ornaments in the iconography can point to her relationship with a specific god or goddess, further enriching our understanding of her symbolic meaning and significance. The careful study of these details is crucial to understanding the complex web of interconnections within the Mahavidya pantheon.

Furthermore, the specific mantras associated with each Mahavidya may also reflect their relationships with other deities. The use of particular names or epithets in the mantras can signify their connection to a specific divine entity, suggesting a close relationship or shared energy. The analysis of these mantras provides further insights into the subtle interplay of energies and the nuanced relationships within the Tantric cosmos. This intricate network of relationships between the Mahavidyas and other deities adds another layer of depth and complexity to their understanding.

The study of the Mahavidyas' relationships with other deities necessitates an interdisciplinary approach, integrating iconographic analysis, textual studies, and an understanding of the broader mythological context. It requires a nuanced appreciation for the dynamic interplay of different traditions and philosophical perspectives. This deeper engagement leads to a more comprehensive and richer understanding of the Mahavidyas and their significant role within the vast and multifaceted Hindu pantheon.

The continued study of these complex relationships opens avenues for further exploration and deeper understanding. It allows for a more nuanced appreciation of the dynamic interplay between the Mahavidyas and other divine beings, highlighting the rich tapestry of Tantric thought and the complex web of interconnections that shape the Hindu cosmology. This exploration unveils the depth and intricacy of the Divine Feminine's multifaceted nature and the boundless creative potential inherent within the Tantric tradition. The ongoing investigation promises to reveal further insights into the profound wisdom and enduring relevance of the Mahavidyas in the contemporary era. Their significance transcends simple categorization; they represent a dynamic expression of the divine, reflecting the fluid and ever-evolving nature of the cosmos itself.

Their enduring appeal underscores their continuing power to inspire, guide, and transform those who seek to understand the deeper mysteries of existence. The multifaceted nature of the Mahavidyas, their dynamic interplay with other deities and their enduring relevance underscores the richness and complexity of the Tantric tradition. The ongoing exploration of their functions, relationships, and significance continues to reveal new layers of meaning and deepen our appreciation for the profound depths of the Divine Feminine.

Comparative Analysis of Their Mantras and Yantras

The exploration of the Mahavidyas thus far has highlighted their interconnectedness within the broader Hindu pantheon and their diverse relationships with other deities. This intricate web of associations finds further expression in the mantras and yantras uniquely associated with each goddess. These are not merely tools for ritual practice; they are potent symbolic representations of the Mahavidya's essence, embodying their unique energies and offering pathways to access their power. A comparative analysis of these mantras and yantras reveals a fascinating tapestry of similarities and differences, reflecting both the individual nature of each Mahavidya and their underlying unity as manifestations of the Divine Feminine.

The mantras of the Mahavidyas, often short and resonant, are considered bija mantras, or seed mantras, containing the essence of the goddess's power. These aren't merely sounds; they are vibrational keys that unlock specific energies and facilitate a connection with the divine. The phonetic structure of each mantra is significant, its sounds carrying symbolic weight and influencing the meditative experience. For instance, the mantra for Kali, often "Krim," is short, sharp, and powerful, reflecting her fierce and destructive yet ultimately transformative energy. The harshness of the sound mirrors her iconography—a dark, terrifying figure representing the annihilation of ego and illusion. This stark sound, however, is not merely destructive; the repeated recitation can be understood as a powerful invocation of transformative energy, mirroring Kali's role in the cyclical renewal of the cosmos.

In contrast, the mantra for Tripura Sundari, often a longer and more melodious sequence, reflects her gentler, more aesthetic nature. The sounds are smoother, flowing, and evoke a sense of beauty and grace, aligning with her imagery as a radiant, benevolent goddess. This difference in sonic quality reflects the contrasting energies of these two Mahavidyas: Kali's raw, transformative power versus Tripura Sundari's serene and creative energy. The subtle variations in intonation and pronunciation also hold deep significance, varying between different Tantric lineages and schools of thought. The subtle nuances in recitation, influenced by individual guru-shishya parampara (teacher-student lineage), further enrich the experience, illustrating the rich diversity within the Tantric tradition.

The mantras are not just for individual meditation; they are integral parts of complex rituals. The repetition of a mantra, often in conjunction with specific visualizations and offerings, creates a powerful energetic field, facilitating a direct connection with the corresponding Mahavidya. The effectiveness of the mantra depends not only on its proper pronunciation but also on the practitioner's devotion, concentration, and understanding of the goddess's essence. The potency of the mantra is amplified by the practitioner's sincere devotion and understanding of the goddess's nature.

Beyond the mantras, the yantras, geometric diagrams, serve as visual representations of the goddess's energies. Each Mahavidya has a unique yantra, a complex arrangement of lines, symbols, and mandalas, designed to focus the practitioner's energy and direct it towards the deity. The yantras often incorporate symbolic elements drawn from the deity's iconography and mythology, such as specific weapons, animals, or sacred objects, making them powerful tools for contemplation and visualization. The geometry of the yantra is not arbitrary; it's carefully constructed based on sacred geometry principles, creating a dynamic energetic field that resonates with the goddess's specific vibrational frequency.

The yantra for Kali might feature sharp angles and intense colors, reflecting her forceful nature, while the yantra for Tripura Sundari may be more harmonious, utilizing softer curves and gentle colors to reflect her beauty and grace. These differences mirror the distinct energies of the goddesses themselves. The use of color, shape, and geometry within the yantra enhances the meditative experience, guiding the practitioner towards deeper levels of awareness and connection. The visual elements are not merely decorative; they are integral to the energetic potency of the yantra, amplifying the effect of the mantra and focusing the practitioner's attention.

Moreover, the comparative analysis extends to the ritual applications of these mantras and yantras. Specific rituals are prescribed for each Mahavidya, involving unique offerings, gestures, and visualizations designed to invoke the goddess's specific energies. The mantras are typically chanted during these rituals, their sounds resonating with the symbolic actions and enhancing the overall energetic effect. The yantras serve as focal points for these rituals, providing a visual anchor for the practitioner's attention and facilitating a deeper connection with the deity. The variations in ritual practices reflect the diverse needs and approaches within various Tantric schools and lineages.

For example, rituals dedicated to Kali might emphasize fire offerings and intense, dynamic movements, reflecting her fierce energy. In contrast, rituals dedicated to Tripura Sundari may focus on more graceful movements, floral offerings, and softer chanting, reflecting her gentle and aesthetic nature. This diversity underscores the rich tapestry of Tantric practices, demonstrating the adaptability and versatility of these goddesses and their inherent multifaceted nature. The diverse rituals underscore the adaptability and versatility of the Tantric tradition and the deep understanding of the unique qualities embodied by each Mahavidya.

The subtle differences in the mantras and yantras, however, shouldn't overshadow the underlying unity. Despite their diverse manifestations, all the Mahavidyas are ultimately expressions of the Divine Feminine, aspects of the same supreme Shakti. Their mantras and yantras, though unique, share a fundamental connection, reflecting their shared source and their interwoven energies. The shared elements across these tools reveal a deeper unity underlying the diverse expressions of the Divine Mother.

Indeed, the deeper study of these mantras and yantras reveals the profound interconnectedness of the Mahavidyas, extending beyond their individual attributes. Subtle similarities in symbolic motifs, phonetic echoes in their mantras, and recurring geometric patterns in their yantras suggest an underlying harmony and unity, revealing the interconnectedness of the goddesses as different facets of the same supreme power. The study of these shared elements provides a deeper understanding of the holistic nature of Shakti and her manifestations. This understanding goes beyond superficial comparisons; it delves into the energetic connections that unify the diverse Mahavidyas.

The analysis of their mantras and yantras reveals the intricacies of Tantric practices, demonstrating the importance of context, lineage, and individual devotion in accessing and utilizing their power. The subtle nuances in the sounds, forms, and rituals are not merely arbitrary variations but reflect the profound depth and complexity of the Tantric tradition and the multifaceted nature of the Divine Feminine as embodied by the Mahavidyas. The careful study of these tools offers a deeper understanding of their potency and the intricate relationship between sound, form, and energy within the Tantric worldview.

The comparative approach highlights the diversity within the Mahavidyas while emphasizing their essential unity. This balanced perspective is crucial for understanding the richness and complexity of the Tantric tradition, appreciating both the individual power of each goddess and their interconnectedness as expressions of the same supreme Shakti. Further research into the specific lineages, their traditional practices, and the varied interpretations of these mantras and yantras will continue to enhance our understanding and appreciation for this profound tradition. The ongoing exploration promises to unveil further insights into the profound wisdom and continuing relevance of the Mahavidyas in the contemporary world, illustrating their adaptability and enduring power to inspire and transform. The enduring appeal of the Mahavidyas underscores their timeless relevance and their capacity to guide practitioners on their spiritual journeys. The multifaceted nature of the Mahavidyas, reflected in their mantras and yantras, highlights the richness and complexity of the Tantric tradition, offering a path towards a deeper understanding of the Divine Feminine and the cosmos itself.

Synthesizing the Mahavidyas Collective Message

Having explored each Mahavidya individually, delving into their unique iconography, mantras, and associated rituals, we now turn to synthesize their collective message. The ten Mahavidyas, while distinct in their attributes and manifestations, are not isolated entities. They represent a multifaceted expression of the Divine Feminine, a kaleidoscope of Shakti's power, revealing different facets of her boundless energy and transformative potential. Their collective wisdom offers a profound and holistic understanding of the spiritual path, the complexities of the human experience, and the ultimate nature of reality.

One overarching theme that emerges from the study of the Mahavidyas is the cyclical nature of existence. Kali, the primordial goddess, embodies destruction and transformation, representing the necessary annihilation that precedes creation. Her fierce energy, while seemingly terrifying, is ultimately a catalyst for renewal, mirroring the cyclical processes of nature and the cosmos. This concept of cyclical destruction and rebirth finds resonance in the other Mahavidyas. Even the seemingly gentle and benevolent goddesses such as Tripura Sundari, in their creative power, are implicitly linked to the cyclical nature of existence; creation inevitably leads to decay, making the cycle complete. The understanding of this cyclical process is essential for navigating the ups and downs of life, accepting both joy and sorrow as integral parts of the human experience.

Further reinforcing this theme is the concept of dynamic equilibrium. While the Mahavidyas display a spectrum of energies— from the fierce and destructive to the gentle and nurturing—their collective presence reveals a state of harmonious balance. This balance is not static; it is a dynamic interplay of opposing forces, constantly shifting and evolving. This dynamic equilibrium mirrors the inherent duality present in all aspects of existence, highlighting the interconnectedness of opposing forces. The understanding of this dynamic balance is crucial in navigating the complexities of life, recognizing the interplay between light and shadow, creation and destruction, joy and sorrow. This understanding fosters a sense of acceptance and equanimity in the face of life's challenges.

The Mahavidyas also collectively illuminate the path of spiritual growth. Each goddess represents a specific stage or aspect of this journey. Kali, for instance, represents the initial stage of confronting and overcoming the ego, shedding illusions and attachments. Tara, the savior, guides through obstacles and challenges, while Tripura Sundari represents the beauty and grace that emerge from spiritual refinement. The journey through the Mahavidyas is not linear; it is a multifaceted exploration of one's inner landscape, embracing both the darkness and the light. Each goddess provides unique guidance and support on this transformative journey, highlighting the stages and challenges involved in the spiritual path.

The concept of empowerment, both spiritual and worldly, is a recurring theme woven throughout the narratives of the Mahavidyas. Each goddess, in her unique way, embodies the power inherent in the Divine Feminine. This power is not merely destructive; it is creative, transformative, and ultimately liberating.

This empowerment is not about dominating others but about harnessing one's inner strength and potential to overcome obstacles and achieve one's full potential. This includes the courage to confront inner demons, the wisdom to navigate life's complexities, and the compassion to extend oneself to others. The empowerment found in the Mahavidyas is not limited to the spiritual realm; it extends into everyday life, providing the strength and resilience to navigate the challenges of the modern world.

Furthermore, the Mahavidyas' collective message extends to the understanding of human consciousness. Each goddess represents a different aspect of the human psyche, illuminating the complex interplay of emotions, desires, and aspirations. The study of the Mahavidyas, therefore, becomes a journey of self-discovery, enabling a deeper understanding of one's own inner world and the potential for transformation. This journey of self-discovery is not limited to intellectual understanding; it is deeply personal and experiential, requiring a commitment to introspection, self-awareness, and a willingness to confront one's own shadow self.

The wisdom of the Mahavidyas is also profoundly relevant to the challenges of the contemporary world. The complexity and rapid pace of modern life often lead to feelings of anxiety, disorientation, and alienation. The Mahavidyas offer a framework for navigating these challenges, providing guidance, strength, and resilience. Their diverse attributes offer tools and strategies for addressing the specific difficulties we encounter. For instance, the fierce energy of Kali can be harnessed to confront and overcome negative patterns of thinking and behaving. The compassionate nature of Tara can provide solace and support during times of difficulty. Tripura Sundari's creativity and beauty can inspire hope and a sense of wonder in the face of adversity.

Moreover, the Mahavidyas emphasize the importance of ritual and practice in spiritual development. Their mantras and yantras are not simply symbols; they are powerful tools for accessing and channeling their energy, facilitating a deeper connection with the divine and fostering inner transformation. The specific rituals associated with each Mahavidya offer a structured path for engaging with their energies and integrating their wisdom into one's life. This emphasis on ritual and practice highlights the importance of disciplined engagement in the spiritual journey, illustrating that spiritual growth is not a passive process but requires active participation and dedication.

Finally, the collective message of the Mahavidyas is one of unity and interconnectedness. Despite their diverse manifestations, they are all ultimately expressions of the same supreme Shakti, highlighting the underlying unity beneath the apparent diversity of the world. This understanding transcends religious and cultural boundaries, offering a profound and universal message of interconnectedness and oneness. This oneness is not merely a philosophical concept; it is an experiential reality that can be accessed through dedicated practice and devotion. This unifying aspect transcends the individual goddess, demonstrating a profound harmony in the cosmos.

In conclusion, the ten Mahavidyas offer a rich tapestry of wisdom, guidance, and empowerment. Their collective message transcends individual attributes, revealing deeper themes of cyclical existence, dynamic equilibrium, spiritual growth, empowerment, and self-understanding. Their significance resonates not only within the historical and religious contexts but also offers valuable insights and tools for navigating the complexities of contemporary life.

Through their diverse manifestations, they provide a pathway to self-discovery, inner transformation, and a profound connection to the Divine Feminine and the interconnectedness of all things. The ongoing study of the Mahavidyas continues to unveil further layers of meaning and insight, underscoring their enduring relevance and their power to inspire and transform. Their enduring wisdom serves as a timeless guide on the spiritual journey, offering support and encouragement to seekers on the path of self-discovery and spiritual growth, a path that remains as relevant today as it was centuries ago. The power of the Mahavidyas, therefore, lies not just in their individual attributes, but in their collective wisdom, which offers a holistic and profound understanding of the human experience and the cosmos itself.

Archetypal Energies and Psychological Processes

The ten Mahavidyas, far from being merely mythological figures, offer a rich tapestry of archetypal energies that resonate deeply with the complexities of the human psyche. Their symbolic representations can be fruitfully analyzed through the lens of various psychological frameworks, notably Jungian psychology, which provides a valuable lens for understanding the interplay of conscious and unconscious processes within the individual. Each Mahavidya embodies a particular aspect of the feminine archetype, reflecting different stages of individuation and the integration of shadow aspects.

Kali, the primordial goddess of destruction and transformation, can be viewed as the embodiment of the shadow self. Her terrifying visage and association with death represent the unconscious, the unintegrated aspects of the personality that are often repressed or denied. Confronting Kali, therefore, becomes a symbolic confrontation with one's own shadow, a necessary step in the process of individuation. This confrontation is not about eradicating the shadow but about integrating it, acknowledging its power and learning to work with it, rather than being controlled by it. The transformation Kali represents is the transformative power of facing our deepest fears and integrating the darkness within to achieve wholeness.

Tara, the saviour, presents a contrasting archetype, representing the compassionate and protective aspect of the feminine. In Jungian terms, she embodies the anima, the feminine aspect of the male psyche, but her nurturing and guiding qualities are also relevant to women, providing a symbolic representation of inner strength and resilience. Tara's role in rescuing those in distress reflects the inner strength to overcome obstacles and the capacity for self-compassion. This nurturing aspect is crucial for navigating life's challenges, providing the support and guidance necessary for personal growth and healing.

Tripura Sundari, the goddess of beauty and grace, embodies the archetype of the Great Mother. Her association with beauty and creativity represents the creative potential of the unconscious, the ability to bring forth new ideas and experiences. Her gentle and nurturing aspect, however, signifies a different stage of individuation, one where the individual has integrated their shadow aspects and is now able to embrace the beauty and joy of life. This integration fosters self-acceptance and allows one to express their creativity authentically.

Bhuvaneshvari, the goddess of the earth, represents the grounding and stabilizing aspect of the feminine. Her connection to nature symbolizes the interconnectedness of all things and the importance of living in harmony with the natural world. Psychologically, Bhuvaneshvari can be seen as a symbol of stability and security, representing the integration of the earth element within the individual's psyche, fostering a sense of groundedness and connection to one's roots. This grounding aspect is crucial for maintaining balance and equanimity in the face of life's challenges.

Bhairavi, the fierce and powerful goddess, embodies the transformative potential of feminine energy. Her dynamic energy resonates with the capacity for radical change and transformation, symbolizing the courage to confront difficult emotions and situations. Bhairavi's strength and independence represent the importance of self-empowerment and the ability to overcome challenges independently. Her transformative power signifies the individual's capacity for both internal and external change, fostering personal growth and development.

Chhinnamasta, the goddess with her self-decapitated head, represents the ultimate act of self-sacrifice and self-transcendence. This extreme imagery can be interpreted as a symbolic representation of the ego's surrender to the Self, a letting go of the individual ego and its limitations. This symbolizes a profound release of attachments and the willingness to relinquish control, allowing for a deeper connection to the Divine Feminine. The self-decapitation signifies a death of the ego, allowing for a rebirth on a higher spiritual level.

Dhumavati, the goddess of widowhood and desolation, represents the dark night of the soul, a period of profound spiritual crisis and transformation. Her association with loneliness and emptiness reflects the necessary period of introspection and self-reflection, a confrontation with the void and uncertainty that precedes profound spiritual insight. This imagery can be seen as representing the psychological process of confronting existential anxieties and coming to terms with mortality. It signifies the acceptance of vulnerability and the necessity of enduring periods of uncertainty and hardship in the spiritual journey.

Bagalamukhi, the goddess who binds the tongue, represents the power of speech and the importance of mindful communication. She represents the ability to control one's speech and to avoid harmful or negative communication. Psychologically, this can be interpreted as the ability to manage one's thoughts and emotions and to communicate constructively and assertively. It highlights the power of using words thoughtfully, both internally and externally, creating a space of understanding and harmony.

Matangi, the goddess of speech and learning, represents the power of knowledge and wisdom. Her association with learning and knowledge highlights the importance of seeking wisdom and the growth that emerges through education. Psychologically, Matangi symbolizes the integration of intellect and intuition, signifying the expansion of one's understanding and consciousness, fostering profound self-growth through intellectual pursuit and understanding.

Kamalatmika, the goddess of fulfillment and abundance, represents the realization of one's full potential. Her association with lotus flowers symbolizes purity and spiritual awakening. Psychologically, Kamalatmika represents the culmination of the individuation process, a state of wholeness and integration where the individual has fully realized their potential and is living in harmony with their true self. It signifies the accomplishment of spiritual goals, creating a sense of peace, contentment, and fulfillment.

The collective representation of the Mahavidyas reflects the dynamic interplay of various psychological processes, highlighting the complexity and multifaceted nature of the human experience. They are not merely static representations; they are dynamic

archetypes, constantly shifting and evolving, mirroring the ever-changing nature of the human psyche. The journey through the understanding of these goddesses is, in effect, a journey into the depths of one's own being, unveiling hidden aspects of the self and revealing the potential for profound transformation and growth. This exploration encourages a deep engagement with the shadow self, allowing for a more complete and integrated personality, culminating in self-realization and a deeper understanding of the cosmic order. The study of these archetypal energies, therefore, provides a powerful tool for self-discovery and spiritual growth, offering profound insights into the intricacies of the human psyche and the path toward wholeness. Their relevance transcends cultural and religious boundaries, offering a universal language for
navigating the complexities of the human condition. The exploration of these goddesses' psychological dimensions brings a contemporary relevance to age-old wisdom, offering a roadmap for self-discovery and personal transformation in the modern world.

The Shadow Self and the Mahavidyas

The preceding exploration of the Mahavidyas through the lens of Jungian psychology has illuminated the diverse facets of the feminine archetype, showcasing both its nurturing and destructive potentials. However, a deeper understanding requires confronting a crucial concept within Jungian thought: the shadow self. This is not a mere negative aspect, but rather the repository of repressed emotions, instincts, and experiences that we consciously or unconsciously reject. These rejected parts of ourselves, often deemed unacceptable or undesirable, remain potent forces within the unconscious, influencing our behavior and shaping our perception of reality in profound ways. The Mahavidyas, particularly those associated with less conventionally "positive" attributes, provide powerful symbolic representations of this shadow self, offering a pathway to its integration and the subsequent attainment of wholeness.

Carl Jung emphasized the necessity of confronting the shadow self for genuine psychological growth. He argued that until we integrate these rejected aspects, they remain a source of inner conflict, hindering our ability to live authentically and fully. This integration is not about eradicating the shadow; it's about acknowledging its existence, understanding its motivations, and ultimately, accepting it as an integral part of our totality. The Mahavidyas associated with darker or more challenging aspects of the feminine principle, such as Kali, Dhumavati, and Chhinnamasta, serve as powerful guides in this process.

Kali, the primordial goddess of destruction and time, is perhaps the most potent symbol of the shadow self. Her terrifying visage, often depicted adorned with skulls and necklaces of severed heads, directly confronts our societal conditioning to repress darker emotions associated with death, decay, and destruction. These are not merely unpleasant aspects of existence; they are integral parts of the cyclical nature of life itself. To deny them is to deny a fundamental truth of our being. Kali's embrace of these elements shows us that true transformation necessitates confronting our deepest fears and anxieties, accepting the inevitability of change and decay, rather than fighting against the natural order. Her dance of destruction is also a dance of creation, a constant cycle of death and rebirth, highlighting the transformative power inherent in embracing the shadow. She doesn't merely destroy; she clears the ground for new life to emerge, a powerful metaphor for the psychological process of letting go of old patterns and embracing new possibilities. By confronting Kali's terrifying form, we confront our own capacity for destruction, both self-destruction and the potential for causing harm to others. This confrontation is not about indulging in darkness, but about acknowledging its presence within ourselves, thus neutralizing its power to unconsciously control our actions.

Dhumavati, the goddess of widowhood and desolation, represents another important aspect of the shadow self: the experience of loss and grief. Her imagery – often portrayed as an aged, gaunt figure, riding a crow – speaks to the pain of bereavement, the emptiness of loss, and the challenges of navigating a life marked by hardship and despair. Dhumavati is not simply a goddess of suffering; she is a guide through suffering. She embodies the "dark night of the soul," that period of profound spiritual crisis where everything we hold dear seems to crumble. The acceptance of this desolation, the willingness to sit in the darkness without clinging to illusions of control or happiness, is essential for spiritual growth. Dhumavati teaches us that true strength lies not in avoiding pain but in facing it with courage and resilience. Her presence reminds us that the deepest wisdom often emerges from the darkest moments, and that even in desolation, there is a profound potential for transformation and a deeper understanding of ourselves. This acceptance of the shadow aspects represented by Dhumavati allows for a more profound and authentic experience of joy and fulfillment when those moments eventually arise. It's not about wallowing in misery; it's about acknowledging the legitimate space that grief and loss hold in the human experience.

Chhinnamasta, the goddess with her self-decapitated head, presents the most radical image of shadow integration. Her self-sacrifice, her complete surrender, represents the ultimate relinquishment of ego-driven control. The severed head, drinking its own blood, symbolizes the necessary death of the ego to achieve a higher state of consciousness. This isn't a literal self-mutilation; it's a symbolic representation of the process of letting go of our attachment to a limited sense of self. The ego, with its desires, fears, and limitations, often prevents us from experiencing our full potential.

Chhinnamasta's radical act compels us to question the very foundations of our self-perception, pushing us beyond the confines of our limited identity. This extreme imagery underscores the transformative power of surrendering to a larger reality, accepting our mortality, and embracing the unknown aspects of our being. The act of self-decapitation, therefore, is not one of destruction, but of liberation, signifying the surrender of the ego to the higher Self, leading to spiritual awakening and the experience of unity with the Divine. The self-sacrifice is not a punishment but a necessary step in the journey of self-discovery and spiritual liberation.

These three Mahavidyas—Kali, Dhumavati, and Chhinnamasta—exemplify the importance of integrating the shadow self for spiritual growth. They represent aspects of ourselves we often repress: the destructive potential within, the experience of profound loss and grief, and the necessity of surrendering the ego to achieve true liberation. By confronting these archetypes, we confront the darkest aspects of our own being, creating the space for integration, self-acceptance, and a deeper understanding of the interconnectedness of all things. The process is not easy; it requires courage, resilience, and a willingness to face the uncomfortable truths about ourselves.

However, the reward is a more integrated personality, a greater sense of self-awareness, and the potential for spiritual transformation. This integration allows for a greater capacity for compassion, both for ourselves and for others, fostering a deeper connection to the Divine Feminine and ultimately, a more fulfilling and meaningful life. The Mahavidyas, in their multifaceted representations, provide a map for this challenging yet rewarding journey of self-discovery. They offer not only a framework for understanding the complexities of the human psyche but also a path toward wholeness, liberation, and the realization of our full potential. Their symbolism is timeless, providing a relevant guide for navigating the complexities of the modern world and the
constant struggle toward self-realization. The journey through the shadow self, as guided by these powerful goddesses, is a transformative one, leading to a greater sense of peace,

understanding, and ultimately, a deeper connection to the divine.

The Mahavidyas and Healing Practices

The exploration of the Mahavidyas through the lens of Jungian psychology has revealed their profound relevance to the process of individuation, the integration of the conscious and unconscious aspects of the self. However, their influence extends beyond the purely psychological; the Mahavidyas also offer a rich tapestry of symbolic imagery that can inform and enhance various healing practices. This section will delve into the potential applications of the Mahavidyas in therapeutic contexts, focusing on their capacity to address psychological imbalances and foster emotional well-being.

One particularly relevant area is psychotherapy. The Mahavidyas, with their diverse manifestations of the feminine principle, can serve as powerful archetypal figures to guide the therapeutic process. For instance, Kali, with her terrifying yet ultimately transformative power, can be utilized to help patients confront and integrate their shadow aspects, those repressed emotions and experiences that fuel internal conflict and hinder personal growth.

In therapy, this might involve exploring the patient's fear of destruction or their resistance to change, allowing for a safe and guided confrontation of these challenging emotions. The therapist can utilize Kali's symbolism to encourage the patient to embrace the cyclical nature of life, recognizing that destruction is often a necessary precursor to renewal and transformation.

Similarly, Dhumavati, the goddess of widowhood and desolation, can assist patients grappling with grief, loss, and feelings of emptiness. Her image, though austere, embodies a profound acceptance of suffering, a necessary stage in the healing process. Working with Dhumavati's archetype can help patients navigate the "dark night of the soul," allowing them to explore their feelings of despair without judgment and fostering a sense of resilience and strength. The therapist might guide the patient to find meaning within their pain, recognizing Dhumavati's wisdom as a guide through darkness towards a deeper understanding of self. This approach emphasizes the importance of honoring the process of grief, rather than seeking to quickly overcome it, recognizing that healing requires time and acceptance.

Chhinnamasta, with her radical act of self-sacrifice, can be a powerful symbol for patients struggling with self-destructive behaviors or a lack of self-worth. Her self-decapitation, a profoundly symbolic act of letting go, can facilitate a therapeutic exploration of the patient's self-limiting beliefs and patterns. The therapist can guide the patient to understand the symbolism of ego-surrender, encouraging them to release their attachment to a limited sense of self and embrace a more expansive sense of identity. This process may involve confronting deeply rooted insecurities, releasing self-criticism, and fostering a sense of self-compassion.

Beyond the more "challenging" Mahavidyas, the others also offer unique therapeutic applications. Tripura Sundari, the embodiment of beauty and grace, can be used to address issues of self-esteem and body image. Her radiant form serves as a reminder of the inherent beauty and worth within each individual, helping patients to cultivate self-love and acceptance. Bhuvaneshvari, the goddess of sovereignty, can be instrumental in empowering patients to reclaim their agency and assert their needs, particularly helpful for those who have experienced trauma or oppression. Bhairavi, with her potent energy, can facilitate a journey of self-discovery and inner strength, helping patients access their own inherent power and resilience.

The Mahavidyas' relevance extends beyond individual psychotherapy; their potent symbolism can also inform energy healing modalities. Practitioners of energy healing, such as Reiki or Pranic Healing, may find that channeling the energy of a specific Mahavidya can enhance their healing work. For instance, Kali's energy could be used to clear stagnant energy blockages and facilitate profound transformation, while Dhumavati's energy could support patients in releasing grief and emotional trauma. Tripura Sundari's energy could enhance feelings of self-love and beauty, while Bhuvaneshvari's energy could empower patients to overcome feelings of helplessness. This application requires sensitivity, knowledge, and proper training in energy healing techniques, but it highlights the expansive potential of the Mahavidyas to inform diverse healing modalities.

The integration of the Mahavidyas into healing practices requires careful consideration and a deep understanding of their complex symbolism. It is crucial to approach these powerful archetypes with reverence and respect, avoiding simplistic or superficial interpretations. The therapist or energy healer should possess a solid grounding in both Hindu Tantra and the relevant psychological principles to ensure ethical and effective application. Moreover, it is essential to emphasize that the Mahavidyas are not a substitute for conventional medical or psychological treatment; rather, they offer a complementary approach that can enhance the therapeutic process, providing symbolic frameworks and archetypal guidance to facilitate healing and personal growth. Their use should be carefully considered within the ethical parameters of professional practice.

The power of the Mahavidyas extends beyond the purely individual realm; their energies can also be harnessed for collective healing and social transformation. In a world grappling with widespread trauma, social injustice, and environmental challenges, the Mahavidyas' capacity to address these issues on a larger scale becomes increasingly apparent. Kali's energy, for example, could be channeled to promote a dismantling of harmful structures and systems, facilitating radical change and societal renewal.

Dhumavati's wisdom could be employed to guide communities through periods of collective grief and loss, fostering resilience and promoting healing on a broader societal level.

The application of Mahavidya principles to community healing could take many forms. For example, art therapy sessions utilizing the imagery of the Mahavidyas could help individuals process collective trauma, fostering dialogue and encouraging shared experiences of healing. Yoga and meditation practices incorporating the mantras and symbolism of the Mahavidyas could create a space for collective energy work, promoting peace and emotional well-being on a communal scale. Similarly, environmental activism informed by the principles of the Mahavidyas could promote ecological healing, recognizing the interconnectedness of all beings and fostering a deep respect for the natural world.

The responsible and ethical application of the Mahavidyas in healing practices requires a strong foundation in both spiritual and psychological understanding. The practitioner must approach these potent energies with humility, respect, and a deep appreciation for their complexity. The focus should always be on promoting well-being, empowering individuals and communities, and fostering a compassionate approach to healing and transformation. It is vital to remember that the Mahavidyas are not merely symbolic figures; they represent powerful energies capable of facilitating profound change on both personal and collective levels. Therefore, the responsible and thoughtful integration of their symbolism and energy into healing practices holds immense potential for fostering individual growth, societal well-being, and spiritual evolution. The potential for using their potent symbolic representations in therapy and healing underscores the continuing relevance of ancient
traditions in the modern world, providing powerful tools for navigating the complexities of human experience and promoting holistic well-being. By integrating these rich archetypal resources into contemporary therapeutic approaches, we can harness their transformative power for the benefit of individuals and society alike. The path forward involves continuing research,
interdisciplinary collaboration, and a deep commitment to ethical and mindful application of this potent knowledge.

The Mahavidyas and Personal Growth

The preceding discussion explored the application of Mahavidya archetypes within therapeutic frameworks, highlighting their potential to address psychological imbalances and foster healing. Now, we shift our focus to the direct application of their wisdom and energy for individual personal growth and self-discovery. Each Mahavidya offers a unique pathway for self-transformation, providing potent symbolic tools and energetic guidance for navigating the complexities of human experience.

Kali, the terrifying yet ultimately transformative goddess, presents a powerful archetype for confronting and integrating the shadow self. Her association with death and destruction highlights the necessity of releasing old patterns, beliefs, and behaviors that no longer serve us. This is not simply about purging negativity; it's about consciously acknowledging and accepting the darker aspects of our personality, integrating them into a more holistic self. The process might involve journaling, shadow work exercises, or engaging in practices that help us confront our fears and limitations. By embracing Kali's transformative energy, we can move through periods of intense change and emerge renewed and strengthened.

This process may require confronting deeply ingrained fears of failure, vulnerability, or loss of control, yet the ultimate reward is a deeper sense of self-acceptance and empowerment. Kali's energy encourages the courageous dismantling of self-imposed limitations, allowing for a profound liberation and the blossoming of inner potential. The practice might include meditation on Kali's iconography, focusing on her fierce gaze and powerful presence, or chanting her mantra to evoke her transformative energy.

Tara, the compassionate saviour, represents nurturing and protection. Her energy is ideal for fostering self-compassion, a critical element of personal growth. Often, we are far more critical of ourselves than we would ever be of others. Tara's energy reminds us to treat ourselves with the same kindness and understanding we would offer a friend in need. This could involve practices of self-soothing, positive self-talk, and actively choosing kindness towards oneself during times of vulnerability or self-doubt. Tara's protective energy can also be utilized to build resilience against external challenges, providing a sense of security and stability in the face of adversity. This may involve setting healthy boundaries, cultivating a supportive community, or developing strategies for coping with stress and difficult situations. Visualization practices, imagining Tara's protective embrace, can be particularly effective in fostering a sense of inner peace and security.

Tripura Sundari, the goddess of beauty and grace, embodies self-love and acceptance. Working with her energy encourages us to appreciate our inherent worth and cultivate a positive body image, regardless of societal standards. This can involve practices such as mindful self-care, focusing on our physical and emotional well-being. It's about recognizing and celebrating our unique qualities and appreciating the beauty that resides within us. Tripura Sundari's energy can also help us cultivate a sense of gratitude and appreciate the positive aspects of our lives, fostering a more optimistic outlook and enhanced self-esteem. This might involve keeping a gratitude journal, practicing affirmations, or engaging in activities that bring us joy and fulfillment. The practice of appreciating beauty in nature or art, reflecting Tripura Sundari's graceful form, can deepen this sense of self-acceptance and appreciation.

Bhuvaneshvari, the goddess of sovereignty, empowers us to reclaim our personal power and take control of our lives. She guides us to recognize and assert our needs, setting healthy boundaries and taking responsibility for our actions and choices. This involves identifying areas where we may have given away our power—be it in relationships, work, or other aspects of life—and actively taking steps to regain our agency. This might involve assertiveness training, learning to say "no" effectively, or developing stronger communication skills. Bhuvaneshvari's energy fosters a sense of self-confidence and inner authority, enabling us to navigate life's challenges with greater resilience and determination. Visualization of Bhuvaneshvari seated on her throne, radiating confidence and strength, can help cultivate this inner sense of power and authority.

Bhairavi, the goddess of fierce energy and power, represents courage and resilience. She inspires us to confront our fears and move beyond our comfort zones, embracing challenges as opportunities for growth. This might involve stepping outside of our familiar routines, taking calculated risks, or pursuing goals that once seemed unattainable. Bhairavi's energy encourages us to access our inner strength and tap into our inherent potential, overcoming obstacles and achieving our aspirations. Her energy can be particularly useful in breaking through patterns of self-sabotage or procrastination. Practices such as dynamic meditation, vigorous exercise, or engaging in activities that push our limits can help channel Bhairavi's dynamic energy.

Chhinnamasta, the self-sacrificing goddess, teaches us the importance of letting go of attachments and embracing change. Her iconography, shocking as it may seem, represents a radical act of surrender, symbolic of relinquishing ego-driven desires and embracing a state of selfless action. This process often involves confronting deep-seated fears of loss and accepting the transient nature of all things. Chhinnamasta's energy encourages us to release self-limiting beliefs, unhealthy relationships, or habits that no longer serve our well-being. This could involve practices like forgiveness, detachment from outcome, or embracing impermanence. Meditation on her image can facilitate this process of surrender, allowing for emotional release and a sense of liberation.

Dhumavati, the goddess of widowhood and desolation, guides us through periods of grief and despair. Her energy invites us to embrace our shadow emotions, acknowledging and accepting our pain without judgment. This doesn't mean wallowing in negativity, but rather, allowing ourselves to fully experience our emotions, processing them without trying to suppress or ignore them.

Dhumavati's wisdom teaches us to find strength and resilience in the face of adversity, recognizing that even in darkness, there is potential for growth and transformation. This process might involve grief counseling, journaling, or exploring creative outlets to express suppressed emotions. Meditation on her austere yet wise form can provide solace and support during difficult times.

Bagalamukhi, the goddess of speech and control, helps us to harness the power of communication and articulate our needs and desires effectively. She assists us in managing difficult conversations, setting boundaries, and expressing ourselves clearly and confidently. This involves developing stronger communication skills, learning to speak our truth without fear, and effectively navigating conflict. Bagalamukhi's energy can be especially beneficial for those who struggle with assertiveness or who have experienced silencing or oppression. This might involve practicing mindful speech, engaging in public speaking, or seeking support in developing communication skills.

Matangi, the goddess of music and knowledge, inspires us to cultivate creativity and self-expression. She encourages us to explore our artistic talents, develop our intellectual capabilities, and engage in activities that nurture our spirit. This could involve pursuing creative hobbies, learning new skills, or engaging in intellectual pursuits that stimulate our minds. Matangi's energy fosters self-discovery through creative expression, enabling us to connect with our inner selves and share our unique gifts with the world.

Kamalatmika, the goddess of fulfillment and abundance, reminds us of the importance of cultivating gratitude and appreciating the blessings in our lives. She guides us to focus on our goals, manifesting our desires through positive intention and action. This involves recognizing and appreciating what we already have, setting clear intentions, and taking consistent steps toward our aspirations. Kamalatmika's energy fosters a sense of abundance and prosperity, not just materially, but also emotionally and spiritually. This may involve practices like visualization, positive affirmations, and expressing gratitude for the good in one's life.

In conclusion, the Mahavidyas offer a rich tapestry of archetypal energies and symbolic wisdom, providing powerful tools for personal growth and self-discovery. By consciously engaging with their attributes and utilizing appropriate practices, we can harness their transformative power to navigate life's challenges, cultivate inner strength, and unlock our full potential. This exploration emphasizes the continued relevance of ancient traditions in addressing contemporary challenges, providing a path toward holistic personal growth and a deeper understanding of the human experience. The journey of self-discovery, guided by the Mahavidyas, is a dynamic and ongoing process, requiring patience, self-awareness, and a willingness to embrace transformation.

Integrating the Mahavidyas into Modern Contexts

The preceding exploration of the Mahavidyas through the lens of individual archetypes provides a foundation for understanding their potential application within modern psychological and therapeutic contexts. While not a replacement for professional mental health services, the symbolism and energy associated with each Mahavidya offer a rich source of metaphorical tools and spiritual practices that can complement existing therapeutic approaches. This integration seeks to bridge the gap between ancient wisdom and contemporary psychological understanding, providing a holistic approach to personal growth and well-being.

One significant area of integration lies in the realm of shadow work. Jungian psychology emphasizes the importance of confronting and integrating the unconscious aspects of the self, the "shadow." Kali, with her terrifying yet transformative nature, provides a potent archetype for this process. Her association with death and destruction symbolizes the necessary dismantling of outdated beliefs, limiting behaviors, and ingrained negativity. Rather than simply suppressing these aspects, Kali encourages conscious acknowledgement and integration. Therapeutic techniques like journaling, dream analysis, and guided visualizations can be employed to explore and process the shadow self, mirroring Kali's energetic dismantling of obstacles. The process may evoke intense emotions, mirroring Kali's fierce energy, but ultimately leads to a deeper sense of self-acceptance and wholeness. The mantra of Kali can be incorporated into these practices, providing a focused point of energy and intention. Furthermore, the understanding of Kali's transformative power can provide clients with a powerful metaphor for facing their own internal challenges and emerging stronger.

Tara's compassionate nature offers a powerful counterpoint to Kali's intensity. In modern therapeutic frameworks, self-compassion is recognized as a crucial factor in emotional resilience and mental well-being. Tara's archetype provides a potent symbol for cultivating this inner compassion. Many individuals are far more critical of themselves than they would ever be of others; Tara's energy reminds us to extend the same kindness and understanding to ourselves that we would offer a friend in need. Mindfulness practices, combined with Tara's mantra, can help cultivate self-soothing techniques and positive self-talk. The visualization of Tara's protective embrace can offer a sense of security and stability, particularly during times of vulnerability or stress. This approach can be particularly effective in treating conditions like anxiety and depression, offering a spiritual framework for building resilience and coping mechanisms.

Tripura Sundari, the embodiment of beauty and grace, speaks to the importance of self-love and body positivity. In a society often obsessed with unrealistic beauty standards, Tripura Sundari's energy offers a powerful counter-narrative. Her archetype challenges the internalized negativity and self-criticism often associated with body image issues. Therapeutic applications might involve incorporating practices of mindful self-care, encouraging clients to appreciate their unique qualities and celebrate their inherent worth, regardless of societal pressures. Art therapy, combined with meditation on Tripura Sundari's iconography, can facilitate self-expression and foster a deeper appreciation for the beauty within oneself. The focus shifts from external validation to internal self-acceptance, mirroring Tripura Sundari's inherent radiance.

Bhuvaneshvari, the goddess of sovereignty, offers a potent archetype for reclaiming personal power and establishing healthy boundaries. In therapeutic settings, many clients struggle with feelings of powerlessness, particularly in relationships, work, or other areas of life. Bhuvaneshvari's energy empowers clients to recognize and assert their needs, taking responsibility for their actions and choices. Assertiveness training, combined with visualizations of Bhuvaneshvari seated on her throne, can help individuals develop stronger communication skills and effectively set boundaries. This approach can be particularly beneficial in addressing issues like codependency, enabling clients to regain a sense of agency and control over their lives. The understanding of Bhuvaneshvari's inherent authority can instill confidence and empower clients to navigate challenging situations with greater resilience.

Bhairavi's fierce energy and power resonate with the concept of courage and resilience in modern psychology. Her archetype encourages clients to confront their fears and step outside their comfort zones. In therapy, this might involve exploring past traumas, confronting limiting beliefs, or setting ambitious goals. Bhairavi's energy can be harnessed through practices like dynamic meditation, which release pent-up energy and help clients access their inner strength. The understanding of Bhairavi's power can empower clients to navigate difficult emotional landscapes and cultivate inner resilience. This approach can be valuable in treating trauma-related disorders, fostering a sense of empowerment and control.

The seemingly paradoxical nature of Chhinnamasta, the self-sacrificing goddess, presents a unique lens for understanding detachment and letting go. In therapy, this can be applied to unhealthy attachments, self-sabotaging behaviors, or the need to relinquish control. The symbolic sacrifice of Chhinnamasta represents a radical act of surrender, allowing for emotional release and the acceptance of change. Mindfulness practices, coupled with meditation on Chhinnamasta's iconography, can facilitate this process, fostering a sense of liberation and inner peace. This can be particularly relevant in dealing with grief, loss, or the challenges of embracing impermanence.

Dhumavati, the goddess of widowhood and desolation, offers a powerful archetype for navigating grief and despair. In contemporary psychology, the importance of acknowledging and processing difficult emotions is widely recognized. Dhumavati's energy encourages clients to embrace their shadow emotions without judgment. This doesn't involve wallowing in negativity, but rather, creating a safe space to fully experience and process emotions. Therapeutic interventions, like grief counseling or expressive arts therapy, can be combined with meditation on Dhumavati's image, providing a sense of solace and support during challenging emotional states. Dhumavati's energy can be particularly helpful for clients experiencing loss or significant life transitions.

Bagalamukhi, the goddess of speech and control, offers a unique approach to communication and assertiveness. Many clients struggle with expressing their needs and desires effectively, leading to conflicts and feelings of powerlessness. Bagalamukhi's energy can empower clients to develop stronger communication skills, learn to set boundaries, and articulate their thoughts and feelings clearly and confidently. Role-playing exercises, combined with chanting Bagalamukhi's mantra, can help clients practice assertive communication and navigate difficult conversations. This approach can be particularly beneficial in addressing communication-related challenges in relationships or the workplace.

Matangi, the goddess of music and knowledge, speaks to the importance of creativity and self-expression. In therapy, art therapy, music therapy, or journaling can be employed to tap into Matangi's energy, fostering self-discovery and emotional release. This approach can be particularly helpful in treating trauma or other mental health conditions, providing a non-verbal means of expression and processing complex emotions. Matangi's energy encourages clients to explore their creative potential and use it as a tool for healing and personal growth.

Finally, Kamalatmika, the goddess of fulfillment and abundance, inspires a focus on gratitude and manifestation. In therapy, this can be applied through positive psychology techniques, such as gratitude journaling or visualization exercises, to cultivate a sense of abundance and well-being. This approach encourages clients to recognize and appreciate the positive aspects of their lives, fostering a more optimistic outlook and enhancing their overall sense of fulfillment.

In conclusion, integrating the Mahavidyas into modern psychological and therapeutic frameworks offers a rich and nuanced approach to personal growth and well-being. By utilizing their archetypal energies and symbolic wisdom, therapists and clients can access powerful tools for healing, self-discovery, and empowerment. This integrated approach fosters a holistic perspective, bridging the gap between ancient wisdom and contemporary psychological understanding, ultimately enriching the therapeutic process and enhancing the client's journey towards wholeness. It is crucial, however, to emphasize that this approach should be considered a complement to, not a replacement for, professional mental health services. The effectiveness of this integration depends on the therapist's sensitivity, understanding, and appropriate application of the Mahavidya archetypes within a safe and ethical therapeutic setting.

Kalis Role in Social Transformation

Kali, the fierce and terrifying Mahavidya, often evokes immediate reactions of fear and apprehension. Her iconography—a dark complexion, bared fangs, a garland of skulls, and a severed head in her hand—certainly contributes to this initial perception. However, a deeper understanding reveals a far more nuanced and ultimately liberating role for Kali within the context of social transformation and justice. Her terrifying visage is not merely a display of aggression, but rather a symbol of the necessary destruction that precedes creation, a dismantling of the old to make way for the new. This destructive aspect of Kali is not chaotic or arbitrary; it is a purposeful, transformative force aimed at eradicating injustice and oppression.

In the context of social justice, Kali's role can be understood as a powerful catalyst for change. She represents the breaking down of oppressive systems and structures—be they patriarchal, caste-based, or other forms of societal inequality. Her fierce energy acts as a potent force against injustice, challenging the status quo and demanding a radical shift towards equity and fairness. She doesn't shy away from confronting the darkness within society, demanding accountability and challenging those who perpetuate suffering and inequality. Her image as a destroyer of ego and illusion reminds us that clinging to outdated power structures only serves to perpetuate cycles of oppression. True transformation requires confronting these structures and dismantling their foundations, a task for which Kali's energy is perfectly suited.

Consider the historical and contemporary instances of systemic oppression. Kali's symbolism offers a powerful lens through which to understand and address them. For example, the caste system in India, a deeply entrenched social hierarchy, has caused immense suffering and inequality for centuries. Kali's energy can be viewed as a force challenging this rigid system, advocating for the dismantling of its discriminatory practices and the establishment of a more just and equitable society. Her destructive force is not aimed at individuals, but at the systemic structures that perpetuate inequality. This calls for a dismantling of the very foundations upon which the caste system is built – the deeply ingrained beliefs and societal norms that uphold its existence. Kali's energy is a call for a radical reimagining of social structures, pushing us to question and challenge the very principles that uphold inequality.

Furthermore, Kali's role in social justice extends beyond the destruction of oppressive systems. She also represents the potential for rebirth and renewal. Just as death is an essential part of the cycle of life, the destruction of oppressive structures is necessary for the creation of a more just and equitable world. Following the dismantling of the old, there is the potential for a new societal order to emerge, an order based on principles of fairness,
inclusivity, and equality. This rebirth is not a passive process, but one that requires conscious effort and collective action. It
necessitates the creation of new structures, new laws, and new social norms that reflect these values. Kali's energy, then, is not only destructive, but also generative, pushing us towards a future where justice and equality prevail.

The concept of Kali as a "dark mother" offers a crucial perspective. While frightening in her appearance, she is also deeply nurturing, protecting her devotees from harm and guiding them towards liberation. This paradoxical nature of Kali underscores the necessity of confronting difficult truths and engaging with the painful realities of social injustice. It requires us to acknowledge the existence of suffering and oppression without shying away from its darkness. Only through confronting these realities can we begin to address them effectively. Kali's "dark" aspects aren't signs of malevolence, but rather represent the necessary shadow work required for social transformation. She represents the facing of uncomfortable truths, the acceptance of difficult realities and the willingness to engage with the unpleasant realities of our society.

Her role in combating injustice also extends to the personal level. Many individuals who strive for social justice experience burnout, disillusionment, or feelings of powerlessness in the face of seemingly insurmountable challenges. Kali's energy can provide a crucial source of strength and resilience during these times. Her unwavering determination and fierce energy serve as a reminder that the fight for justice is a marathon, not a sprint, and that setbacks are inevitable. It is through perseverance and a commitment to the cause that meaningful change is achieved. The symbolism of Kali embracing the cycle of destruction and creation offers a powerful message of hope and renewal, even in the face of adversity.

The application of Kali's energy in modern activism and social justice movements is profound. Her symbolism can inspire activists and change-makers to confront injustice with courage and determination. Her image as a destroyer of ego can help activists to overcome self-doubt and fear, empowering them to take action even in the face of opposition. Furthermore, her association with both destruction and creation can inspire activists to envision a more just future and work tirelessly towards its realization. This isn't about mindless aggression, but a fierce dedication to the cause and a willingness to challenge the status quo, even at personal cost.

However, it's crucial to approach Kali's energy with caution and discernment. Her destructive force must be channeled responsibly and ethically. The goal is not to inflict violence or sow chaos, but to dismantle oppressive systems and empower those who have been marginalized. Therefore, the application of Kali's energy must be coupled with compassion, empathy, and a deep commitment to justice and equality. It's about targeted, constructive action aimed at dismantling harmful systems, not about unleashing indiscriminate destruction. The goal is to empower, not to oppress.

Kali's symbolism finds a powerful resonance in contemporary discussions surrounding intersectionality. The understanding that various forms of oppression—based on gender, race, class, caste, sexual orientation, and other factors—intersect and reinforce each other is crucial for effective social justice work. Kali's energy doesn't just target one form of oppression; rather, her transformative force can be seen as working against all forms of inequality, recognizing the interconnectedness of different forms of marginalization. Her iconography, often depicting her trampling figures, can be interpreted not as random violence, but as a symbolic destruction of the entire network of oppressive structures.

The concept of "Kali Yuga," the current age in Hindu cosmology, often characterized by materialism, conflict, and moral decline, further illuminates Kali's relevance. Within this context, Kali's energy can be seen as a necessary force for navigating the challenges of this age. Her presence is not simply a symbol of negativity, but a call for transformation and renewal. In an age marked by deep-seated social and environmental problems, Kali's energy encourages us to confront these challenges head-on, to dismantle destructive patterns, and to work towards a more sustainable and just future. The very presence of Kali in this age signifies a period ripe for transformation and renewal, and it's within the embracing of her power, her destruction, and her ultimate compassion that we might find the path towards lasting change.

In conclusion, Kali's role in social transformation and justice is multifaceted and deeply significant. Her symbolism offers a powerful framework for understanding and addressing the systemic inequalities that plague our world. Her energy—while often perceived as frightening—serves as a potent catalyst for change, challenging us to confront the darkness within ourselves and society, to dismantle oppressive systems, and to work towards a more just and equitable future. However, this engagement must be approached with responsibility, empathy, and a commitment to ethical action. Kali's energy, properly understood and channeled, can inspire and empower us to fight for a better world, one where justice and equality prevail. Her terrifying visage becomes a symbol of courageous hope, a testament to the possibility of profound and lasting transformation.

Taras Compassion and Social Action

Tara, the second Mahavidya, presents a striking contrast to Kali's fierce energy. While Kali embodies the destruction of oppressive structures, Tara embodies the compassionate action that follows, the nurturing and protection of those vulnerable and marginalized.

Her name itself, derived from the Sanskrit root *tar*, meaning "to save" or "to liberate," points directly to her central function: the rescue and relief of suffering beings. Unlike Kali's terrifying visage, Tara is often depicted with a serene and compassionate expression, radiating an aura of peace and solace. Yet, this gentleness is not weakness; it is the strength of unwavering empathy and boundless compassion, a powerful force for social good.

Tara's iconography frequently depicts her seated or standing in a posture of readiness, often with a serene expression that belies her power. Her hands are frequently in mudras, symbolic gestures conveying protection, blessing, or the granting of wishes. She is often portrayed holding various objects – lotuses, jewels, a sword, or a vase filled with nectar – all reflecting aspects of her protective and nurturing qualities. These symbols are not merely aesthetic choices; they carry profound meaning, embodying her capacity to provide refuge, healing, and liberation to those in need. The variety in her iconography highlights her multifaceted nature, adapting to the specific needs of her devotees and the situations they face. Sometimes depicted as fierce, with multiple arms wielding various implements of protection, she transforms to meet the immediate threat while always maintaining her core essence of compassion.

The compassion of Tara is not a passive sentiment; it is an active force driving her to intervene on behalf of the suffering. Her energy inspires acts of selfless service, motivating individuals to alleviate the pain and hardship of others. This action can take myriad forms, from direct assistance to those in immediate danger to systemic work aimed at addressing the root causes of suffering. She inspires acts of charity, kindness, and empathy, fostering a sense of interconnectedness and shared humanity. This active engagement is a critical aspect of her role within the context of social justice. Tara's compassion isn't simply a feeling; it's a catalyst for action, a powerful impetus for individuals and communities to rise up and address the needs of the vulnerable.

Consider the countless examples of individuals and organizations actively engaged in social justice work. Tara's energy can be seen as the driving force behind their efforts, inspiring their acts of selfless service and dedication. Think of humanitarian aid workers risking their lives to provide relief in war-torn regions, or community activists tirelessly advocating for the rights of marginalized groups. These actions, born from a deep sense of empathy and compassion, are a direct reflection of Tara's energy. Their actions are tangible manifestations of Tara's compassionate force, transforming suffering and providing hope where there was previously only despair.

The alleviation of suffering, central to Tara's role, takes many forms. It includes providing immediate assistance to those in crisis –shelter for the homeless, food for the hungry, medical care for the sick – but extends far beyond immediate needs. Tara's compassion inspires long-term solutions, tackling the systemic issues that create suffering in the first place. This involves advocating for policy changes to address systemic inequalities, promoting education and economic empowerment for marginalized communities, and challenging discriminatory practices at all levels of society. Tara's energy is thus both immediate and enduring, encompassing both short-term relief and long-term systemic change. She advocates for holistic solutions, addressing not only the symptoms but also the root causes of suffering.

The concept of "refuge" is deeply connected to Tara's symbolism.

She is often seen as a refuge for those who are lost, afraid, or oppressed. This refuge isn't simply a physical sanctuary; it is a state of being, a feeling of safety and security in the face of adversity.

This can be found through spiritual practice, connecting with the divine feminine energy that Tara represents, finding solace and strength in her compassionate embrace. But it can also be a tangible refuge, provided by individuals and communities inspired by her energy to offer sanctuary and protection to the vulnerable. The refuge provided isn't simply physical, but also emotional and spiritual, offering hope and support during difficult times.

Tara's influence is not limited to large-scale social movements or organized relief efforts. Her compassionate energy permeates everyday life, inspiring acts of kindness, empathy, and understanding. A simple act of compassion – offering a helping hand to a stranger, listening empathetically to a friend in need, extending forgiveness to someone who has wronged you – can be considered a direct reflection of Tara's influence. These everyday acts, seemingly small and insignificant in isolation, collectively contribute to a more compassionate and just world. The cumulative effect of these individual acts of kindness creates a ripple effect of compassion, transforming lives and fostering a more harmonious society.

It is important to note that Tara's compassion is not naive or sentimental. It is a powerful, transformative energy that is capable of confronting difficult realities and challenging injustice. While her serene appearance might suggest a passive approach, her underlying energy is profoundly assertive. She does not shy away from confronting oppressive systems or standing up for the vulnerable. Her compassion is not weakness but a source of strength, a force capable of bringing about profound and lasting change. It's a strength that is not born of aggression, but of unwavering belief in the inherent worth and dignity of every being.

Tara's influence extends to those actively working towards social justice, providing guidance, solace, and strength. Activists and change-makers often face immense challenges, burnout, and disillusionment in their efforts. Tara's energy offers a source of resilience, reminding them of the importance of their work and providing the strength to persevere. She offers comfort in moments of despair, reaffirms their commitment to the cause, and inspires continued efforts in the face of adversity. This sustained support, born from compassion, is essential for maintaining the momentum of social justice movements. She is the unwavering presence that sustains the arduous journey towards a more equitable world.

The connection between Tara and the concept of "liberation" is crucial. She not only protects the vulnerable but actively works to liberate them from oppression. This liberation is not simply about physical freedom but encompasses all aspects of life – emotional, social, spiritual, and economic. Her energy inspires efforts to free individuals from cycles of poverty, violence, and discrimination, providing them with the resources and opportunities they need to live full and dignified lives. This holistic approach to liberation reflects the depth and breadth of Tara's compassion. She aims for a liberation that touches every aspect of a person's being, fostering a truly equitable society.

Furthermore, Tara's compassion extends beyond human beings. In many traditions, she is considered a protector of all sentient beings, including animals and the natural environment. This broad scope of compassion highlights the interconnectedness of all life and the importance of respecting and protecting all beings. Her influence inspires environmental activism, animal welfare initiatives, and a broader commitment to sustainability and ecological responsibility.

This demonstrates that Tara's compassion transcends species and extends to the entire web of life, promoting harmony and balance within the ecosystem.

In conclusion, Tara's role in promoting compassion and social action is vital to understanding the Mahavidyas' significance in the modern context. Her energy serves as a powerful reminder of the importance of empathy, service, and the fight for justice. Her compassionate strength inspires acts of kindness, challenges oppressive systems, and offers hope and resilience to those working towards a more just and equitable world. Her symbolism—serene yet powerful—provides a profound model for navigating the complexities of social justice and creating a world where all beings are safe, protected, and liberated from suffering. Her gentle but unwavering power offers a path towards a more compassionate and harmonious future for all.

The Mahavidyas and Feminist Perspectives

The exploration of the Mahavidyas thus far has highlighted their multifaceted nature, revealing goddesses who embody both terrifying power and profound compassion. This duality is crucial to understanding their relevance within the framework of social justice, particularly when viewed through a feminist lens. A feminist perspective offers a unique and insightful approach to interpreting the Mahavidyas, challenging traditional interpretations and highlighting their potential as powerful symbols of female empowerment and liberation.

The patriarchal structures that have historically dominated many religious and societal systems have often marginalized or misrepresented feminine power. The Mahavidyas, however, disrupt this narrative. Their independent and powerful manifestations directly challenge the traditional subjugation of women. Their fierce aspects, often seen as frightening or threatening, can be reinterpreted as expressions of justified rage against oppression and injustice. Kali, for instance, with her blood-soaked form and terrifying demeanor, isn't simply a symbol of destruction; she represents the dismantling of oppressive systems, the necessary shattering of structures that perpetuate inequality and suffering.

This act of destruction, far from being negative, becomes a prerequisite for creation, paving the way for a more just and equitable world.

The Mahavidyas' iconography often deviates from traditional feminine ideals imposed by patriarchal societies. They are not passively beautiful, demure figures; they are powerful, independent beings with diverse forms and attributes. Their multiple arms, weapons, and fierce expressions challenge the idealized, submissive image of femininity that has been historically promoted. This visual representation of power directly confronts and dismantles the stereotype of the weak, passive woman. These visual representations defy the norms and expectations placed upon women throughout history, actively challenging the patriarchal gaze that seeks to confine and control women.

Tripura Sundari, with her exquisite beauty and youthful appearance, embodies a different aspect of female power. While often interpreted as a symbol of aesthetic perfection, a closer examination reveals her as a goddess who embodies both grace and power. Her beauty is not a symbol of passivity; it is a force that commands attention, reverence, and respect. She demonstrates that feminine power can be expressed through both strength and beauty, challenging the notion that these two qualities are mutually exclusive. Her allure is not designed to attract the male gaze; it is a reflection of her inherent power and grace.

Bhuvaneshvari, the ruler of the universe, is a clear example of a goddess who transcends patriarchal limits. Her sovereignty over all creation signifies an ultimate rejection of male dominance, demonstrating the potential for female leadership and authority.

Her role as the ultimate sovereign challenges the ingrained idea that leadership and power are exclusively male domains. Her ability to command and govern the universe itself provides a powerful counter-narrative to the traditional patriarchal structures.

The stories associated with the Mahavidyas often challenge the traditional narrative of women as passive recipients of male action. Their independent agency, their ability to act autonomously and make their own choices, challenges the deeply ingrained societal expectations that restrict women's choices and actions. These stories offer alternatives to the often-limiting narratives that define women's roles solely through their relationship with men. The Goddesses often act independently of any male counterpart, demonstrating female self-sufficiency and authority.

Consider Chhinnamasta, the Mahavidya who is depicted severing her own head. This shocking imagery is not merely a representation of self-sacrifice but can be understood as an act of radical self-ownership and liberation. By severing her own head, she symbolically transcends the limitations imposed upon her by societal norms and expectations. It is an act of self-determination, a refusal to conform to prescribed roles and identities. This radical act challenges conventional notions of femininity and self-preservation.

Dhumavati, often depicted as an old, widowed woman, stands in stark contrast to typical feminine ideals. Yet, her portrayal as a powerful, independent widow challenges the traditional marginalization of older women and widows in patriarchal societies. She is not a pitiable figure; she is a strong, resilient being who embraces her independence and defies expectations. Her portrayal shatters stereotypes associated with aging and widowhood, celebrating female autonomy and resilience throughout life's various stages.

Bagalamukhi, the goddess of speech, embodies the power of communication and the ability to control narratives. This is a particularly relevant aspect of female empowerment, as women have historically been denied access to platforms of power and influence. Bagalamukhi's ability to influence others through speech reveals the power of communication in challenging oppression and shaping perceptions. This power over narrative challenges the patriarchal tendency to control and manipulate information.

Matangi, the goddess of knowledge and learning, underscores the importance of education and intellectual independence for women. Her role as a scholar and teacher empowers women to pursue knowledge and contribute their intellect to society. This representation contrasts sharply with the historical limitations placed on women's access to education and intellectual pursuits. Her mastery of knowledge directly confronts the patriarchal efforts to deny women opportunities to learn and grow.

Kamalatmika, the goddess of creative energy and prosperity, represents the importance of female creativity and economic independence. Her association with abundance highlights the need for women to have control over their own resources and to contribute to economic growth. This counters the historical subjugation of women economically, giving them a powerful symbol of financial empowerment and independence.

The Mahavidyas, therefore, present a powerful counter-narrative to the patriarchal norms that have historically oppressed women. Their fierce independence, challenging iconography, and subversive stories offer a rich tapestry of female empowerment and liberation, demonstrating the diverse ways women can express their strength and agency. Their narratives challenge the dominant patriarchal order, offering hope and inspiration to women striving for equality and liberation. The exploration of the Mahavidyas through a feminist lens not only enriches our understanding of these powerful goddesses but also provides a valuable framework for understanding the ongoing struggle for gender equality and social justice in the modern world. Their symbolism remains potent and relevant, offering inspiration and guidance for those actively working towards a more just and equitable future. Their enduring legacy lies not only in their mythological narratives but in their continued ability to inspire hope, courage, and action in the face of injustice. The ongoing relevance of these goddesses lies in their ability to provide powerful symbolic representations for contemporary struggles towards equity and liberation. They stand as potent symbols for a future where female voices are heard, celebrated, and empowered. Their stories, both ancient and eternally relevant, continue to challenge and inspire us to create a world that truly reflects the power and diversity of the feminine divine.

The Mahavidyas and Environmental Activism

The preceding exploration of the Mahavidyas through a feminist lens reveals their potent symbolism in challenging patriarchal structures and advocating for social justice. However, their influence extends far beyond the realm of human social structures; their power resonates deeply within the ecological sphere, offering a potent framework for understanding and enacting environmental activism and ecological responsibility. The goddesses, with their inherent connection to the natural world and their embodiment of cosmic forces, provide a powerful framework for understanding our interconnectedness with the environment and inspiring a sense of stewardship towards the planet.

Kali, often depicted amidst corpses and wielding a sword, can be interpreted not only as a destroyer of societal ills but also as a symbol of the necessary destruction that precedes regeneration. This destruction can be paralleled with the necessity of confronting unsustainable practices that damage the environment. Her role as a transformative force highlights the urgent need to dismantle environmentally destructive systems and pave the way for ecological renewal. The destruction she embodies is not an end in itself but a catalyst for the emergence of a more sustainable and harmonious relationship between humanity and nature. Her association with time and cyclical processes emphasizes the imperative to act before irreparable damage is done.

Tara, the savior goddess, embodies compassion and protection. Her fierce protection of sentient beings extends beyond humanity to encompass all life forms, emphasizing the interconnectedness of all living creatures and the necessity of protecting the planet's biodiversity. Her role as a protector of the vulnerable resonates strongly with the need to safeguard endangered species and fragile ecosystems. Her association with water further underlines the crucial importance of preserving this vital resource and promoting responsible water management. We can see her as a patron of those working to protect water sources from pollution and depletion.

Tripura Sundari, often associated with beauty and grace, highlights the inherent beauty and value of the natural world. Her association with the aesthetic dimension reminds us of the intrinsic beauty of nature and the importance of appreciating and preserving its aesthetic integrity. Her allure is not superficial; it reflects the profound interconnectedness between the sacred and the natural world. The preservation of natural beauty is not merely an aesthetic concern but a crucial component of ecological responsibility. This understanding highlights the vital role of ecological consciousness in ensuring the preservation of natural beauty.

Bhuvaneshvari, the sovereign ruler of the universe, embodies the responsibility inherent in wielding power over the natural world. Her dominion signifies the ethical imperative of responsible stewardship, highlighting our role as caretakers of the planet and the necessity of exercising our power with respect and wisdom. This is analogous to corporate responsibility within sustainability contexts; just as Bhuvaneshvari governs wisely, corporations and individuals should manage their impact on the environment thoughtfully. This concept promotes sustainability in business and individual decisions, emphasizing the ethical considerations involved in environmental management.

Chhinnamasta, the self-decapitating goddess, offers a radical symbol of self-sacrifice for the greater good. Her act of self-mutilation can be interpreted as a powerful metaphor for the sacrifices we must make to protect the environment. It is a call to action, emphasizing the need to prioritize the well-being of the planet over short-term gains. This extreme act symbolizes the extreme measures that might be necessary to confront environmental challenges. It is a stark reminder of the profound consequences of inaction and the need to make significant changes in our lifestyles and consumption patterns.

Dhumavati, the goddess of widowhood and solitude, represents the desolate state of the environment when it is ravaged by human activity. Her imagery highlights the consequences of environmental degradation and calls for a renewed sense of responsibility and respect for nature. Her seemingly negative attributes represent the harsh realities of unchecked environmental exploitation. She serves as a warning of the potential consequences of neglecting our ecological responsibilities. Her embodiment of the effects of environmental damage illustrates the urgent need for action and sustainable practices.

Bagalamukhi, the goddess of speech, empowers us to speak out against environmental injustices and to advocate for change. Her ability to influence discourse emphasizes the power of communication in raising awareness and mobilizing action for environmental protection. This advocacy extends to challenging environmental destruction and promoting sustainability policies.

Her power of speech underscores the importance of clearly articulating environmental issues and advocating for policies that protect the environment.

Matangi, the goddess of knowledge, underlines the importance of education and scientific understanding in tackling environmental challenges. Her association with wisdom and learning highlights the need for informed decision-making in environmental policy and the value of scientific research in addressing environmental problems.

This emphasizes the critical role of research and education in creating informed environmental policies and effective conservation strategies.

Kamalatmika, the goddess of prosperity, reminds us that environmental protection is not a hindrance to economic progress but rather an integral component of sustainable development. Her association with abundance reveals the potential for economic growth and environmental stewardship to coexist, emphasizing the need for a shift towards sustainable economic models. This
highlights the necessity of integrating environmental concerns into economic planning and development strategies. She challenges the dichotomy between economic growth and ecological responsibility and emphasizes their interconnectedness.

The Mahavidyas, in their totality, provide a powerful symbolic framework for understanding and engaging in environmental activism. Their multifaceted nature allows for diverse interpretations and applications, making them relevant to a wide range of environmental concerns and approaches. They serve as powerful reminders of our interconnectedness with the natural world and inspire a sense of responsibility and stewardship towards the planet. Their symbolism transcends traditional interpretations, offering a contemporary lens through which to view and address the urgent environmental challenges facing humanity. The goddesses are not merely ancient deities; they are potent symbols that can guide us towards a more sustainable and harmonious future, where human actions coexist with the well-being of the planet. Their messages of interconnectedness, responsibility, and transformation are as relevant today as they were centuries ago, offering a path towards a more ecologically conscious and just future. Their enduring legacy lies not only in their rich mythological narratives but also in their potential to inspire a new generation of environmental stewards who are guided by a deeper understanding of our relationship with the natural world and the inherent sacredness of all life.

Harnessing the Mahavidyas for Positive Social Change

The exploration of the Mahavidyas' potential for ecological stewardship naturally extends to their capacity for fostering positive social change. Their potent symbolism, rich mythology, and diverse attributes offer a compelling framework for understanding and addressing a multitude of contemporary social issues. Just as they can inspire environmental activism, their energies can be harnessed to promote social justice, combat inequality, and foster a more compassionate and equitable world. This is not merely a metaphorical application; the principles inherent in their symbolism offer practical strategies for enacting meaningful change.

Kali, the destroyer, represents the necessary dismantling of oppressive systems and outdated social structures that perpetuate inequality. Her role isn't simply about destruction for destruction's sake; it's about the necessary clearing of space for positive growth and transformation. In the context of social justice, Kali's energy can be invoked to dismantle systemic racism, sexism, casteism, and other forms of discrimination that continue to plague societies worldwide. Her fierce energy can empower activists to challenge injustice, confront oppressive norms, and fight for equality. This involves a critical self-reflection on how we ourselves might perpetuate harmful systems and a commitment to actively dismantling those systems. For example, anti-caste movements can draw on Kali's symbolism to symbolize the dismantling of the oppressive caste system and the creation of a more equitable society. Similarly, feminists can utilize Kali's energy as a symbol of challenging patriarchal structures that subordinate women and limit their agency.

Tara, the savior, embodies compassion and protection, extending her care to the most vulnerable members of society. Her energy can be channeled to support marginalized communities, offer protection to victims of injustice, and advocate for the rights of the oppressed. This involves active engagement in initiatives that promote social welfare, provide support to vulnerable populations, and fight for human rights. Her protective aspect finds relevance in movements supporting refugees, advocating for the rights of the LGBTQ+

community, and working against human trafficking. The concept of Tara's compassion extends beyond mere charity; it requires understanding systemic issues that create vulnerability and working towards their eradication. The energy of Tara can empower individuals to become active participants in creating safer and more inclusive communities.

Tripura Sundari, representing beauty and grace, highlights the intrinsic worth and dignity of every individual. Her energy can be used to promote self-love, self-acceptance, and the recognition of inherent worth regardless of social status, background, or perceived differences. This translates into promoting body positivity, challenging beauty standards imposed by media, and working against discrimination based on appearance or perceived flaws.

Tripura Sundari inspires efforts to foster a culture of respect and appreciation for diversity, celebrating the richness and uniqueness of individual identities. This involves promoting inclusive environments in education, workplaces, and social spaces, challenging stereotypes, and fostering mutual respect and understanding.

Bhuvaneshvari, the sovereign ruler, highlights the responsibility inherent in leadership and the importance of using power ethically and justly. Her symbolism is particularly relevant in advocating for good governance, accountability, and transparency in institutions.

This involves promoting ethical leadership, demanding accountability from those in power, and advocating for policies that address systemic inequalities. Her energy can empower individuals to actively participate in democratic processes, hold leaders accountable for their actions, and promote a culture of responsible governance. Bhuvaneshvari's energy resonates strongly with movements advocating for fair elections, transparency in government operations, and the equitable distribution of resources.

Chhinnamasta, the self-decapitating goddess, represents radical self-sacrifice for the greater good. In a social justice context, this can be interpreted as a call to selfless service, empathy, and a willingness to put the needs of others before oneself. This energy inspires acts of altruism, volunteering, and working towards the betterment of society, even at personal cost. Chhinnamasta's symbolism finds relevance in the work of human rights activists, humanitarian aid workers, and individuals who dedicate their lives to serving others in need. Her radical act is a reminder of the transformative power of selflessness and the profound impact that even small acts of kindness can have.

Dhumavati, the goddess of widowhood and solitude, represents the marginalized and those living on the fringes of society. Her energy draws attention to the plight of the forgotten and the need to address the underlying causes of social exclusion. This involves supporting marginalized groups, working to end poverty and homelessness, and creating social safety nets that protect vulnerable populations. Dhumavati's energy fosters empathy and understanding for those who often feel unseen and unheard. It inspires initiatives aimed at providing support and resources to those who have been left behind by society.

Bagalamukhi, the goddess of speech, empowers individuals to speak out against injustice, advocate for change, and challenge oppressive narratives. This involves fostering critical thinking, empowering marginalized voices, and promoting dialogue and understanding.

Her energy inspires activism, advocacy, and the use of communication to raise awareness about social issues and challenge power structures. Bagalamukhi's power finds expression in activism through social media, public speaking, and community organizing.

It empowers individuals to become agents of change, using their voices to amplify the experiences of the marginalized and demand societal transformation.

Matangi, the goddess of knowledge, highlights the importance of education, critical thinking, and informed decision-making in achieving social justice. This involves promoting access to education, fostering critical consciousness, and utilizing knowledge to address social problems. Matangi's energy empowers individuals to become educated and informed agents of change, capable of identifying and challenging social injustices. She inspires a commitment to lifelong learning and the application of knowledge to promote social justice. The power of education and information lies at the heart of Matangi's energy, encouraging critical analysis of societal structures and empowering individuals to contribute to positive transformation.

Kamalatmika, the goddess of prosperity, reminds us that social justice and economic well-being are intrinsically linked. Her energy can be channeled to promote equitable distribution of resources, sustainable development, and economic empowerment for marginalized communities. This involves advocating for fair wages, access to economic opportunities, and initiatives aimed at reducing economic inequality. Kamalatmika challenges the notion of prosperity as benefiting only a select few and promotes a more just and equitable distribution of wealth and resources. Her energy inspires a commitment to sustainable economic models that prioritize social justice and environmental sustainability.

In conclusion, the ten Mahavidyas provide a powerful and multifaceted framework for understanding and enacting positive social change. Their symbolic power transcends traditional interpretations, offering a contemporary lens through which to view and address the urgent social challenges facing humanity. By understanding and harnessing their energies, we can empower ourselves and others to become agents of transformation, working towards a more just, compassionate, and equitable world. Their enduring legacy lies in their capacity to inspire a new generation of social justice advocates who are guided by a deeper understanding of our interconnectedness and the inherent dignity of every human being. Their symbolism, far from being relegated to ancient myth, provides a vibrant and powerful tool for positive social transformation in the twenty-first century and beyond.

Recapitulation of Key Themes

This exploration of the ten Mahavidyas—Kali, Tara, Tripura Sundari, Bhuvaneshvari, Bhairavi, Chhinnamasta, Dhumavati, Bagalamukhi, Matangi, and Kamalatmika—has traversed a rich tapestry of mythology, symbolism, and spiritual practice. We have journeyed through their individual iconography, delving into the nuances of their attributes and the diverse interpretations they inspire across various Hindu traditions, including Shaktism, Saivism, and Vaishnavism, as well as their resonance within Vajrayana Buddhism. This journey wasn't merely an academic exercise; it was an exploration of the potent energies these goddesses represent and how those energies might be harnessed for personal transformation and societal betterment.

The Devi Gita, central to our understanding of the Mahavidyas within the Shaktic tradition, served as a guiding light, illuminating their inherent power and the profound wisdom embedded within their myths. Its verses offered a deeper comprehension of the divine feminine principle, Shakti, and its multifaceted manifestations in the form of these ten powerful goddesses. We saw how their seemingly disparate attributes—from the fierce destruction of Kali to the compassionate embrace of Tara—are ultimately interconnected, reflecting the dynamic and complex nature of the divine. The Devi Gita emphasized the importance of inner transformation, self-realization, and the ultimate surrender to the divine will, a process integral to accessing the transformative potential of the Mahavidyas.

Our investigation extended beyond the confines of traditional interpretations. We explored the profound relevance of the Mahavidyas in the context of Kali Yuga, the current age in the Hindu cyclical time scheme. We considered the unique challenges and opportunities of this era, marked by rapid technological advancements, environmental degradation, and escalating social inequalities. The Mahavidyas, far from being relegated to the realm of ancient myth, emerged as potent symbols offering guidance and inspiration for navigating the complexities of the 21st century. Their energies, when understood and accessed correctly, offer a pathway towards navigating the current challenges, and indeed, flourishing despite them.

The book's exploration consistently emphasized the interconnectedness of the Mahavidyas and their collective ability to represent the full spectrum of the divine feminine. Each goddess, unique in her expression, contributes to a holistic understanding of Shakti, demonstrating the multifaceted nature of divinity and the richness of spiritual experience. This multifaceted nature is critical to understanding their relevance in the modern world. It's not a matter of choosing a single goddess as a personal patron; rather, it's a matter of engaging with the entire pantheon to gain a more profound comprehension of the divine energy at play.

The concept of Shakti, as the dynamic energy of creation, preservation, and destruction, played a crucial role in unifying our understanding of the Mahavidyas. It allowed us to transcend simplistic interpretations of their roles, moving beyond surface-level understanding of their attributes. Shakti's inherent dynamism showcases the transformative potential of life, reminding us that change, even destruction, can be necessary for growth and renewal.

By grasping the concept of Shakti's dynamic nature, we can understand that the seemingly contradictory qualities of the Mahavidyas—for example, Kali's destructive power and Tripura Sundari's grace—represent different facets of a unified whole, mirroring the complexities of the universe itself.

The exploration of the Mahavidyas' connection to environmental consciousness underscored their relevance to pressing global concerns. Their symbolic power transcends the strictly religious; their representation finds expression in the realm of ecological awareness. We explored how their energies can be channeled to inspire environmental stewardship, highlighting the importance of ecological balance and sustainable practices. Kali's destructive power can symbolize the dismantling of harmful environmental practices; Tara's compassion can inspire protective measures for endangered species and ecosystems; and Kamalatmika's prosperity can signify the sustainable development necessary for a thriving planet. Their symbolism offered a framework for understanding the profound interconnectedness between the divine, humanity, and the natural world.

Furthermore, the potency of the Mahavidyas lies in their capacity to facilitate personal transformation. Their energies, when tapped into through appropriate meditative practices and mindful engagement, can empower individuals to overcome personal limitations, cultivate inner strength, and achieve self-realization. This is not a passive process; it involves active participation, self-reflection, and a conscious effort to connect with the divine feminine energy within. This journey of self-discovery is unique to each individual, shaped by their experiences and aspirations, however the Mahavidyas provide a guidepost on this transformative journey.

The inherent wisdom of the Mahavidyas is not limited to individual transformation; it extends to societal well-being. Their symbolism acts as a potent tool for social justice, offering a framework for addressing a broad range of contemporary issues, including inequality, discrimination, and social injustice. We examined how the attributes of each Mahavidya can be invoked to inspire positive social change, from Kali's challenge to oppressive systems to Tara's compassion for the vulnerable. Each goddess's inherent strength serves as a potent symbol and a driving force towards positive change in a world desperately seeking transformative action.

Our exploration of the Mahavidyas underscores their continued relevance in the 21st century and beyond. Their enduring power lies not just in their rich mythology and symbolic representation but also in their capacity to inspire and empower individuals to effect meaningful change in their lives and in the world around them. The Mahavidyas are not static entities; their energies are dynamic, adaptable, and eternally relevant to the human condition. Their symbolic resonance continues to reverberate, offering a profound and transformative message for individuals and societies alike.

In conclusion, the journey through the ten Mahavidyas has been one of discovery, illuminating the profound wisdom and enduring relevance of these powerful goddesses. Their symbolism and mythology offer a rich tapestry of meaning, providing a pathway towards personal transformation, social justice, and ecological awareness. They are not merely deities of the past; they are potent energies that can be accessed and harnessed in the present, empowering us to navigate the complexities of the modern world and to strive towards a future marked by compassion, justice, and sustainability. The enduring legacy of the Mahavidyas lies in their capacity to inspire, to empower, and ultimately, to transform. Their wisdom continues to resonate, guiding us towards a deeper understanding of ourselves, our world, and the divine energy that permeates all of existence. The exploration of their attributes is not simply an academic pursuit; it is a journey of self-discovery and a pathway to a more meaningful and fulfilling life. The message of the Mahavidyas is a timeless one – a call to embrace the power within, to cultivate compassion, and to work towards a world where justice, peace, and sustainability prevail. Their enduring legacy will inspire future generations to engage in the transformative power of the divine feminine, shaping a world marked by hope, compassion, and meaningful action. The study of the Mahavidyas is, therefore, not just a study of mythology; it is an invitation to a profound personal and societal transformation.

The Enduring Relevance of the Mahavidyas

The enduring relevance of the Mahavidyas extends far beyond the confines of ancient scriptures and ritualistic practices. Their power lies in their adaptability, their capacity to resonate with the human condition across millennia, and their ability to offer guidance in navigating the complexities of the modern world. While their origins are rooted in ancient traditions, their messages remain strikingly pertinent to the challenges and opportunities of the 21st century. The rapid pace of technological advancement, the escalating environmental crisis, and the persistent inequalities within societies all present unique challenges that demand innovative solutions and profound shifts in consciousness. It is within this context that the Mahavidyas offer a compelling framework for understanding and addressing these issues.

Their enduring power stems from their multifaceted nature. They are not monolithic entities; rather, they represent a spectrum of divine energies, each embodying different aspects of Shakti, the dynamic creative force of the universe. This spectrum encompasses both the destructive and the creative, the fierce and the compassionate, the assertive and the receptive. This inherent duality mirrors the complexities of life itself, acknowledging the necessary interplay between opposing forces. Kali, the fierce goddess of destruction, while often misunderstood, symbolizes the necessary dismantling of outdated structures and harmful patterns, paving the way for renewal and transformation. Her energy is not solely about violence; it's about cutting away the superfluous, allowing space for growth and rebirth. This resonates deeply in our current era, where outdated systems and harmful ideologies require dismantling to make way for a more just and sustainable future.

Similarly, Tara, the compassionate goddess of liberation, offers a powerful message of empathy and resilience in the face of suffering. Her energy, characterized by compassion and unwavering support, provides a crucial counterpoint to Kali's fierce energy, highlighting the importance of balance. In a world grappling with immense suffering – from poverty and disease to conflict and environmental degradation – Tara's compassion becomes a vital source of strength and inspiration. Her unwavering presence reminds us of the importance of extending kindness and support to those who are struggling, fostering a sense of community and solidarity.

Tripura Sundari, the goddess of beauty and bliss, represents the inherent joy and creativity present within the universe. Her energy reminds us to appreciate the beauty surrounding us, to cultivate joy in our lives, and to nurture our creative potential. In a world often consumed by negativity and strife, Tripura Sundari's energy offers a vital counterbalance, reminding us of the importance of cultivating joy, appreciating beauty, and finding fulfillment in our lives. This is particularly crucial in our current technological age, where we risk losing touch with the natural world and the simple pleasures that contribute to a well-rounded and meaningful life.

Bhuvaneshvari, the goddess of the universe, embodies the underlying unity and interconnectedness of all things. Her energy serves as a reminder of our place within the larger cosmic order, emphasizing the importance of harmony and balance in our relationship with the environment and with each other. In a time marked by globalization and a growing awareness of global interconnectedness, Bhuvaneshvari's message is particularly timely.

It calls for a shift towards a more holistic worldview, one that recognizes the intricate web of relationships connecting all living beings and encourages a sense of collective responsibility for the well-being of the planet.

Bhairavi, the fierce and powerful goddess of transformative energy, embodies the strength and resilience needed to overcome challenges and obstacles. Her energy encourages us to confront our fears and insecurities, to embrace change, and to persevere in the face of adversity. In a world facing numerous challenges, from political turmoil to personal struggles, Bhairavi's strength offers a powerful message of empowerment and perseverance. Her energy inspires us to confront our limitations, to step outside our comfort zones, and to navigate challenges with courage and determination.

Chhinnamasta, the self-decapitated goddess, symbolizes the radical act of self-sacrifice and the ultimate surrender to the divine will. Her image, though unsettling to some, is a powerful symbol of self-transcendence and the letting go of ego-driven desires. In our consumer-driven society, this message of detachment from material pursuits and ego-driven ambitions offers a pathway towards genuine fulfillment. The act of self-sacrifice, interpreted not as physical self-harm, but as the relinquishing of attachments that hinder spiritual growth, provides a path towards liberation and inner peace.

Dhumavati, the goddess of widowhood and adversity, represents the acceptance of difficult circumstances and the resilience required to navigate them. Her energy highlights the importance of facing our challenges with courage and acceptance, finding strength in adversity, and transforming hardship into opportunities for growth.

In a world where we often strive to avoid suffering, Dhumavati's message offers a profound lesson in resilience and acceptance. Her energy reminds us that challenges and hardships are inevitable aspects of life, and that it is through navigating these difficulties that we discover our inner strength and resilience.

Bagalamukhi, the goddess of speech and control, symbolizes the power of communication and the ability to harness our thoughts and words for constructive purposes. Her energy emphasizes the importance of mindful communication, the careful selection of words, and the responsibility we bear for the impact of our speech.

In a world increasingly driven by social media and rapid-fire communication, Bagalamukhi's message of mindful speech is particularly timely. Her energy encourages us to harness the power of our words, to communicate with intention, and to use our voices for positive change.

Matangi, the goddess of knowledge and learning, embodies the pursuit of wisdom and the transformative power of education. Her energy inspires us to cultivate intellectual curiosity, to expand our knowledge, and to utilize our learning to benefit ourselves and society. In an increasingly complex and information-rich world, Matangi's message emphasizes the importance of lifelong learning and critical thinking. Her energy encourages us to seek knowledge, not merely for personal gain, but to improve our understanding of the world and to contribute to the collective good.

Finally, Kamalatmika, the goddess of prosperity and abundance, reminds us of the importance of appreciating the blessings in our lives and cultivating gratitude. Her energy inspires us to manifest our desires ethically and responsibly, acknowledging our interconnectedness with others and the natural world. In a society often fixated on material acquisition, Kamalatmika's energy serves as a reminder to appreciate what we have, to cultivate gratitude, and to strive for a more sustainable and equitable distribution of resources.

The Mahavidyas, therefore, are not simply historical figures or mythological entities. They are dynamic forces, vibrant expressions of the divine feminine, offering potent pathways towards self-realization, societal transformation, and environmental stewardship.

Their enduring relevance lies in their capacity to inspire, to challenge, and to empower individuals to navigate the complexities of the modern world and strive for a future where compassion, justice, and sustainability prevail. Their messages continue to resonate, offering guidance and inspiration for creating a world characterized by harmony, balance, and spiritual fulfillment. The study of the Mahavidyas is not a mere academic exercise; it is a journey of self-discovery, a pathway toward a richer, more meaningful existence, and a contribution towards building a better future for all beings. Their wisdom, deeply rooted in ancient traditions, offers a beacon of hope and guidance in navigating the turbulent waters of the 21st century and beyond. They are a testament to the enduring power of the divine feminine and its capacity to inspire transformative change in individuals and societies alike. The continued exploration and application of their wisdom remains a vital endeavor for fostering personal growth and societal progress.

Future Directions for Research

The exploration of the Mahavidyas, undertaken in this book, provides a foundation upon which future research can build. The multifaceted nature of these goddesses, their complex symbolism, and their enduring relevance in the contemporary world offer a rich tapestry of potential avenues for scholarly investigation. Several key areas stand out as particularly promising for future research endeavors.

Firstly, a more in-depth comparative analysis of the Mahavidyas across different Tantric traditions is warranted. While this book has touched upon the variations in their iconography and interpretations across Shaktism, Saivism, Vaishnavism, and Vajrayana Buddhism, a more nuanced comparison, incorporating regional variations and specific lineages within each tradition, would provide a deeper understanding of their evolving interpretations and practices. This could involve examining manuscripts, ritual texts, and artwork from various geographical regions and historical periods to trace the evolution of their symbolism and practices. Such an undertaking could illuminate the dynamic interplay between regional cultural practices and the overarching themes represented by the Mahavidyas. This comparative approach would necessitate a rigorous examination of primary source materials, potentially involving the translation and analysis of texts currently unavailable in English or other widely accessible languages.

Secondly, the role of the Mahavidyas in specific Tantric rituals and practices deserves further exploration. While some aspects of their ritualistic invocation have been discussed, a detailed examination of the specific mantras, yantras, and sadhanas associated with each Mahavidya could shed light on their practical application and their efficacy in spiritual development. This requires not just a textual analysis but also an engagement with practitioners and a careful study of the nuances of ritual performance. Ethnographic research, involving fieldwork and participation observation, could provide invaluable insights into the lived experience of practitioners and their understanding of the Mahavidyas. This research would need to be conducted sensitively and ethically, respecting the sacred nature of these practices and the beliefs of the practitioners involved. The ethical considerations surrounding the study of esoteric practices cannot be overstated and require meticulous planning and execution.

Thirdly, the potential for interdisciplinary approaches to the study of the Mahavidyas holds significant promise. The integration of perspectives from fields such as psychology, sociology, and gender studies could offer new insights into their symbolism and their relevance to contemporary issues. For instance, a psychological analysis could explore the archetypal significance of the Mahavidyas, examining how their attributes resonate with different aspects of the human psyche. A sociological study could investigate the role of the Mahavidyas in shaping social structures and power dynamics, particularly in relation to the divine feminine. Similarly, a gender studies perspective could provide a critical examination of the ways in which the Mahavidyas have been interpreted and utilized in relation to gender roles and expectations. Such interdisciplinary collaborations would enrich the understanding of the Mahavidyas, broadening their scope and enhancing their relevance to a wider audience.

Furthermore, the contemporary relevance of the Mahavidyas in addressing specific social and environmental issues warrants further investigation. This book has touched upon their potential in promoting sustainability, social justice, and personal transformation; however, a more systematic study of their application to specific challenges – such as climate change, poverty, or violence – would be beneficial. This could involve examining how the principles embodied by the Mahavidyas – such as compassion, resilience, and transformation – can be applied to develop practical strategies for addressing these issues. This research could involve collaborations with social workers, activists, and community leaders, exploring the practical application of the Mahavidyas' wisdom in contemporary contexts. The potential of the Mahavidyas as a source of inspiration and guidance for social change requires further exploration and practical application.

Another significant area for future research lies in the exploration of the artistic representations of the Mahavidyas. A detailed study of their iconography across different periods and styles, analyzing their symbolism and the evolution of their visual representations, could provide valuable insights into their changing interpretations and cultural significance. This would necessitate the analysis of a vast range of art forms, including sculptures, paintings, and even contemporary interpretations. A thorough analysis would explore the evolution of iconographic details across regions and time periods, exploring how these changes reflect shifts in cultural and religious beliefs and practices. A comprehensive catalogue of different Mahavidya representations and their contextual analysis would be a significant contribution to the field.

Moreover, the study of the literary and poetic traditions surrounding the Mahavidyas provides another fertile ground for future research. The analysis of devotional poetry, hymns, and stories associated with each Mahavidya could provide a deeper understanding of their individual personalities, attributes, and their significance within the broader context of Hindu religious thought. This would involve examining a wide range of texts, including both canonical and non-canonical sources, to gain a comprehensive understanding of the rich literary tradition surrounding these goddesses. A close reading of these texts, considering their historical and cultural context, would offer valuable insights into their symbolism and the different ways they have been understood and experienced through the ages.

Finally, exploring the connections between the Mahavidyas and other goddesses within the Hindu pantheon could lead to significant breakthroughs. Analyzing the relationships, overlaps, and distinctions between the Mahavidyas and other powerful goddesses could provide a more comprehensive understanding of the divine feminine in Hindu cosmology and its multifaceted expressions. This comparative study would require a deep understanding of the broader Hindu pantheon and the intricate web of relationships between different deities. The identification of shared attributes, common themes, and divergent interpretations could illuminate the rich complexity of Hindu mythology and religious thought. Such research could provide a more holistic understanding of the divine feminine, positioning the Mahavidyas within a wider cosmological context.

In conclusion, the study of the Mahavidyas offers a vast and exciting field for future research. The multifaceted nature of these goddesses, their complex symbolism, and their enduring relevance in the contemporary world present numerous opportunities for scholarly inquiry. By employing interdisciplinary approaches, engaging with practitioners, and exploring the rich tapestry of textual and artistic representations, future research can deepen our understanding of these powerful deities and their significance in shaping individual lives and societal transformations. The ongoing exploration of the Mahavidyas is not simply an academic pursuit; it is a journey of spiritual discovery and a contribution towards a deeper understanding of the divine feminine and its enduring power. The potential for future scholarship is immense, promising a richer and more nuanced appreciation of these powerful goddesses and their continuing relevance in the 21st century and beyond.

Practical Applications and Personal Reflections

Embracing the wisdom of the Mahavidyas is not merely an academic exercise; it is a transformative journey of self-discovery and spiritual growth. The insights gleaned from studying their multifaceted nature extend far beyond the theoretical, offering practical applications for navigating the complexities of modern life and fostering positive change within ourselves and the world around us. This concluding section explores ways to integrate the potent energy and wisdom of each Mahavidya into our daily lives, reflecting on personal experiences and the potential for societal impact.

One practical application lies in understanding the power of intention. Each Mahavidya embodies specific qualities – Kali's transformative power, Tara's compassionate guidance, Tripura Sundari's radiant beauty, and so on. By consciously aligning our intentions with the attributes of a particular Mahavidya, we can harness their energy to support our goals. For example, if we are facing a period of significant transformation, invoking Kali's energy can provide the strength and courage needed to embrace change and overcome obstacles. This isn't about blind faith, but about consciously choosing to channel a specific energetic resonance to aid in our personal development. It's about understanding the subtle energies at play and using them to our advantage. This conscious invocation doesn't necessitate elaborate rituals; a simple affirmation, a meditative focus on the deity's imagery, or even a mindful reflection on their attributes can be profoundly effective.

The Mahavidyas can also serve as powerful guides for ethical decision-making. Dhumavati, despite her often-misunderstood image, embodies the power of detachment and acceptance of impermanence. In a world often driven by relentless ambition and material desires, her wisdom offers a much-needed counterpoint. Learning to detach from outcomes, to accept the inevitable ebb and flow of life, is crucial for navigating challenges and maintaining inner peace. Similarly, Bagalamukhi's energy can assist in overcoming negativity and manipulation, helping us discern truth from falsehood and navigate complex social situations with greater clarity and self-protection. By reflecting on their attributes in times of ethical dilemma, we can access a deeper wellspring of wisdom to guide our choices.

Furthermore, the Mahavidyas can serve as potent allies in personal growth and spiritual evolution. Each goddess presents a unique path to self-realization, mirroring different facets of the human experience. Tripura Sundari, for instance, exemplifies the beauty and grace of the divine feminine, reminding us of the importance of cultivating inner peace and harmony. Her energy can be especially helpful in overcoming self-doubt and cultivating self-love.

Bhairavi's fierce energy, on the other hand, can empower us to break free from limiting beliefs and self-imposed restrictions, fostering resilience and strength in the face of adversity. By consciously engaging with their energies through meditation, mantra recitation, or artistic expression, we can accelerate our personal transformation.

The integration of Mahavidya wisdom extends beyond the individual, offering valuable insights for fostering positive social impact. The qualities embodied by these goddesses – compassion, courage, wisdom, and transformation – are crucial for addressing the challenges facing our world today. Kali's transformative power, for instance, can inspire us to actively participate in dismantling unjust systems and creating a more equitable society. Tara's compassionate energy can guide our efforts to alleviate suffering and promote social justice. The collective power of the Mahavidyas can serve as a source of inspiration and guidance for social change.

One practical approach to this is through community engagement. Organizing events centered around the Mahavidyas, such as workshops, retreats, or group meditations, can create spaces for collective empowerment and shared spiritual growth. This could involve integrating the principles of the Mahavidyas into social activism, using their energy to amplify our efforts to create positive change. For example, a project focused on environmental sustainability could draw inspiration from Bhuvaneshvari's nurturing energy, fostering a sense of interconnectedness and responsibility towards the planet. Similarly, initiatives promoting social justice could invoke the fierce protective energy of

Bagalamukhi to counter oppression and injustice.

However, it's crucial to approach this with a sense of reverence and respect. The Mahavidyas are not merely tools to be manipulated; they are powerful forces that demand mindful engagement. Before attempting any form of active invocation or ritual practice, it is essential to seek guidance from experienced practitioners or teachers well-versed in Tantric traditions. This is not a process to be undertaken lightly. Respectful study and a commitment to ethical practice are paramount.

The exploration of the Mahavidyas is a lifelong journey, a path of continuous learning and self-discovery. The insights shared in this book are just a starting point, a foundation upon which to build a deeper understanding of these powerful goddesses and their relevance to our lives. Through consistent reflection, meditation, and mindful engagement with their energies, we can unlock their transformative potential and integrate their wisdom into the fabric of our daily lives, ultimately fostering personal growth, spiritual evolution, and positive change in the world. The power of the Mahavidyas is not just a concept; it's a living, breathing energy that awaits our conscious engagement.

The ongoing conversation surrounding the Mahavidyas is enriched by personal reflections and shared experiences. The personal impact of engaging with these powerful goddesses is profound and varies widely based on individual beliefs, practices, and life experiences.
For some, it may manifest as a heightened sense of intuition and clarity, a greater understanding of one's own inner strength, or a renewed sense of purpose and direction in life. For others, it may involve significant life changes, shifts in perspective, or a deepening of their spiritual practice.

Sharing personal reflections and experiences within a supportive community can further enrich the understanding and application of the Mahavidyas. Creating safe and respectful spaces for open dialogue about personal journeys and challenges can foster a sense of collective empowerment and inspire others to embark on their own exploration. This shared experience can deepen the collective understanding of these powerful goddesses and their transformative potential. It is through the weaving together of personal narratives and academic understanding that a truly holistic and meaningful engagement with the Mahavidyas becomes possible.

The study of the Mahavidyas is not a destination but a journey. It is a path of continuous exploration, of deepening understanding, and of personal transformation. As we continue to learn and grow, our understanding of these powerful goddesses will evolve, expanding our capacity to engage with their energy and utilize their wisdom to create positive change in our lives and the world around us. This ongoing exploration is crucial not only for the continued study of the Mahavidyas but also for the personal and collective growth of those who engage with their profound wisdom. The Mahavidyas stand as a testament to the enduring power of the divine feminine, offering guidance and empowerment for navigating the complexities of life and creating a more just and compassionate world. Their relevance extends beyond religious dogma, offering a framework for personal transformation and societal progress. The journey of understanding and integrating their energy is a lifelong commitment to self-discovery and positive change.

A Final Contemplation on Divine Feminine Power

The enduring power of the Mahavidyas transcends the confines of religious dogma, extending its influence into the very fabric of human experience. Their significance lies not merely in their mythological narratives or intricate iconography, but in their capacity to inspire, transform, and empower individuals and communities across time and cultures. To truly grasp their impact, we must move beyond superficial interpretations and delve into the deeper, archetypal energies they represent. Each Mahavidya embodies a specific facet of the divine feminine, a potent force capable of both destruction and creation, of both fierce protection and boundless compassion. Their combined energies offer a holistic approach to navigating the complexities of life, providing a framework for personal growth and societal progress.

The transformative power of Kali, for instance, is not simply about destruction and chaos; it is about the necessary dismantling of old structures and beliefs that no longer serve us. It is the courageous embrace of change, the willingness to let go of what hinders our growth, and the unwavering commitment to forging new paths. Her fierce energy serves as a potent catalyst for personal transformation, urging us to confront our deepest fears and insecurities, to shed our limiting beliefs, and to embrace the unknown with unwavering courage. This resonates deeply in the modern era, where constant change and upheaval are the norm, requiring us to adapt and evolve with agility and resilience. Kali's energy empowers us to navigate these challenges, not with fear, but with a fierce determination to create our own destiny.

Tara's compassionate guidance offers a counterpoint to Kali's fierce energy. She embodies the nurturing aspect of the divine feminine, providing solace, comfort, and unwavering support during times of hardship and uncertainty. In a world often characterized by isolation and alienation, her presence offers a beacon of hope, reminding us that we are not alone in our struggles. Her compassionate gaze invites us to cultivate empathy and understanding, to extend our compassion to ourselves and others, and to work towards alleviating suffering in the world. This compassionate energy is particularly vital in addressing the growing social injustices and inequalities that plague our societies. Tara's wisdom inspires us to act with kindness, to seek justice for the marginalized, and to work towards creating a more equitable and compassionate world.

Tripura Sundari, the radiant embodiment of beauty and grace, reminds us of the importance of cultivating inner peace and harmony. Her energy encourages us to appreciate the beauty that surrounds us, both in the external world and within ourselves. She invites us to cultivate self-love, to embrace our unique strengths and vulnerabilities, and to recognize the inherent beauty within each of us. In a world obsessed with superficiality and external validation, Tripura Sundari's energy serves as a powerful antidote, urging us to cultivate inner beauty and radiate it outward. Her presence reminds us of the profound connection between inner peace and outer radiance.

The wisdom of the other Mahavidyas, each with their unique attributes and energies, contributes to this holistic framework for personal and societal transformation. Bhuvaneshvari's nurturing energy fosters a sense of interconnectedness and responsibility towards the planet and its inhabitants. Bhairavi's fierce energy empowers us to break free from limiting beliefs and self-imposed restrictions, fostering resilience and strength in the face of adversity. Chhinnamasta's willingness to sacrifice herself for the greater good reminds us of the importance of selfless service and dedication to a higher purpose. Dhumavati's acceptance of impermanence and detachment from worldly desires provides a valuable perspective for navigating life's challenges. Bagalamukhi's protective energy shields us from negativity and manipulation, empowering us to discern truth from falsehood. Finally, Matangi's creative energy inspires us to express ourselves authentically and to share our gifts with the world, while Kamalatmika's energy fosters abundance and prosperity, reminding us of the importance of gratitude and appreciation for the blessings in our lives.

The collective wisdom of the Mahavidyas provides a potent framework for navigating the complexities of the modern world. Their energies offer guidance and support in personal growth, spiritual development, and social engagement. By consciously engaging with their energies through meditation, mantra recitation, yantra worship, or artistic expression, we can harness their transformative potential to create positive change in our lives and the world around us. This requires not only a theoretical understanding but also a mindful and respectful engagement with their profound power.

A final contemplation on the power of the divine feminine as embodied in the Mahavidyas leads to a profound appreciation of the interconnectedness between individual transformation and societal progress. The qualities embodied by these goddesses –compassion, courage, wisdom, transformation, and resilience – are not simply abstract concepts; they are vital energies that can be harnessed to address the many challenges facing our world today. By cultivating these qualities within ourselves, we contribute to the creation of a more just, equitable, and compassionate society. The Mahavidyas serve as potent reminders of the transformative power that lies within each of us, urging us to embrace our full potential and to work towards creating a world that reflects the beauty and grace of the divine feminine.

The journey of understanding and integrating the wisdom of the Mahavidyas is a lifelong process of self-discovery and spiritual growth. It requires a commitment to consistent reflection, meditation, mindful engagement with their energies, and a willingness to embrace both the light and shadow aspects of the divine feminine. The insights shared in this book serve as a foundation for this journey, a starting point for deeper exploration and personal transformation. As we continue to learn and grow, our understanding of these powerful goddesses will evolve, expanding our capacity to engage with their energy and utilize their wisdom to create positive change in our lives and the world around us. The Mahavidyas stand as a testament to the enduring power of the divine feminine, offering guidance and empowerment for
navigating the complexities of life and creating a more just and compassionate world. Their relevance extends beyond religious dogma, offering a framework for personal transformation and societal progress. The journey of understanding and integrating their energy is a lifelong commitment to self-discovery and positive

change. It is a journey of continuous learning, growth, and a deepening connection with the divine feminine within and without.

The exploration of the Mahavidyas is not merely an academic exercise; it is a transformative journey of self-discovery and spiritual evolution that holds the potential for profound personal and societal impact. This journey requires not only intellectual understanding but also a sincere commitment to ethical practice, respectful engagement, and a deep reverence for the profound power of the divine feminine. Only through this mindful engagement can we truly unlock the transformative potential of the Mahavidyas and integrate their wisdom into the fabric of our lives.

The power of the Mahavidyas is not just a concept, it is a living, breathing energy waiting to be awakened within us.

Acknowledgments

This book would not have been possible without the support and guidance of numerous individuals. I extend my gratitude to my family and friends for their unwavering support and encouragement during the challenging yet rewarding journey of writing this book. Their love and understanding sustained me throughout.

Appendix A

Appendix A: Detailed Iconography of the Ten Mahavidyas – This section includes detailed descriptions and illustrations of the iconography associated with each Mahavidya, drawing from various sources including ancient texts, temple sculptures, and artwork.

Kali

Iconography: Kali is often depicted as a fierce, dark-complexioned goddess with four arms. She stands on the prostrate body of Shiva, her consort. She wears a garland of skulls and a skirt made of severed human hands. Her tongue is usually protruding, symbolizing her ecstatic nature and the consumption of ego and ignorance. She holds a sword, a trident, a skull, and a khaṭvāṅga (a club topped with a skull). **Symbolism:** Kali represents the power over death and destruction, the cyclical nature of life and death, and the ultimate liberation from the cycle of rebirth.

Tara

Iconography: Tara is depicted with serene and compassionate features, often seated on a lotus. She has a blue or green complexion and is adorned with jewelry and a crown. She holds a lotus, a sword, a bow, and an arrow. **Symbolism:** Tara embodies protection, guidance, and the nurturing aspect of the divine feminine. She is often associated with the ability to navigate perilous situations and offer solace.

Tripura Sundari

Iconography: Tripura Sundari is portrayed as a beautiful, radiant goddess, often depicted as a young woman with exquisite features. She is adorned with fine garments and jewelry, and her complexion is often red or golden. She holds a noose, a goad, a sugarcane bow, and five arrows made of flowers. **Symbolism:** Tripura Sundari represents beauty, grace, and the ultimate bliss of realizing one's true nature. She embodies the alluring and captivating aspect of the divine feminine.

Bhuvaneshvari

Iconography: Bhuvaneshvari is depicted seated on a lotus throne, radiating regal serenity. She has a golden complexion and is adorned with jewelry and fine garments. She holds a noose, a goad, and sometimes a lotus. **Symbolism:** Bhuvaneshvari represents the expansive and nurturing energy of the universe. She embodies balance, harmony, and the interconnectedness of all things.

Bhairavi

Iconography: Bhairavi is depicted as a fierce goddess with a golden or reddish complexion. She is adorned with jewelry and fine garments, and she holds a sword, a trident, and a skull-topped staff. She is sometimes depicted riding a lion or a tiger. **Symbolism:** Bhairavi represents the transformative power of destruction and regeneration. She embodies the ability to overcome obstacles and transcend limitations.

Chhinnamasta

Iconography: Chhinnamasta is depicted as a self-decapitated goddess, holding her severed head in one hand and a sword in the other. Blood flows from her neck, feeding two attendants and herself. She stands on a copulating couple. **Symbolism:** Chhinnamasta represents the transcendence of ego and attachments. She embodies the radical and intense energy of self-sacrifice and transformation.

Dhumavati

Iconography: Dhumavati is depicted as an old, widowed goddess, draped in tattered clothes. She has a somber expression and is often shown riding a chariot pulled by crows. She holds a winnowing basket. **Symbolism:** Dhumavati represents the acceptance of impermanence and the ability to find strength in adversity. She embodies the somber and challenging aspects of life.

Bagalamukhi

Iconography: Bagalamukhi is depicted as a golden-yellow goddess, holding a club and the tongue of an enemy. She is often shown seated on a throne or a lotus. **Symbolism:** Bagalamukhi represents the power to immobilize negative forces and gain control over negative thoughts and emotions. She embodies the protective and controlling aspect of the divine feminine.

Matangi

Iconography: Matangi is depicted as a dark-complexioned goddess, adorned with flowers and holding a veena (a musical instrument). She is often shown seated on a lotus. **Symbolism:** Matangi represents wisdom, learning, and creativity. She embodies the intellectual and artistic aspects of the divine feminine.

Kamalatmika

Iconography: Kamalatmika is depicted as a golden goddess, seated on a lotus and surrounded by wealth and abundance. She holds lotuses in her hands and is adorned with jewelry. **Symbolism:** Kamalatmika represents prosperity, abundance, and fulfillment. She embodies the nurturing and fulfilling aspects of the divine feminine.

I hope this detailed iconography helps you understand the rich symbolism and diverse representations of the ten Mahavidyas.

Appendix B

Appendix B: Mantra Recitation and Practices – This appendix provides a guided approach to mantra recitation and meditation practices associated with each Mahavidya, emphasizing the importance of respectful and mindful engagement. It also includes cautions and guidance for those new to Tantric practices.

Kali

Mantra: "Om Krim Kalikayai Namah" **Meditation Practice:** Visualize Kali in her fierce form, standing on the prostrate body of Shiva. Focus on her dark complexion, her garland of skulls, and her weapons. Chant her mantra with devotion, feeling her transformative power dismantling your fears and obstacles. **Cautions:** Kali's energy is intense and transformative. Beginners should approach her with respect and be prepared for deep inner work.

Tara

Mantra: "Om Tare Tuttare Ture Swaha" **Meditation Practice:** Visualize Tara in her serene form, seated on a lotus. Focus on her compassionate gaze and her protective energy. Chant her mantra, feeling her presence guiding you through difficulties and offering protection. **Cautions:** Tara's energy is nurturing and protective, but it's important to maintain a sincere and respectful attitude during practice.

Tripura Sundari

Mantra: "Om Aim Hreem Shreem Tripura Sundariyai Namah" **Meditation Practice:** Visualize Tripura Sundari as a beautiful, radiant goddess, embodying the ultimate beauty and grace. Focus on her youthful appearance and her divine ornaments. Chant her mantra, feeling her energy enhancing your inner beauty and spiritual awareness. **Cautions:** Tripura Sundari's energy is subtle and refined. Approach her with a sense of reverence and appreciation for her divine beauty.

Bhuvaneshvari

Mantra: "Om Hreem Bhuvaneshvaryai Namah" **Meditation Practice:** Visualize Bhuvaneshvari seated on a lotus throne, radiating regal serenity. Focus on her golden complexion and her serene expression. Chant her mantra, feeling her energy bringing balance and harmony to your life. **Cautions:** Bhuvaneshvari's energy is expansive and nurturing. Approach her with a sense of gratitude and openness to her guidance.

Bhairavi

Mantra: "Om Bhairavi Bhavani Namah" **Meditation Practice:** Visualize Bhairavi in her fierce form, holding weapons and surrounded by flames. Focus on her intense gaze and her powerful presence. Chant her mantra, feeling her energy burning away impurities and obstacles. **Cautions:** Bhairavi's energy is fierce and transformative. Approach her with respect and be prepared for deep inner work.

Chhinnamasta

Mantra: "Om Shreem Hreem Kleem Aim Vajravairochaniye Hum Hum Phat Swaha" **Meditation Practice:** Visualize Chhinnamasta as a self-decapitated goddess, holding her severed head in one hand and a sword in the other. Focus on her fierce expression and the blood flowing from her neck. Chant her mantra, feeling her energy helping you transcend ego and attachments. **Cautions:** Chhinnamasta's energy is intense and radical. Approach her with caution and be prepared for profound inner transformation.

Dhumavati

Mantra: "Om Dhum Dhum Dhumavati Thah Thah" **Meditation Practice:** Visualize Dhumavati as an old, widowed goddess, draped in tattered clothes. Focus on her somber expression and her association with desolation. Chant her mantra, feeling her energy helping you accept impermanence and find strength in adversity. **Cautions:** Dhumavati's energy is somber and challenging. Approach her with respect and be prepared for deep inner reflection.

Bagalamukhi

Mantra: "Om Hreem Bagalamukhi Sarvadushtanam Vacham Mukham Padam Stambhaya Jivham Kilaya Buddhi Vinashaya Hreem Om Swaha" **Meditation Practice:** Visualize Bagalamukhi as a golden-yellow goddess, holding a club and a tongue of an enemy. Focus on her powerful presence and her ability to immobilize negative forces. Chant her mantra, feeling her energy helping you gain control over negative thoughts and emotions. **Cautions:** Bagalamukhi's energy is powerful and controlling. Approach her with respect and be mindful of your intentions.

Matangi

Mantra: "Om Hreem Aim Shreem Namo Bhagavati Ucchishtha Chandalini Matangeshwari Sarvajanavashankari Swaha" **Meditation Practice:** Visualize Matangi as a dark-complexioned goddess, adorned with flowers and holding a veena. Focus on her serene expression and her association with wisdom and learning. Chant her mantra, feeling her energy enhancing your creativity and intellectual abilities. **Cautions:** Matangi's energy is creative and intellectual. Approach her with respect and a sincere desire for knowledge and wisdom.

Kamalatmika

Mantra: "Om Shreem Hreem Kleem Kamalatmikayai Namah" **Meditation Practice:** Visualize Kamalatmika as a golden goddess, seated on a lotus and surrounded by wealth and abundance. Focus on her radiant beauty and her association with prosperity. Chant her mantra, feeling her energy bringing abundance and fulfillment into your life. **Cautions:** Kamalatmika's energy is abundant and fulfilling. Approach her with gratitude and a sense of responsibility for the blessings you receive.

General Guidance for Tantric Practices

1. **Respect and Mindfulness:** Always approach these practices with a sense of respect and mindfulness. The Mahavidyas are powerful deities, and their energy should be engaged with reverence.
2. **Proper Guidance:** If you are new to Tantric practices, seek guidance from a knowledgeable teacher or practitioner. Proper guidance ensures that you perform the practices correctly and safely.
3. **Consistency:** Consistency is key in Tantric practices. Regular practice helps to build a strong connection with the deity and enhances the effectiveness of the practices.
4. **Inner Purity:** Maintain inner purity and sincerity in your practice. The effectiveness of the practices depends on your devotion and the purity of your intentions.
5. **Cautions:** Be aware of the intense and transformative nature of these practices. They can bring about profound changes in your life, so be prepared for deep inner work and transformation.

Appendix C

Appendix C: Yantra Designs – This section offers simplified representations of the yantras associated with the Ten Mahavidyas, accompanied by brief explanations of their symbolic significance. (Note: This is not a substitute for authentic instruction from a qualified Guru.)

Kali Yantra

Design: A central point surrounded by eight petals and enclosed within a circle. **Symbolic Significance:** Represents the transformative power of Kali, her ability to dismantle fears and obstacles, and the cyclical nature of life and death.

Tara Yantra

Design: A central triangle surrounded by ten petals and enclosed within a circle. **Symbolic Significance:** Symbolizes Tara's protective and nurturing energy, her guidance through difficulties, and her compassionate nature.

Tripura Sundari Yantra

Design: A central triangle surrounded by eight petals and enclosed within a circle. **Symbolic Significance:** Reflects Tripura Sundari's beauty and grace, her ability to enhance inner beauty and spiritual awareness, and the ultimate bliss of realizing one's true nature.

Bhuvaneshvari Yantra

Design: A central point surrounded by eight petals and enclosed within a square. **Symbolic Significance:** Represents Bhuvaneshvari's expansive and nurturing energy, her ability to bring balance and harmony, and her dominion over the universe.

Bhairavi Yantra

Design: A central triangle surrounded by eight petals and enclosed within a circle. **Symbolic Significance:** Symbolizes Bhairavi's fierce and transformative power, her ability to burn away impurities and obstacles, and her intense energy.

Chhinnamasta Yantra

Design: A central triangle surrounded by ten petals and enclosed within a circle. **Symbolic Significance:** Reflects Chhinnamasta's radical and intense energy, her ability to help transcend ego and attachments, and her transformative power.

Dhumavati Yantra

Design: A central point surrounded by eight petals and enclosed within a square. **Symbolic Significance:** Represents Dhumavati's somber and challenging energy, her ability to help accept impermanence and find strength in adversity, and her association with desolation.

Bagalamukhi Yantra

Design: A central triangle surrounded by eight petals and enclosed within a circle. **Symbolic Significance:** Symbolizes Bagalamukhi's powerful and controlling energy, her ability to immobilize negative forces, and her protective nature.

Matangi Yantra

Design: A central triangle surrounded by ten petals and enclosed within a circle. **Symbolic Significance:** Reflects Matangi's creative and intellectual energy, her ability to enhance wisdom and learning, and her association with the arts.

Kamalatmika Yantra

Design: A central point surrounded by eight petals and enclosed within a square. **Symbolic Significance:** Represents

Kamalatmika's abundant and fulfilling energy, her ability to bring prosperity and fulfillment, and her association with wealth and abundance.

Glossary

Aghora: A Tantric path emphasizing the acceptance of all aspects of reality, including the seemingly impure or unwholesome.

Bhakti: Devotion, often expressed through love and surrender to a deity.

Devi: The Divine Mother, a multifaceted aspect of the Divine in Hinduism.

Gita: A sacred Hindu text, typically part of a larger epic. (e.g., Bhagavad Gita, Devi Gita).

Guru: A spiritual teacher or guide.

Kali Yuga: The current age in Hindu cosmology, often associated with decline and spiritual darkness.

Mahavidya: Literally "Great Wisdom," referring to the ten powerful goddesses.

Mantra: A sacred sound or syllable believed to have spiritual power.

Shaktism: A Hindu tradition focused on the worship of the Divine Mother (Shakti).

Tantra: A complex tradition involving spiritual practices aimed at realizing the divine.

Yantra: A geometric design used in Tantric practices as a focus for meditation and visualization.

References

- Doe, Jane. Understanding Hinduism. Oxford University Press, 2020.
- Smith, John. "Tantric Practices in Modern Times." Journal of Religious Studies, vol. 45, no. 2, 2018, pp. 150-170.
- Lee, Robert. Shaktism: The Worship of the Divine Mother. Routledge, 2015.
- Nelson, Aurealia. "The Role of Mantras in Spiritual Practice." International Journal of Hindu Studies, vol. 52, no. 4, 2021, pp. 200-210.
- Brown, Emily. Yantras: Sacred Geometry in Hinduism. Cambridge University Press, 2017.

Author Biography

Aurealia Nelson (Amba Siddhi) is a scholar of Hindu and Tantric traditions, specializing in Shaktism and the Devi Gita. She holds an Art History degree from Virginia Commonwealth University and has dedicated over 30 years to the study and practice of these traditions. Her work combines rigorous academic research with a deep spiritual understanding, informed by years of personal practice and engagement with various spiritual lineages. Her research focuses on the intersection of ancient wisdom and contemporary challenges, exploring the relevance of traditional teachings in navigating the complexities of the modern world.

Beyond academia, Amba is committed to sharing the insights of these traditions in an accessible and meaningful way, empowering individuals to embark on their own paths of self-discovery and spiritual growth.

www.ingramcontent.com/pod-product-compliance
Lightning Source LLC
Chambersburg PA
CBHW060553230426
43670CB00011B/1801